STUDIES IN AFRICAN AMERICAN HISTORY AND CULTURE

edited by

GRAHAM HODGES
COLGATE UNIVERSITY

A GARLAND SERIES

THE PAN-AFRICAN IDEA IN THE UNITED STATES 1900–1919

African-American Interest in Africa and Interaction with West Africa

MILFRED C. FIERCE

GARLAND PUBLISHING, Inc.
New York & London / 1993

Library of Congress Cataloging-in-Publication Data

Fierce, Milfred C., 1937–
    The Pan-African idea in the United States, 1900–1919 : African-American interest in Africa and interaction with west Africa / by Milfred C. Fierce.
        p.   cm. — (Studies in African American history and culture)
    Includes bibliographical references (p.   ) and index.
    ISBN 0–8153–1460–4 (alk. paper)
    1. Afro-Americans—Relations with Africans. 2. Afro-Americans—History—1877–1964. 3. Pan-Africanism. I. Title. II. Series.
E185.625.F54   1993
320.5'49'08996073—dc20   93–28751
                                                                            CIP

Printed on acid-free, 250-year-life paper
Manufactured in the United States of America

To Helen

Contents

Preface

This study investigates the major forms of African-American interest in Africa and interaction with West Africa during the first two decades of the twentieth century, between the Pan-African Conference of 1900 in London and the Pan-African Congress of 1919 in Paris. Moreover, the study considers how this interest was manifested and to what extent its expressions metamorphosed and stimulated interaction. This inquiry also focuses on the development of the Pan-African idea among African-Americans during the time of two of the most significant gatherings in the evolution of Pan-Africanism in the twentieth century.

This book is essentially thematic or topical in approach. That is, the subject treatment conforms to the following basic themes: Black intellectual interest (chapter 2), missionary interest (chapters 3, 4), back-to-Africa movements (chapter 5), interest in Liberia (chapter 6) and what falls into the category called "other secular interests" (chapters 7, 8) such as the case study of African-Americans growing cotton in Togo and Pan-African conferences. Consequently, some chronological overlap occurs. Because the "themes" are of paramount concern, the time periods covered often vary from chapter to chapter.

The first chapter provides the nineteenth century background of the African-American involvement in Africa. It was a period dominated by colonization and emigration schemes. However the missionary interest, particularly after the Civil War, was quite pronounced. Africa before 1900 also engaged the attention of a score of nineteenth century Black intellectuals. The Congress on Africa (1895) was the last important conference of the century related to Africa and therefore is discussed. Chapter

2 illustrates the variety of ways in which twentieth century Black American intellectuals waged an indefatigable campaign to restore Africa's dignity and the proud heritage of people of African descent in the United States. Chapters 3 and 4 describe the missionary interest in Africa. The overriding concern is Black missionaries in Africa beginning with a consideration of the White-sponsored Stewart Foundation for Africa. Most of Stewart's missionaries in Africa were Black Americans. The second part of the missionary section investigates the Africa interest and activities of the independent Black churches.

The back-to-Africa movement of "Chief Sam" is the subject in chapter 5. The emigration movement led by Bishop Henry McNeal Turner reached its limits in the 1890s and began to decline by the early part of the twentieth century. Wide spread despair among Blacks in the southwestern portion of the United States, especially Oklahoma, made it possible for Chief Sam to recruit his following. Before the movement ran its course, only twenty-seven African-Americans were transported to Africa in the one ship supported by the Chief Sam movement. However, that number was not indicative of the greater Black support for the Chief Sam movement in the United States.

The relationship between Black American elites and Liberia, which is a significant part of the African-American past, is investigated in chapter 6. Since some African-Americans made efforts to assist Liberia, through diplomacy (a dramatic departure from the traditional interest), during a period of severe crisis, those efforts receive much attention. Chapters 7 and 8, take up additional selected aspects of the non-religious, secular interest. The Tuskegee Institute cotton-growing expedition in Togoland is a lesser-known example of African-American interaction with Africa. It is an experience characterized by high expectations, disappointment and tragedy. The final chapter treats the three significant conferences inspired by a concern for Africa held between 1900 and 1919: the Pan-African Conference in London (1900), the Tuskegee Institute-sponsored

Conference on the Negro (1912), and the Pan-African Congress in Paris (1919).

The Social/Historical Milieu

At the opening of the twentieth century, the United States of America, in so far as Black men, women and children were concerned, was in an ugly mood. One scholar, professor Rayford Logan, described the early years of the new century as a central period in the "nadir" of Black life and history in America. There is some agreement among historians regarding when this post-emancipation low point began (1890), but little consensus on its terminal date. However it is difficult to find a period in United States history with more evidence of Negrophobia, extreme racism and rigid segregation than the first nineteen years of this century.[1]

In so many respects the events in American society that punctuated the period 1900–1919 were carried over from the last decade of the previous century. The infamous "Mississippi plan" signaled the onset of disfranchisement for southern Black voters. Shortly after Mississippi set the pace by amending its constitution, as part of an effort to deprive Black citizens of the suffrage, most other southern states, and some outside the South, unveiled a stream of artifices to eliminate Black political involvement. There were grandfather clauses, literacy tests, poll taxes, intricate registration requirements, unannounced relocation of polling places and White primaries. And, of course, the White South also turned to intimidation and violence.[2]

By the last decade of the nineteenth century as well, both White and Black opinion, North and South, agreed that the transition from a slave system to the caste system that replaced it was complete. The new peonage arrangement relegated most Blacks in the South to the lives of sharecroppers, cropliners and tenant farmers. By 1900 three-fourths of all Black farmers were croppers or tenants.

The convict lease system, which was operating full steam in the South during the last ten years of the nineteenth century, claimed a disproportionate number of Blacks. This system allowed for the leasing of convicts to individuals or private business for ten, twenty and thirty years and was the foundation for huge fortunes in the South. Leasing convicts to private entities who had sole responsibility for regulating hours, working conditions and medical treatment for prisoners, quickly became a vicious and sinister business. A parallel for the southern convict lease system, according to one student of the subject, can only be found in Nazi Germany or the persecutions in the Middle Ages.[3]

In the ominous Plessy Decision of 1896, in which the nation's highest court confirmed the doctrine of "separate but equal," it was claimed that "legislation was powerless to eradicate racial instincts." This opinion was not struck down until 1954. The walls of discrimination erected by Jim Crow and racial caste, and raised higher and higher by custom and by law, were now strengthened by judicial sanction.

Southern Populism, encouraging at first with the possibility of Black and White farmer cooperation, yielded to the rhetoric of racism as expounded by James K. Vardaman of Mississippi and "pitchfork" Ben Tillman of South Carolina, and in doing so sealed its own fate. Vardaman's view that he was "just as opposed to Booker T. Washington as a voter, with all his Anglo-Saxon re-enforcements, as I am to the coconut-headed, chocolate-covered, typical little coon Andy Dotson, who blacks my shoes every morning" revealed more than just his antipathy for Black voting. It suggested opposition to every level of social and political intercourse between Blacks and Whites, for which Black suffrage represented a potential Pandora's box. Very soon Blacks became the scapegoats for the failure of Populism and, ironically, as C. Vann Woodward has noted, the social and political proscription of southern Blacks increased in inverse proportion to the expansion of political democracy among White yeoman farmers. There was little relief in sight for the aggravation of racial tensions brought on by Populism.[4]

The Blair bill for federal assistance to public education and the Lodge bill for federal management of national elections were defeated in Congress early in 1890 and 1891 respectively because southern Whites, who were mainly democrats, perceived each initiative as an attempt by the Republican Party to once again aid Blacks. The rate of Black lynchings and race riots were increasing during this era and despite pronouncements to the contrary, Blacks were being excluded from the country's major labor unions. Noteworthy was Samuel Gompers, who as president of the American Federation of Labor suggested that it was impractical to insist on the acceptance of Black members in White unions; therefore, separate unions should be organized for them. Later Gompers was quoted as supporting the elimination of Blacks from labor unions altogether because they did not "understand the philosophy of human rights."

The emergence of Social Darwinism, "White man's burden" and American imperialistic adventures overseas is significant for an understanding of the racial climate in the United States at the dawn of the twentieth century. Darwin's theories of ascendance of the fittest and disappearance of the unfit was attractive to those who believed in the superior-subordinate relationship among different members of the human family. Although Darwin's research was done primarily on the animal kingdom, his findings were now applied to people. Social Darwinists also combined the late nineteenth and early twentieth century theories of Count Arthur de Gobineau, the "Father of Racism" and others, about the inferiority of races and Herbert Spencer's assertions of "survival of the fittest" to prove White superiority over Blacks. Under the earlier influence of Thomas R. Malthus, Darwin contended that those living things that lost out in the struggle for existence were inferior specimens who adapted poorly to their environment. The survivors, the higher races, formed the foundation for an improved stock, banishing the lower races to eventual extinction. When these principles were applied to humans, as most of them were during this period, the notion of Blacks and other people of color as subject races became widely accepted.[5]

Further corroboration for these corrupt ideas was found in the European scramble for Africa (1885–1915) and in U.S. imperialism. At the conclusion of the Spanish-American War (1898), millions of "colored people" in the Pacific and Caribbean were brought under the jurisdiction of the United States. The nation as a whole adopted the southern attitude that since Whites were the stronger and more capable race they were free to impose their will on "backward races" whether in the Philippines, the West Indies, Africa, Brazil or Mississippi and Alabama. This was the doctrine of White supremacy, and its propaganda contaminated and pervaded an American society so willing to accept it, especially in the late nineteenth and early twentieth centuries. In the northern mind as well as the southern, the concept of innate Black inferiority was an acceptable explanation for eschewing African-Americans and Africans and non-Whites in general.

At the turn of the twentieth century, the new hope that came with Theodore Roosevelt's rise to the presidency in 1901 was soon dashed by some of the president's actions. Roosevelt, to the chagrin of southern Whites, had invited Booker T. Washington to dine at the White House, but by his second term in office Blacks began to understand that his friendship would be neither genuine nor lasting. Roosevelt's insensitive handling of the "Brownsville Affair" (Texas) in August of 1906 was the "nail in the coffin" in convincing many Blacks that they had no real friend in Washington. The president dismissed an entire battalion, on the flimsiest of evidence, without honor for their alleged involvement in a riot in that small Texas town, and disqualified all its members from service in either the military or civil service of the United States. Blacks were, to say the least, piqued but to no avail. Six years later, when southern delegates in the Progressive Party, with Roosevelt's knowledge, barred Blacks from their convention, earlier suspicions of Roosevelt's capitulation to White supremacy were substantiated and Black Americans realized that the Bull Moose movement would not be responsive to their interests.[6]

There were other outstanding events and issues during the period 1900–1919 that persuaded most Blacks they would be better advised to conserve their energy and best efforts for a survival strategy, not an interest in Africa. During the first decade of the new century, for example, race extremism may have reached a wider audience than ever before. Thomas Dixon's series of historical novels on the race conflict, including his bitter indictment of Blacks in *The Clansman* (later the basis for the widely seen motion picture, "Birth of a Nation"), contributed much to contemporary Negrophobia. In this novel published in 1905, Dixon intensified his effort to demonstrate the bestiality of Blacks. The attempt actually began with the publication of Dixon's first novel in 1902, entitled *The Leopard's Spots*. This book by the former Baptist minister, turned novelist, projected White hysteria regarding allegations of degeneracy, animality, and, "sexual madness." Described also was Dixon's view of how the Civil War and Reconstruction had transformed Blacks from chattel into beasts. This new would-be Black menace, called a veritable "Black Death" by Dixon, purportedly threw a shadow over all future generations in the United States and, therefore, Whites were justified in using any means at their disposal to control it, perhaps even eliminate it.

In the wider media Blacks were portrayed, in stereotypic fashion, as "wretched freedmen," "comic," "brutelike," "tragic mulattoes" and "exotic primitives." All of these stereotypes were marked by exaggeration and omission. Conspicuous was the African-American's deviation from the Anglo-Saxon norm, to the flattery of the latter. Newspapers in particular cooperated in circulating anti-Black propaganda through feature stories, cartoons, photographs and posters. One absurd extreme to which these vilifying claims went was the suggestion of "sexual madness" among African-Americans, in the respectable journal *Medicine* in 1903 in an article by a Dr. William L. Howard. He contended that the "frequent" attacks on White women by Blacks were best explained by peculiar "Racial instincts" among African-Americans. The large size of the Black American's penis and the lack of sensitiveness of the terminal fibers, according to Howard, explained that the "African's birthright was sexual madness and excess."[7]

The race riots in Atlanta, Georgia (1906), Springfield, Illinois (1908) East St. Louis (1917) and Chicago, Illinois (1919) were by far the most ruthless of the period. Dozens of Blacks were killed, hundreds were injured and many, out of fear for their lives, were forced to abandon their property and possessions and leave town. In almost every single case the guilty parties went unpunished.

From 1900 to 1919 segregation and Jim Crow continued uninterrupted and virtually unchallenged. The number of lynchings soared from approximately 100 in 1901 to more than 1,100 just before the outbreak of World War I. And during the war itself Black soldiers, notwithstanding the call by W.E.B. DuBois to "close ranks" behind the United States and subordinate race agitation and protest during this period of national crisis, were the subjects of the most shameful treatment by the United States government simply because of the color of their skin.

During the Great War, Blacks in military service were discriminated against in the draft, in training, and in assignment. They were recruited and inducted into a rigidly segregated army with disabilities that exempted White men from service. Black troops were denied adequate medical attention, supplies and recreational facilities. And in spite of a commendable fighting record in the Civil War and the Spanish-American War, 70 percent of all Black soldiers were placed in stevedore and labor units and were appointed to duties considered unsuitable for White troops. Despite undeniably inferior treatment, preparation and leadership (usually White), Black troops were expected to perform at least as well as their White counterparts.

In Europe, a document entitled "Secret Information Concerning Black American Troops," circulated by an American colonel attached to American Expeditionary Force Headquarters, counseled the French population on how to treat Blacks and why. French citizens were advised that "whether they agreed or not," fifteen million Blacks in the United States presented the threat of race mongrelization unless strict separation of Blacks and Whites was maintained. The French were also told that White Americans considered Blacks to be ignorant and devoid of civil and professional morals. It was necessary, therefore, to avoid association with African-Americans; the French were asked not to eat or shake hands with Blacks, and not to praise them, especially in the presence of Whites. French authorities were requested "*qu'elles ne gatent pas les negres.*" Black American troops were not even permitted to march in the ceremonious Allied Victory Parade in Paris after the armistice although that parade included the Black troops of England and France. The height of brutal paradox was reached after the war when in Europe, investigations revealed several illegal, cowardly executions and lynchings of Black soldiers, there to "make the world safe for democracy."

The organized Black response to these desperate times manifested itself in the emergence of the Niagara Movement (1906), subsequently absorbed by the formation of the National Association for the Advancement of Colored People (NAACP) in 1909, and the establishment of the National Urban League in 1911. Booker T. Washington, the guru of accommodation and conciliation, died in 1915, leaving a temporary void in Black leadership until Marcus Garvey's bold program of Black nationalism captured the imagination of the masses. Forced by White rejection to exploit their own potential and resources, and develop their own institutions, Black communities constructed carbon copies of the White world within their clearly defined borders. This became the turf of the Black middle and upper classes; they launched and dominated churches, schools, banks, theaters, the professions, small businesses and the services. The

"Year of the Jubilee" (1913), celebrating fifty years of emancipation, was marred by economic deprivation, political exploitation and social degradation. Two years later when southern Blacks joined the "exodus fever" it was as much for political and social reasons as for economic ones. In the cities of the North, even though more African-Americans there met fewer obstacles to voting and office-holding, they faced restrictive covenants that limited housing, the omnipresence of segregation, and were often thrown into competition with Whites for jobs and used as strikebreakers.

Such was the social-historical climate that prevailed in the United States between 1900 and 1919. Little wonder that many Blacks considered their plight to be not far removed from slavery. Man-constructed obstacles to voting, education, employment housing and social intercourse abounded. The United States of America was pregnant with race bigotry, hypocrisy and duplicity.

The most surprising factor about the limited interest in Africa at this time is that there was any at all. Africa was described by European travelers, imperial anthropologists and missionaries as depraved, barbaric, degenerate and repulsive. Sensationalized and presented in lurid detail, without context and with relish, were such practices as human sacrifice, paganism and polygamy. Virtually anything that did not fit the contemptuous stereotype such as African art, indigenous crafts or the efficient organization of African societies, some copied by Europeans, was suppressed or ignored altogether.

The influential historian Joseph Tillinghast applied the Darwinian concepts of racial heredity and Black inferiority to African and African-American history in his 1902 study, *The Negro in Africa and America*. His work substantially influenced a generation of scholars, his essential argument was that the only way racial heredity could be changed was in "slow infinitesimal degrees." This would be done through a selection process of accumulating advantageous variations in offspring, thereby eliminating unfavorable ones. Tillinghast further suggested that climate was an important factor in the "unfortunate biological inheritance" of Africans and their descendants. Black character had been shaped in Africa, which was purportedly a continent with an inglorious history of "stagnation, inefficiency, ignorance, cannibalism, sexual license and superstition."

In sum, almost everything about Africa was considered odious and portrayed with derision. U.S. citizens of African descent could not escape the strong impact such a scornful image of Africa had on their perceptions of that continent. By and large they wanted little association or identification with a place considered so objectionable and a people so maligned. The fact that any African-Americans defended Africa or had even the most minimal interest in it, in the face of so much condemnation, coupled with extreme duress in the United States, was remarkable.

Pan-Africanism

The November 16, 1974 issue of the New York *Amsterdam News*, that claimed at the time to be "Americas' largest weekly" and the Black newspaper with the largest circulation, declared in bold, glaring, red headlines, "South Africa is Kicked Out of U.N." The story below the headlines consumed most of the front page and referred to the unprecedented decision to oust the White-minority, apartheid-inclined government of South Africa from the General Assembly of the United Nations. South Africa was barred from "sitting, speaking or voting" as well as participating in the deliberations of the world organization, despite the efforts of the United States, France and Great Britain to block such a move. The movement to expel South Africa was led by an African-Arab coalition with substantial support from several socialist governments. The crusade to deny South Africa membership in the General Assembly was closely watched by the Black American press and the successful effort generally delighted the Black American community. African-American interest in Africa is still more sentimental than active (notwithstanding the Leon Sullivan-led African-American African "summits" and the "Sullivan principles" for U.S. companies operating in South Africa), but Africa consciousness in the final quarter of the twentieth century was at an all-time high and interaction between African-Americans and Africa is likewise undergoing unparalleled activity (for example African Liberation Day programs, mobilization of support for the Somalia crisis and drought in the region earlier, Black and Africana Studies programs in schools and universities, the formation of Trans Africa and its leadership of the Free South Africa Movement). Therefore, the *Amsterdam News* headlines two decades ago were symbolic of Black America's concern for Africa, which has not always been as pronounced.[8] Moreover, this sensitivity of African-Americans to events in the African world is indicative of the Pan-African idea, and the idea's popularity is enjoying its apogee in the history of Black people in the Americas.

Interest in Pan-Africanism has enjoyed rapid growth among Black Americans, especially college students, since the early 1970s. This factor is an outgrowth of the modern civil rights movement, and one manifestation of this phenomenon is the recent renaissance in the study of African and African-American history, culture and heritage, all of which emphasize Africa. In addition, the burgeoning political potential of Africa and its people on the world stage, despite setbacks by civil wars, famine, drought and debt still attracts considerable attention. Definitions and descriptions of Pan-Africanism[9] are available but confusing.[10] Immanuel Geiss, a German scholar, in a work translated from German to English attempts to define Pan-Africanism but compounds the issues instead of clarifying them.[11] Perhaps this equivocation is not entirely the fault of writers and students of this subject. Pan-Africanism has been an evolving ideology that encouraged uncertainty. Part of the problem in the past has been the failure to make distinctions between the idea and the movement.

For purposes of this study, the Pan-African idea is distinguished from the movement. The *movement* refers to an organized set of activities designed to relieve Black people (especially but not exclusively Africans) from various kinds of exploitation and oppression on the path to bonafide Black nationalism: social, political, and economic. The *idea* is the extent to which, if any, an African kinship or brotherhood consciousness exists among African-Americans, irrespective of the steps taken. Providing the stimulus for most of the action generated such as conferences, lobbying, demonstrations and petition campaigns, was a sense of the reciprocal bond of Blackness. All through the eighteenth and nineteenth centuries, the idea of ebony kinship among Africans and African-Americans was expressed in parts of the African-American community. Therefore, by 1900 the idea was not brand new. However, this study presents a preponderance of evidence that after the turn of the twentieth century the Pan-African idea became more acceptable among Black Americans than it had ever been.

In their broadest sense, references to Pan-Africanism have included all those Blacks who expressed an interest in uplifting of Africa and Africa's people, for whatever reason. The early Pan-Africanists were drawn, in the main, from the ranks of Blacks in mainland North America and the Caribbean—prior to the twentieth century.[12] At different times and under a wide variety of circumstances, these pioneer proto-Pan-Africanists included people like Paul Cuffe, Lott Cary, Daniel Coker, John B. Russworm, Martin Delaney, Edward Blyden, Alexander Crummell and Henry M. Turner.[13]

A more parochial or exclusive definition of Pan-Africanism confines it to a strict interest in political unity, cooperation or development on the African continent. This brand of Pan-Africanism was inspired greatly by the Manchester Congress (1945), after which Pan-Africanism as an idea and a movement coalesced and concentrated on independence and self-determination among African elites from European colonies in Africa. Pan-Africanism as outlined here emphasized the leadership role to be played by continental Africans, which contrasted with the leadership role played by "New World" Africans until 1945. Since 1957 this later phase of Pan-Africanism also highlighted the need for regional and it was hoped, continental unity and cooperation, mainly in economic and political affairs.

Between these two extremes of Pan-Africanism several other definitions can be accommodated. All of these, however, borrow generously from one or both of the extremes while adding or deleting appropriate nuance. In this discussion the definition of Pan-Africanism continues as a view, notion or ideology that promotes the global cooperative struggle for dignity and self-reliance among Black people and the complete stripping away of colonial and neo-colonial legacies. This species of Pan-Africanism transcends national and geographic boundaries. It is racial in orientation and, therefore, includes primarily the behavior of members of the African family on the continent and people of African descent in the diaspora. Ideologically, unity and cooperation are promoted between Black people of the world. And Africa, with its plentiful supply of human and material resources, is recognized as the center of gravity in the Black world. Consequently, complete liberation from and removal of all remnants of alien intrusion in Africa and its legacy, along with unencumbered self-determination, are an early priority.[14] The objective of this brand of Pan-Africanism is intended to be accomplished peacefully but resorting to violence and armed struggle cannot be ruled out as a possibility. It is expected that when Africa is totally free and assumes a leadership role in a new international order, the economic, political and social quality of life for the sons and daughters of Africa everywhere will be raised proportionately because newly conscientized African leadership will accept no less for their diasporic cousins. At the same time, Blacks in diaspora are obligated, wherever they are, to contribute to Africa's elevation. No local, short-range Black struggles would need to be abandoned anywhere a need for a struggle exists (for example in the United States, where the demand for adequate housing, more equitable employment opportunities, and basic human rights continues). These efforts would, however, be clearly recognized as transitory endeavors. According to Columbia University political scientist Charles V. Hamilton, it may be difficult to appreciate the relationship between the imperatives for Blacks in Africa and Blacks in the diaspora.[15] Nevertheless, the links are there and "a correct Pan-African ideology will illuminate the relationship both in its short-term and long-range dimension."[16] The particular role that Black Americans would play in the Pan-African scheme is also noted by Hamilton:

> Black Americans, living in the midst of the strongest western nation, have a vital function in the modern political struggle. That function is to utilize the resources of land, economics and ideology to maximize Black political power in this country in order to influence (reverse, neutralize) western intervention in revolutionary, developing Africa. This can only be done by an economically and politically powerful force within this country. It is difficult to imagine any force other than Blacks taking the initial interest and the lead in this struggle. The admonition of President Nyerere will only be heeded if Black Americans—organized and powerful— take the lead in reversing policies of this country. This will be Pan-Africanism moved beyond anticipation and pronouncement to act and progress.[17]

It is not altogether clear to what degree an interest in Pan-Africanism was influenced by early pan-movements.[18] A few of these early pan-movements seem to have enjoyed their peak in the late nineteenth and early twentieth centuries. This is the exact period when several writers argue that Pan-Africanism had its most concrete origins. W.E.B. DuBois, an eminent figure in the Pan-African movement, was engaged in graduate study at the University of Berlin in the mid 1890s when Pan-Germanism began to flower. There is little question that DuBois was conscious of and familiar with the propaganda of a growing Pan-German movement, designed to ignite the racial consciousness of the German people. George Shepperson asserts that , "Out of these European experiences, in a classical period of Pan-Nationalism, the father of Pan-Africanism [DuBois] must have contributed more than nuance's to not only the 1900 Pan-African Congress but also to the formative conferences of 1919 and 1927."[19]

Following closely on the heels of Pan-Germanism was the appearance of other pan-nationalist movements, also in the 1890s, which mobilized people along political, racial and cultural lines: Pan-Africanism, Pan-Slavism, Pan-Islamism, Zionism, Pan-Nordism, Pan-Hispanism, Pan-Arabism, Pan-Asianism and Pan-Latinism. Pan-Africanism is the relative late-comer compared with these other pan-movements. Nevertheless, its origin too is most identified with this period, the turn of the twentieth century.

Many writers consider the Pan-African Conference called by the Trinidad barrister, Henry Sylvester Williams, in London (1900), to be the twentieth century launching pad for Pan-Africanism. Others argue that the 1919 Pan-African Congress promulgated by W.E.B. DuBois in Paris was the take-off point for the development of Pan-Africanism. Still others assert that the Pan-African idea in the United States between the two forums was dormant. Most of those who support the latter position are substantially influenced by DuBois's own statements, since he was a participant at the 1900 assembly.

> This meeting [1900] had no deep roots in Africa itself, and
> the movement and the idea died for a generation.[20]

It is the contention of the author and the argument of this study that the Pan-African idea was perhaps unconventional, sporadic, and ephemeral but it certainly was not dead between 1900 and 1919. The Africa interest, such as it was, during this ominous period in African-American history, was part of an ongoing and persistent phenomenon, that materialized principally through those mediums described above and which is the overarching subject here. If this book sufficiently establishes such a view its objective will be realized.

NOTES

1. The literature on the three decades, 1890 to 1920, that Rayford Logan labeled the "nadir" is extensive and fairly well known. Consequently no effort is made here to simply list the top fifteen or twenty books on the period although some are noted in other endnotes or in the bibliography. Logan's analysis of the period can be found in his, *The Betrayal of the Negro: From Rutherford B. Hayes to Woodrow Wilson* (London, 1969).

2. One older and one newer survey of this "tragic era" is C. Vann Woodward, *Origins of the New South 1877–1913* (Baton Rouge, Louisiana, 1951) and Nell Irvin Painter, *Standing at Armageddon: The United States, 1877–1919* (New York, 1987).

3. There is no modern single volume study of the southern convict lease system. Several are underway with different foci including one by the author of this book.

4. The "inverse proportion" argument is persuasively presented in C. Vann Woodward, *The Strange Career of Jim Crow* (New York, 1974), who also argues the racial politics of Southern Populism and the movement's transformation to racism in this book and in *Origins of the New South 1877–1913*.

5. The literature on pseudo-scientific race thought is massive. Two, among many, works that I found useful are Idus A. Newby, *Jim Crow's Defense: Anti-Negro Thought in America, 1900–1930* (Baton Rouge, Louisiana, 1965), and George M. Frederickson, *The Black Image in the White Mind: The Debate on Afro-American Character and Destiny, 1817–1914* (New York, 1971). Charles Darwin's *The Origin of Species* (London, 1859) and *The Descent of Man* (New York, 1874) are very important. Individuals new to the subject however might begin with Gertrude Himmelfarb, *Darwin and the Darwinian Revolution* (London, 1959). The

"Father of Racism," Count Arthur de Gobineau was a Frenchman. Therefore much of his writing is in the French language and sometimes German although there are selected English translations. A good start for broadening one's knowledge of Gobineau and his influence can be made in English with Michael D. Biddiss, ed., *Gobineau: Selected Political Writings* (New York, 1970).

6. A short introduction to the larger significance of "Progressivism" and the Progressive movement, and party, can be found in Richard Hofstadter, ed., *The Progressive Movement 1900–1915*, "Introduction," 1–15 (Englewood Cliffs, New Jersey, 1963).

7. Cited in Frederickson, *The Black Image*, 279.

8. Also reflecting a positive interest in Black America toward Africa in the 1970s was an interview with Black New York Congressman Charles Rangel, then Chairman of the Congressional Black Caucus, published in *Africa: An International Business, Economic and Political Monthly* (March, 1975) 7, 42–44. Further reflecting Black American leadership's attitude toward Africa policy in the 1970s was the article by Congressman Charles Diggs entitled "The Afro-American Stake in Africa" in *Black World* (January, 1976), 4–9. More significant was the announcement that the U.S. Congressional Black Caucus would have what amounts to precedent-setting influence in the formulation of American foreign policy toward Africa. The high point in African-American influence on U.S. foreign policy toward Africa and in general occurred during the presidency of Jimmy Carter (1976–1980), with Andrew Young and Donald McHenry serving respectively as United States ambassadors to the United Nations. This argument could be challenged by General Colin Powell serving as the chairman of the Joint Chiefs of Staff under President George Bush, and Edward Perkins, serving as the first Black U.S. ambassador to South Africa under Ronald Reagan and later as ambassador to the United Nations under Bush. All previous African-American foreign policy influence could be exceeded during the administration of President Bill Clinton. Elliott Skinner has captured African-American influence on United States Africa foreign policy in the nineteenth and twentieth centuries "through symbolic modes as well as formal structure" in *African Americans and U.S. Policy Toward Africa* (Washington, D.C., 1992). For a survey of African-American opinions toward South Africa in the 1980s, and a view on African-American elites and organizations on the same subject see Milfred C. Fierce, "Black and White American Opinions Towards South

Africa," *Journal of Modern African Studies*, Vol. 20, No. 4 (1982), 669–687, and "Selected Black American Leaders and Organizations and South Africa, 1900–1977: Some Notes," *Journal of Black Studies*, Vol. 17, No. 3 (1987), 305–326. For a perspective on the early 1990s consider Edwin Dorn and Walter Carrington, "Africa in the Minds and the Deeds of Black American Leaders," Joint Center for Political and Economic Studies, Inc., 1991, 48 pages.

9. The most scholarly pioneer effort to elucidate the differing components of Pan-Africanism was George Shepperson, "Pan-Africanism and 'Pan-Africanism': Some Historical Notes," *Phylon* (Winter, 1962), 346–358. Shepperson argues that Pan-Africanism with a capital "P" is a "clearly recognizable movement," with W.E.B. DuBois as its prime mover. Pan-Africanism with a small "p" cannot be recognized, he continues, and is "rather a group of movements, many very ephemeral." Since this study deals with Pan-Africanism as an idea rather than a movement, all references to Pan-Africanism are capitalized in an attempt to reduce confusion. Moreover, because the different varieties of Pan-African thought that fed into what Shepperson and others consider a formal movement, it is much more difficult to separate out the ephemeral from the continual than Shepperson has suggested.

10. Cf. the following essays and articles: Peter Duignan, "Pan-Africanism: A Bibliographic Essay," *African Forum* Vol. 1, No. 1 (Summer, 1965), 105–107; Rayford Logan, "The Historical Aspects of Pan-Africanism: A Personal Chronicle," *African Forum*, Vol. 1, No. 1 (Summer, 1965), 90–104; "Pan-Africanism: New Aspirations of an Old Movement," *Round Table*, Vol. 49 (Summer, 1959), 345–350 (no author listed); St. Clair Drake, "Pan-Africanism": What is it?" *Africa Today* (January–February, 1969), 6–10; George Shepperson, "Notes on Negro American Influences on the Emergence of African Nationalism," *Journal of African History* (1960), 299–312; Charles Hamilton, "Pan-Africanism and the Black Struggle in the U.S.," *The Black Scholar* (March, 1971), 10–15; Immanuel Geiss, "Notes on the Development of Pan Africanism," *Journal of the Historical Society of Nigeria*, Vol. 3, No. 4, 719–740. Charles F. Andrian, "The Pan-African Movement: The Search for Organization and Community," *Phylon*, Vol. 23, No. 1 (Spring, 1962), 5–17. The following monographs discuss Pan-Africanism: American Society of African Culture (ed.), *Pan-Africanism Reconsidered* (Berkeley, 1962), *passim;* Colin Legum, *Pan-Africanism: A Short Political Guide* (New York, 1965 rev. ed.); George Padmore, *Pan Africanism, or Communism* (New York, 1971) and

Padmore (ed.) *History of the Pan-African Congress* (London, 1963); Imamu A. Baraka (ed.), *African Congress: A Documentary of the First Modern Pan-African Congress* (New York, 1972), *passim*, especially the introduction; Adekunle Ajala, *Pan-Africanism; Evolution, Progress and Prospects* (New York, 1974); J.R. Hooker, *Black Revolutionary: George Padmore's Path from Communism to Pan-Africanism* (London, 1967); J.A. Langley, *Pan-Africanism and Nationalism in West Africa, 1900–1945* (New York, 1973); Ras Makonen, *Pan-Africanism from Within* (London, 1973); Vincent Thompson, *Africa and Unity: The Evolution of Pan-Africanism* (New York, 1969); Robert Christman and Nathan Hare (ed.), *Pan-Africanism* (New York, 1974); P. Olisanwuche Esedebe, *Pan-Africanism: The Idea and the Movement, 1776–1963*, (Washington, D.C., 1982); Opoku Agyeman, *The Pan Africanist World View* (Independence, Missouri, 1985). An interesting perspective in the literature is that of a scholar from the former USSR and one each from Czechoslovakia and Poland. See: N.G. Scherbakov, "PanAfrikanizm I PanAfrikanskaia Konferenfsiia 1900 G.," *Narody Azii i Afriki* (USSR), 1983, I, 81–89; Vladimir Klima "Duboisuv Pan Afrikanism," *Novy Orient* (Czechoslovakia) 1983, XXXVIII, (5), 138–143; Ewa Nowicka, "Historia Pan Afrikanizmu a Ruchy Umyslowe Wsrod Czarnet Ludnosci Stanow Zjednoczonych Ap," *Kultura i Spoleczenstwo* (Poland) 1980, XXIV (24), 271–290.

One important doctoral dissertation dealing specifically with Pan-Africanism as an idea, and therefore central to the discussion in this book is, John Markakis, "Pan-Africanism: The Idea and the Movement" (Columbia University, 1965). Others that are worth seeing, although slightly tangential are: Abiola Ade Lipede, "Pan-Africanism in Southern Africa, 1900–1960" (University of York, U.K., 1960); Dennis Paul Kimbro, "Towards a Model of Pan Africanism" (Northeastern University, 1984); Karefah Marah, "Social History of Practical Pan Africanism and the Education of Teachers in Africa including a Pilot Study of Factors Affecting Najala University College Teacher Trainees to Teach in Other African Countries" (Syracuse University, 1982).

11. Immanuel Geiss, *The Pan-African Movement: A History of Pan-Africanism in America, Europe and Africa* (New York, 1974), 3–15. In all fairness to Geiss, he states from the outset, "It is still difficult, perhaps even impossible, to provide a clear and precise definition of Pan-Africanism." However, the feeling here is that he makes it a little more complex than it is, even though his discussion is very stimulating.

12. Hollis R. Lynch, "Pan-Negro Nationalism in the New World Before 1862," *Boston University Papers on Africa*, II, 1966, 149–179; Howard Bell, "Introduction," in Martin Delaney, Robert Campbell, *Search for a Place: Black Separatism and Africa, 1860*, 1–22; Robert Weisbord, *Ebony Kinship: Africa, Africans and the Afro-American* (Westport, Connecticut, 1973), 1–87.

13. *Ibid*. On Cuffe see: Lamont Thomas, *Rise to Be a People: A Biography of Paul Cuffe* (Urbana, 1986). For Crummell see: Wilson J. Moses's *Alexander Crummell: A Study of Civilization and Discontent* (New York, 1989) and Moses's edited volume of Crummell's writings entitled *Crummell: Destiny and Race: Selected Writings 1840–1890* (Amherst, Massachusetts, 1992); Gregory U. Rigsby, *Alexander Crummell: Pioneer in Nineteenth-Century Pan-African Thought* (New York, 1987).

14. This definition of Pan-Africanism appeared in slightly edited form in Milfred C. Fierce, "Defining and Dating Pan-Africanism," *Africa: An International Business, Economic and Political Monthly* (August, 1975), 56–57.

15. Charles V. Hamilton, "Pan-Africanism and the Black Struggle in the U.S.," *Black Scholar* (March, 1971), 10.

16. *Ibid*.

17. *Ibid.*, 14.

18. Hans Kohn, "Pan-Movements," *Encyclopedia of the Social Sciences* (New York, 1933), XI, 544–554; P. Kazemzadea, "Pan-Movements," *The International Encyclopedia of the Social Sciences* (New York, 1968), II, 365–370; *Encyclopedia Britannica* (New York, 1957), XXIII, 950–957; R.L. Buell, *International Relations* (New York, 1929), 72–95.

19. Shepperson, "Pan-Africanism," 353. For more on Shepperson's writings relative to Pan-African thought see, "The African Diaspora or the African Abroad," *African Forum* (1966), 76–91 and less important but useful, "Abolitionism and African Political Thought," *Transition* XXII (1964), 22–26.

20. W.E.B. DuBois, *The World and Africa* (New York, 1946), 8.

Acknowledgments

As anyone who has ever written a book knows all too well, rarely is such an undertaking completed without incurring substantial debt along the way. I certainly have not departed from that reality. Mentioning individuals by name is precarious at best because, invariably and almost inevitably, a name or names are omitted. Nevertheless, the compulsion, indeed the obligation, to acknowledge those institutions, organizations, and individuals without whose assistance books would seldom see the light of day is appropriately too great to resist.

The library staffs at the various manuscript collections, archives, and university and general libraries listed in the bibliography, or cited in endnotes throughout, were very helpful. There was not a single instance in which I did not receive valuable assistance. In the finals stages of the project, the library staff at the Ford Foundation, especially Mary Jane Ballou, and at the Woodruff Library on the campus of the Atlanta University Center, in Atlanta Georgia, particularly Dovie T. Patrick, were indispensable with bibliographic checks and other tedious matters.

Kathy Semble at Garland Publishing efficiently input the manuscript and made many changes. Alice Tufel did a superb copy editing job, and when I elected not to follow her advice, it was for reasons too numerous and detailed to mention here.

My colleague George Cunningham, in the Department of Africana Studies at Brooklyn College (CUNY), gave the manuscript its most substantive read, corrected several errors, and rescued me from what would have been obvious embarrassment, omission, and oversight. However, the author did not always follow Professor Cunningham's good advice either. Professor Hollis Lynch of Columbia University saw the book in an earlier incarnation and receives my gratitude for his guidance and wise counsel.

Susan V. Berresford, Vice President of the Program Division at the Ford Foundation, deserves more credit than I can ever give her in these pages, for this exercise being brought to fruition.

Without the support of Franklin A. Thomas, President of the Ford Foundation, publication of this book would simply not have been possible. He is simultaneously a mentor, a colleague, and a friend. Even though he did not see the manuscript prior to its publication, Frank Thomas is almost as responsible for its existence as I am, in ways that only he and I will ever know.

Whatever strengths this book has must be shared with all of the individuals named above, and some unnamed. The shortcomings, however, rest solely with MCF.

The Pan-African Idea
in the United States
1900–1919

CHAPTER I

Nineteenth Century Antecedents to Twentieth Century Africa Interest

African-American interaction with Africa is not at all a brand new phenomenon.[1] It is not even of recent origin. In point of fact, the nexus between Black America and Africa—especially West Africa—has been an ordered theme in African-American history, dating from the onset of the first direct traffic in slaves from West Africa to the Americas in the early part of the sixteenth century. According to John Hope Franklin, an acknowledged scholar of African-American history, there was hardly a time when some Blacks in the Americas did not hope to return to the land of their forebears. Floyd J. Miller, a student of Black colonization and emigration, writes that Blacks in "Boston and in Newport and Providence, Rhode Island, all formulated emigration plans in the 1780's."[2]

Colonization and Emigration

The action phase of the African-American's engrossment with Africa when they were doing things rather than simply thinking or dreaming about Africa, most of the time, took the form of Black nationalist or back-to-Africa movements. However, the nineteenth century Africa interest, also included, to a much lesser extent, bringing small groups of African students to study at Black American universities and colleges, mainly in the American South, plus African-American missionaries evangelizing in Africa, and occasionally fanciful

3

episodes involving African-Americans engaged in commercially inspired enterprises in Africa. In addition, an Africa consciousness and the activities of various individuals and organizations in the United States with a particular affinity for Africa inspired a limited amount of African-American writings and intellectual activities. Not to be overlooked in any consideration of African-American expressions of interest in Africa is the influence West Africa has always had on the emergence of a uniquely fashioned African-American culture: folklore, diet, dance, music, language, religion, and family life.

The first Black individual to actually carry a group of African-Americans back to Africa from what is now the United States, was Paul Cuffe, the offspring of Native American mother and Black father. Ottobah Cugoano, Gustavas Vassa, Phyllis Wheatley (all born in Africa), and Benjamin Banneker each had early, albeit different, connections with Africa or the Africa interest as well. But it is most often Cuffe's actions that serve as the starting point for an investigation of African-American interest in Africa as well. Cuffe was born free in Massachusetts in 1759 and eventually became a relatively wealthy shipowner there. During the War for U.S. independence, Paul Cuffe refused to pay his taxes because of his disillusionment with the plight of free Blacks in Massachusetts regarding the franchise.

Following the war and smarting from worsening conditions for Blacks in the United States generally, Cuffe turned to Africa. In 1811, with a particular interest in emigration possibilities and a labored concern for the destruction of the Atlantic slave trade, Captain Cuffe sailed to the new British West African colony of Sierra Leone. Upon his return to the United States, this devout Quaker concentrated his energy and resources on his intention to stimulate the development of legitimate commerce among Sierra Leone, England, and the United States. It was hoped that this kind of commercial intercourse would accelerate the demise of the slave trade and eventually supplant it. With that in mind, Cuffe became instrumental in the formation of the African Institution of Boston and the Friendly

Society of Sierra Leone. Cuffe also hoped to settle desirable emigrants in West Africa who would aid the growth and development of Sierra Leone while at the same time meliorating the negative image of Africa. His motives, like so many who would later follow his lead, were bound up in the Christianizing–civilizing perception he had of the role that African-Americans would play in Africa.

In December of 1815, Cuffe carried seven pioneering-emigrant families to settle in Sierra Leone, largely at his own expense. After some initial delay and confusion, the emigrants were welcomed by the Governor of Sierra Leone and the group was given fifty acres of land and a year's rations. Cuffe himself remained in Sierra Leone for two months, supervising the new settlement, before returning to the United States in May of 1816. He hoped to lead other contingents of Blacks to Sierra Leone but met an untimely death on September 9, 1817.[3]

The chief organizational effort regarding colonization in Africa was undertaken by the American Colonization Society (ACS) founded during the winter of 1816–1817, by an interesting, seemingly antipodal combination of clergymen and slaveholders. Brought together in what apparently was a marriage of convenience, they sought to inaugurate a private program for the removal of the free Black population from the United States. The motives of these two antithetical groups were allegedly different, but they shared an interest in accomplishing the same end. In any event, the American Colonization Society drew heavily on the experiences of Paul Cuffe and the two unprecedented voyages by a Black from the Americas to West Africa.[4]

The American Colonization Society was beset with controversy from its origin, since Blacks expressed immediate skepticism regarding what they considered its sinister motives.[5] Richard Allen, James Forten, and Absolom Jones, among others, led the denunciation. They charged that force would be used to remove free Blacks from the United States and that the formation of the ACS was inspired by a slaveholder's conspiracy that wanted all free Blacks discharged from the country. The ACS rejoined this excoriation by defending what it considered to be the purity and altruism of its motives. It offered that Paul Cuffe himself had advised them on the organization of the ACS and they produced evidence from Black settlers in Africa confirming the initial success of colonization. Despite the fact that Paul Cuffe and Absolom Jones do appear to have been convinced of some merit in colonization, by and large, free Blacks remained in opposition to the ACS and its efforts to colonize Blacks in Sierra Leone and, later, in Liberia.

The American Colonization Society,[6] like much else in nineteenth century United States, appears to have been rife with paradox. The religious wing is celebrated as a group of unselfish, divinely inspired individuals whose greatest interest was the salvation of Blacks. According to a leading student of the ACS, "the American Colonization Society was not a conspiracy to strengthen the chains of slavery. Colonizationists, like *most* Americans of the early nineteenth century, were troubled by slavery and wished to end it"[7] (emphasis added). Certainly it would be easy enough to be persuaded of the charity of some of the founders of the ACS. At the same time, in examining the statements of some others, clerics especially in this case, it is possible to draw an altogether different conclusion. Samuel J. Mills, chief fund-raiser during the initial period of the ACS, was clearly influenced by what he considered the degradation that the presence of free Blacks brought to American society. Hence, he came to support colonization not from beneficence but because it was his conviction that the moral decay of the United States could only be avoided if Blacks were removed from the presence of Whites. In Mills's view, it was Blacks who provoked the immorality of Whites, but rather than attack the cause of the wickedness (pejorative White attitudes toward Blacks that might have incited further hostility and more immorality by Whites), a few members of the ACS were able to salve their consciences by concentrating on a symptom or consequence of the immorality by promoting the removal of the accused irritant, free Blacks.

"We must save the Negroes *or the Negroes will ruin us*,"[8] opined Mills (emphasis added). Elias B. Caldwell, Secretary of the ACS between 1817 and 1823, was in the same camp as Mills. He declared on one occasion, "It [colonization] was expedient because the free Blacks have a demoralizing influence on our civil institutions."[9] The salvation of White America, in other words, in the opinion of some of these early colonization supporters, was measured in direct proportion to the distance and extent to which free Blacks were removed from the White population. It had little or nothing to do with their humanistic concern for the welfare of free Blacks and the suffering they experienced in the United States. This ideological mind-set had a sizable following and might have been more the rule than it was the exception.

During the first thirty years of the nineteenth century four outstanding Black American nationalists were advocating a return to Africa; Cuffe, John B. Russwurm, Lott Cary and Daniel Coker. Each of these individuals envisioned Black nations emerging in Africa that would symbolize Black progress and exemplify Black nationalism at this time. All except Cuffe played a role in Liberia's early history. Coker, "Dignified in manner, almost regal in appearance, [and] near white in color,"[10] was among the first contingent of eighty-eight African-Americans sent to Liberia by the ACS in 1820. The early years of hardship at Cape Mesurado (of which Liberia was an outgrowth) indicate that Coker eventually assumed the leadership role in the new colony over the White agents of the ACS.

Lott Cary arrived in Liberia with the second group of African-American colonizationists sent there by the ACS in March, 1821. Cary increasingly took on the leadership role in Liberia, occupied earlier by Daniel Coker, in shaping the new settlement. Rev. Cary was a well-to-do Baptist preacher from Richmond, Virginia, who had, decided to abandon the United States in order to preach the gospel to indigenous Africans.[11]

Jamaican-born John B. Russwurm was co-founder of the first Black newspaper in the United States, *Freedom's Journal*

(1827), and is sometimes touted as the first Black college graduate.[12] Like Cuffe, Coker, and Cary, he encouraged emigration to West Africa. Formerly anti-emigration and anti-American Colonization Society, by 1830 Russwurm converted to colonization and departed for Liberia.[13] Between 1830 and 1851, Russwurm held a variety of governmental and private posts in Liberia. He was editor of the *Liberia Herald*,[14] Superintendent of Emigration, and Colonial Secretary. In 1836 he became governor of the Maryland Colony,[15] which was founded by the Maryland Colonization Society in 1834 and was located adjacent to Liberia, with which it merged in 1857. He held the post of governor until his death in 1851.[16]

The twenty-year period 1830–1850 represents a time of ebbing interest both in colonization and Africa among African-Americans. One explanation for this decline was the militant anti-colonization/emigration[17] stand taken by the American Society of Free Persons of Colour early in the 1830s.[18] The Free Black Convention Movement, of which the Society was a vital part, commenced a series of meetings, sometimes annual and sometimes irregular, that lasted until 1864 and then continued after slavery was abolished. Generally the conventions were concerned with the abolition of slavery and improving the lot of free Blacks throughout the United States. A tertiary concern of theirs, however, was mobilizing opposition to the American Colonization Society and discouraging colonization. No pronounced expression of interest in Africa per se emanated from these early conventions, and those who might have held Africa sentiments were understandably reluctant to be more outspoken. They eschewed identification with the Colonization Society out of fear of providing Whites with the necessary ammunition to purge the land of its free Black population.

It was at the Philadelphia convention of 1835 that the question of the continued use of the term "African" came up. During the morning session of June 5, 1835, on the motion of a William Shipper, seconded by Robert Purvis, both delegates from Pennsylvania, it was recommended, insofar as possible, that Blacks in the United States "remove the title of African from their institutions, the marbles of churches and C [*sic*]."[19] At the afternoon session, following a brief debate, the motion was called up and adopted. Ostensibly, this motion suggested that African-Americans at this time decried public identification with Africa. On the other hand, this limited reference to the use of the term "African," a single motion, might indicate that the concern, such as it was, was not persistent or widespread, nor was it acted upon. The use of the term "African" was not discontinued by any major Black American institutions that had adopted it, such as the African Methodist Episcopal (A.M.E.) and African Methodist Episcopal Zion (A.M.E.Z.) churches.

The appearance of "militant abolitionism" by 1831, led by the crafty, celebrated William Lloyd Garrison, is not without significance in this colonization–emigration scenario. Garrison had initially supported colonization but later abandoned the ACS and went on to become an incessant nuisance to the colonization scheme. His *Thoughts on African Colonization* only partially reveals Garrison's enmity for colonization. Using the Society's own publication, *The African Repository*, Garrison effectively disrupted the ideological base of the ACS and uncovered its underlying anti-Black intent. Garrison traveled throughout the eastern and midwestern states hurling assaults at the ACS. Oftentimes he purposely followed spokespersons for colonization to various cities to refute and discredit their claims. This energetic White militant openly challenged and attacked the leadership, aims and motives of the Colonization Society before Black audiences. His forays were especially vitriolic at the 1832 Free Black Convention meeting in Philadelphia. Garrison also used the pages and editorials of *The Liberator* to direct insulting, sometimes savage invective at the Society and often at its Secretary himself, Ralph Gurley.[20] Garrison even carried his vendetta against colonization to England during the summer of 1833, and challenged the Society's agent, Elliot Cresson, who was touring the British Isles on a fund-raising junket, to debate the merits of colonization. Subsequently, Cresson was harried out of

Great Britain when Garrison got wind of his contrivance to recruit British support in an effort to unite Sierra Leone and Liberia in a grandiose "Empire of Liberia."[21]

By the middle of the nineteenth century several events had begun to spark a relative groundswell in emigration sentiment among African-Americans. Of course, emigration still dominated the Africa interest, but now more Blacks than ever before, thoroughly disgusted by all the humiliation they continued to suffer in the United States, began to opt for removal to a land where the heavy hand of the Caucasian would no longer be felt.

The first new attraction for emigration was Liberia's independence in 1847. Here now was a Black Republic in West Africa that stood as an example to Blacks and Whites as well, of the potential capacity for Black people to govern themselves. Liberia therefore epitomized an advanced phase of Black nationalism. There were great expectations for the new Republic that had a "pull" effect among Black Americans, who, heretofore, had wound up in Africa largely as a consequence of the "push" effect. In 1847 there were fifty-one emigrants to Liberia and one year later there were 441, an increase of over 800 percent.[22] Because of what it represented, euphoria over Liberia was widespread but short-lived in the African-American community, and only the most perspicacious of individuals were able to forecast the reverses for Blacks that would come in the next decade.

The earliest example of harder times to come for Blacks in the 1850s and indicative of the "push" effect that drove Blacks reluctantly into the ranks of emigration, was the passage of a new Fugitive Slave Law as part of the Compromise of 1850. It was undeniable evidence of the eroding situation for Blacks who remained in the United States, because it dramatized the possibility that free Blacks could be remanded to bondage wholesale.[23] The law encouraged cooperation in the return of runaways, and created federal commissioners who were empowered to hear all cases and render a decision. Jury trials were ignored for alleged fugitives and the law was *ex post facto* in nature.

Second only to the Fugitive Slave Law for its impact on increasing emigration sentiments during this decade was the Kansas Nebraska Act (1854). This act nullified the earlier Missouri Compromise (1820), that had prohibited slavery's extension into part of the Louisiana Territory. Now reopened was the possibility of slavery's extension by the declaration that the principle of squatter sovereignty would prevail in the Kansas and Nebraska territories. This was a signal to Blacks that in spite of the abolitionist crusade, there would be no early end to slavery in the United States. Some Blacks now felt that the safest place to be was outside the United States. Many went to Canada. Others felt that even Canada was too close and decided on Liberia.

The infamous Dred Scott Decision (1857) and the repercussions from the abortive John Brown's Raid (1859) were the two final episodes, prior to the outbreak of the Civil War, that convinced still more Blacks to abandon the United States for Africa, primarily Liberia. However, the conversion of two important former "stay-at-homes," Martin Delany and Henry H. Garnet, also served to provoke considerable interest in an exodus to West Africa.[24] Delany, the better known of the two, and a kind of "nineteenth century *uomo universale*,"[25] did not at this time support emigration to Liberia but rather to what is now Nigeria. Actually, in 1859 Delany led an exploring party to the Niger Delta and negotiated a treaty with several Egba chiefs in Yorubaland for the cession of land to him as a representative of "the African race of the United States and the Canadas in America."[26] In return for the land, African-Americans were obligated to bring to the Egbas ". . . intelligence, education, a knowledge of the arts and sciences, agriculture and other mechanical and industrial occupations, which they shall put into immediate operation, by improving the lands, and in other useful vocations."[27] Soon after Delany returned to the United States from this West African expedition most, if not all, interest in emigration ceased.[28] The coming of the Civil War was encouraging to Black Americans, who impatiently anticipated the abolition of slavery with a Union victory and an attendant improvement in the quality of life for all Blacks. Delany himself joined the army, recruited Blacks for the Union war effort, and attained the rank of Major before the war ended in 1865. Nevertheless, before he died in 1885 at seventy-three years of age, Martin Delany was once again engaged in an exciting scheme promoting Black emigration beyond the borders of the United States, this time to Liberia. Like many others Delany now knew that the expectation for a better life in the United States would be realized more in the breach than in the observance.

Support for emigration also came from one of Black America's leading clergymen and intellectuals, Alexander Crummell. Crummell was a close associate of Edward W. Blyden, quintessential black intellectual, and during the middle of the nineteenth century both were promoting African-American emigration to Liberia. In the summer of 1861, Crummell and Blyden journeyed from Liberia to the United States in order to make a personal appeal for settlement there.

Crummell was born in 1819 and received his early education in New York, completing secondary school at Oneida Institute in Whitesborough, New York. Like many of his Black contemporaries, he pursued higher education through religious studies one of the very few educational opportunities available to Blacks at this time was training for the ministry. He was ordained a minister in 1844 but was unhappy with the small number of Blacks in the parishes to which he was assigned. By 1853, Crummell had completed his Bachelor of Arts degree at Queens College, Cambridge University (England), and headed for Liberia. He remained in Liberia for twenty years and during that time became very interested in emigration.[29]

Emigration, Crummell argued, would be voluntary and would involve primarily educated and skilled Blacks but would never entail a mass exodus of African-Americans back to Africa. He was not enthusiastic about emigration to areas other than

Liberia but he did not condemn the efforts of other emigrationists such as James T. Holly, Martin Delany, or Henry H. Garnet and his African Civilization Society. Crummell's highest priority was race solidarity, and he therefore believed that fragmented settlement in West Africa or elsewhere would handicap the best efforts of the race.[30] He urged African-Americans to support emigration, missionary efforts, and trade with Africa, all of which had some benefits for the continent, its people, and African-Americans.[31]

Back to Africa

Africa did not significantly return to the consciousness of African-Americans until the "exodus fever" in the South during the late 1870s. The excitement of the Civil War and Reconstruction era had substantially short-circuited the emigration-based Africa interest. However, the failures of this period to improve the Black American condition only threw into bolder relief for some African-Americans the earlier wisdom of a return to Africa. The desperation and persecution of the post-Reconstruction years produced a handful of would-be back-to-Africa aspirants, the most colorful of whom was Benjamin "Pap" Singleton. Singleton, at different times, was advocating flight to Kansas, Liberia, or even Cyprus. Pap Singleton is given credit for leading thousands of southern Blacks into Kansas, but he never realized his Africa plan and died disillusioned and impoverished at eighty-three years of age in 1892.[32]

In 1880 South Carolina was the state with the largest Black population. Indeed, Blacks outnumbered Whites. Because of the sizable free Black population in Charleston before the Civil War, that city was an appealing recruiting center for colonization. Moreover, the argument has been advanced that by dint of South Carolina's "close" proximity to Liberia, its accessibility enhanced its attractiveness as an entrepot for West African settlement.[33] However, emigration sentiments had already been revived before 1880 because of the acute state of recrudescent Black despair following the downfall of the Radical Republican administration. In fact, South Carolina became unofficial headquarters for emigration from the United States to West Africa. Late in the 1870s it was a Black Congressman-minister-newspaperman, Richard H. Cain, who led exodus sentiment. The Liberian Exodus Joint Stock Steamship Company (LEJSSC) was organized to transport Blacks from South Carolina to Liberia, and the aging Martin R. Delany was persuaded to support it. As interest in emigration swelled, there was some opposition from local Whites, who feared the loss of cheap Black labor, but it did not offset the magnetic effect of the preposterous rumors circulating about Liberia. Potatoes were believed to grow large enough to feed an entire family. Sugar, syrup, and bacon could be obtained directly from trees, without the need to be processed, and cooking was done by the heat from the sun.[34] In 1878, the Liberian Exodus Joint Stock Steamship Company vessel *Azor*, with 206 emigrants aboard (two hundred were left behind because the ship was overloaded), sailed for Liberia. The voyage, like others to come in the 1890s and early part of the twentieth century, was plagued by disease, disappointment, deception, and some trouble in West Africa—especially Sierra Leone. Some emigrants died, some returned disgruntled to the United States, and some others enjoyed the "promised land" success that prompted them to head for Liberia in the first place. There were plans by the LEJSSC to send out another shipload of Black settlers to Liberia but these were never realized. The project eventually was destroyed by the accumulation of unanticipated debts, relentless pressure from creditors, adverse propaganda from the press, and by lengthy and devious litigation. This South Carolina exodus, nevertheless, represents the first organized effort in the post-Civil War period independent of the American Colonization Society to settle African-Americans in Liberia. It set the precedent, in a sense, for several other back-to-Africa movements that would follow. Not the least important of these was the effort led by the dynamic Henry McNeal Turner.

The penultimate decade of the nineteenth century, much like the decade 1850–1860, represented incertitude and despair for Black Americans. This ten-year period, and beyond, was characterized by widespread intimidation, violence, race discrimination, penury, and the *coup de grace* for many Blacks—systematic, legal, and constitutional disfranchisement. The infamous Mississippi Plan of 1890, race demagogery, the Convict Lease System, and the onerous Plessy decision all occurred in this period. Consequently, it should come as no surprise that this was an era of increased interest in emigration to Africa. This period produced the back-to-Africa movement's most eloquent United States-born exponent, Bishop Turner. Under Turner's influence, interest in emigration escalated and continued to dominate the Africa interest from 1890 to the close of the century.

Bishop Turner occupies a position of special significance in the history of African-American interaction with Africa.[35] He was a man of character, zeal, energy, influence and intelligence. He was also an uncompromising critic of the United States and its failure to protect and provide for the interests and needs of its Black citizens, which made him both compelling and galling. He would not hesitate to smite the canard of what he considered the failures of American duplicity or its apologists "scullion Blacks." It would be a mistake to conclude that Bishop Turner's concerns were exclusively Africa or emigration—his domestic interests and activities were substantial indeed. But once he swung over to emigration he did not falter in his insistence that a return to Africa, preferably to Liberia, offered the best possibility for Black Americans ever achieving national identity, dignity, and self-determination.

Turner was born free in South Carolina in 1834. Around mid-century he was a traveling evangelist for the Methodist Church in the South, where he made quite a name for himself. Upon discovering the existence of the Black-controlled African Methodist Episcopal Church, he immediately joined it. During the Civil War he recruited Black troops to fight for the Union and became the first Black chaplin to serve in the United States Army. During Reconstruction, Turner saw duty with the Freedman's Bureau and was very active in Georgia politics. By the time Reconstruction ended, Turner was devoting most of his time, effort, and energy to church work. In 1880 he was elevated to the position of Bishop in the A.M.E. Church, a position he held with ever-increasing influence until his death in 1915. Bishop Turner, made four separate visits to Africa, in 1891, 1893, 1895, and 1898. He never settled in Africa and he gave credit for his transformation to promoting African-American emigration to Africa to another veteran emigrationist from the United States, the Rev. Alexander Crummell.

Interestingly, Bishop Turner accepted a position as honorary Vice President of the American Colonization Society even though he was aware of the fact that the Society was rebuked by many Blacks who questioned its motives. He was also at his oratorical best articulating the reasons why emigration was the best solution for the problems confronting Blacks in a White-dominated United States. Turner added currency to his emigration argument by directly attacking the injustices Blacks faced in the land of his birth. Sometimes Turner was contradictory; at other times he was condescending and paternalistic toward Africa. Often he was even presumptuous and ill-informed. On occasion he was guilty of perpetuating pseudo-scientific notions about race, and his remarks were frequently couched in the platitudes of the day. Turner stated more than once that "American Negroes were made up of the most inferior portion of the African tribes, and that no 'big blood,' first class Africans had been sold to Europeans during the slave trade, only small blood, second class ones."[36] Black Americans, he also remarked, "were the tail-end of the African races."[37] Yet he would come right back supporting the position that the uplift and resurgence of Africa would be led by African-Americans. Apparently he was unable to appreciate this inconsistency or he used this irreconcilable argument for tactical or strategic reasons, or in response to one detractor or another.

Bishop Turner's fascination with Africa, unlike some of his contemporaries, went far beyond the sentimental to the active. In his relentless pursuit of translating ideas into action, Turner headed for Africa in 1891. His mission to Africa was supported by funds from the A.M.E. Church and his objective was to establish new A.M.E. churches as well as to assist with the organization and administration of existing ones in Sierra Leone and Liberia. When he went to South Africa in 1898 he set a precedent by ordaining African ministers, a privilege theretofore reserved for White clergymen. In general, Africa confirmed and even on occasion surpassed the Bishop's expectations. What he saw in Africa was in concord with this romanticized African dream, although there were a few times when he reflected disappointment in Africa and Africans. Most of the time, however, Turner managed to conceal or subordinate any disappointment he had with Africa. Following his visits he wrote letters to the *Christian Recorder* and other periodicals, which revealed, in hyperbolic terms, his satisfaction with his experiences and observations in Africa. To Turner, Liberia in particular, after having visited it was "one of the most paradisical portions of the earth my eyes ever beheld."[38] The United States could not compare with Liberia, Turner felt, and "any man who would run down Liberia . . . is a fool and an ass; I am not talking about what I have heard either, I am speaking of what I have seen with my own eyes."[39]

The active phase of Bishop Turner's romance with Africa included his enthusiastic support for the ephemeral Afro-American Steamship Company (AASC) headed by a Daniel E. Johnson. His major interest in the AASC was to establish regular steamship routes between Africa and the United States which to him was essential for the renascence of Africa. The *Voice of Missions* was launched in January, 1893 and although it was supposed to be a publication to promote church activities it quickly became Turner's personal forum for broadcasting African emigration propaganda. After Bishop Turner's second visit to West Africa, a visit which sharpened his perceptions about Africa, he sent out a call for a National Black Convention. This was the last convention of the century to consider the desirability of emigration. The convention delegates, mainly northern middle-class Blacks, did not confirm Turner's interest in emigration to Africa, notwithstanding individual statements of qualified support from Black notables such as Ida B. Wells, P.B.S. Pinchback, and John Mercer Langston. Turner's spirits must have been dampened, but this setback did not noticeably affect his zeal for emigration or Liberia. He returned from this Cincinnati convention to his home in Atlanta, proclaiming that "at least two million of colored people here in the South are ready to start to Africa at any moment."[40]

In 1894 Bishop Turner's persistence in seeking to establish a steamship line between the United States and Africa began to reap some dividends. It took the backing of four White Alabama businessmen, but the International Migration Society was announced to the world in January. Support from the veteran American Colonization Society was invited immediately. During its five years of existence, the International Migration Society generated an unparalleled amount of excitement for emigration. After an auspicious start it was hamstrung by a paucity of funds and opposition from middle-class, stay-at-home Blacks, who by now included two former advocates of emigration, Alexander Crummell and Edward W. Blyden. The critics crowded one upon the other, foretelling of troublous times for those who joined the ranks of emigration. Bishop Turner was more than equal to the task of flailing one critic after another as interest in emigration continued to grow. When the steamship *Horsa* sailed for Liberia with a shipload of two hundred emigrants on March 19, 1894 it signaled a long-awaited victory for emigration and a personal triumph for emigration's most resolute supporter. The publicity attending the departure of the *Horsa* was a boon to emigration and its critics were stunned and silent, momentarily. When the dust cleared and the opposition regrouped, they had merely been recharged for stepping up anti-emigration activity. Attempts were made to discredit the International Migration

Society. The Black press threw the weight of its influence behind anti-emigration sentiment and circulated the disgruntled complaints of some *Horsa* passengers. Despite the opposition, which by now had recruited none other than Booker T. Washington, plans for the sailing of a second steamship, the 1,200 ton *Laurada*, were announced; within two years of the *Horsa's* departure, on March 2, 1896, the *Laurada* steamed out of Savannah, Georgia, with a second contingent of 321 emigrants headed for Liberia. Liberia never did meet all of the expectations of these wide-eyed escapees from the United States. There were shortages in rations, general discontent, disease, and some deaths which prompted a modified reverse exodus to the United States later in 1896. The International Migration Society, Bishop Turner, and even the American Colonization Society attempted to explain away and apologize for the condemnation of the returnees. But the frequently exaggerated, slanderous reports of those who returned, combined with traditional opposition and the coming of the Spanish-American War, sounded the death-knell for this phase of the Africa interest and emigration. For all intents and purposes, by December 1899 the International Migration Society was dead. However, Bishop Turner was still very much alive and full of industry. In 1900 he spearheaded the formation of the Colored National Emigration Association to promote commerce and emigration to Africa. He lost some of his energy in his twilight years (but none of his enthusiasm), and right up until his death in 1915 he continued to be Africa's champion.

African-American interaction with Africa in the nineteenth century was monopolized by one kind of emigration/ colonization scheme or another. Prior to 1865 the views of Black America were articulated mainly by the small class of free Blacks in places like New Orleans, Louisiana; Charleston, South Carolina; Washington, D.C. or Philadelphia, Pennsylvania. Outside of the few free Blacks returning to West Africa and a handful of Black missionaries evangelizing there, little other evidence of interaction with Africa is identifiable. And given the

nature of the slave system in the United States South, the
isolation of slaves who by now had mostly been born in the
United States, and the high percentage of illiteracy, it is most
difficult if not impossible to measure the level of Africa
consciousness among that population. After the Civil War this
same pattern continued with some slight modifications. Of
course, slavery was outlawed, but Blacks remained relatively
isolated as sharecroppers, tenant farmers, and crop lieners in the
South. The illiteracy rate remained high and the periodic efforts
by some Blacks to get back to Africa punctuated the Africa
interest. The articulate few, as before, claimed to represent the
views of the inarticulate many. Insofar as African-American
letters were concerned, between Phyllis Wheatley and Paul
Lawrence Dunbar, the protest genre was outstanding and the ex-
slave autobiographies and other literature were very important,
but despite the publication of such books as *Blake; or The Huts of
Africa* and other works, there was little of major consequence
regarding intense Africa interest.

Missionary Interest

In the nineteenth century the missionary interest in Africa
was subordinate to emigration interest. White and Black
churches did not begin in earnest to evangelize in Africa until
after the Civil War. However, there is evidence that a few Blacks
in the United States hoped to Christianize Africans as far back as
the last quarter of the eighteenth century. These Blacks wanted
to share their religion and their view of a better life through
religion, with Africans. One early Black missionary in Africa was
sent out in 1787 to what became Liberia by the Rev. Samuel
Hopkins of Newport, Rhode Island.[41] David George organized a
Baptist church in Sierra Leone in 1792, and Lott Carey, the
prudent Virginian, was a Baptist minister in West Africa in the
1830s and '40s. Daniel Coker was a leading exponent of
Methodism in Sierra Leone and Liberia in the 1820s.[42]

At the time of the outbreak of the Civil War, the versatile Episcopalian Divine, Alexander Crummell, was also a peerless exponent of the Black missionary obligation to Africa. He believed that it was the responsibility of westernized Blacks, more than anyone else, to take the lead in the regeneration of Africa. "It is the duty of Black men to feel and labor for the salvation of the mighty millions of their kin all through the continent," stated Crummell.[43] He expounded on this role repeatedly because he saw African-Americans as the agents of Africa's second rise.[44]

Commerce and Christianity, according to Crummell, would bring civilization and prosperity to Liberia and Africa. Crummell argued further that "New World" Blacks should initiate trade between Africa and America, and Black American missionaries should help lift the hinterland out of the depths of "paganism" and bring them up to the prevailing world standard of civilization through Christianity.[45] Like Martin Delany, Alexander Crummell believed that a serious blow could be dealt to slavery in the United States by underselling southern cotton on the world market.

Some of the early assumptions about Black missionaries in Africa vis-à-vis Whites tended to favor the presence of African-Americans on the continent. Black and White missionaries believed, for example, that Black Americans were better able to withstand the ravages of climate and diseases unique to Africa. Moreover, there was the feeling that the commonality of Blackness would make the Gospel more welcome in Africa if preached by other Blacks. However, by the last quarter of the nineteenth century the fear began to grow among White settlers in Africa and colonial officers that Black missionaries were "subversives." It was the activities of the African Methodist Episcopal (A.M.E.) and African Methodist Episcopal Zion (A.M.E. Zion) churches that provoked accusations of politicizing or radicalizing Africans, charges that were largely unfounded. However, the very presence of Black missionaries in Africa alone, much like the presence of free Blacks in the antebellum

South, inspired unrest among Africans and slaves alike. The missionaries were symbols of available opportunities if and when European control over Africans was eliminated. Nevertheless, the charges of political organizing and stirring up revolt were generalized to include all Black missionaries in Africa regardless of denomination and whether they were sponsored by White or Black mission boards.

The first decades of the nineteenth century represent a period of expansion in foreign mission for the three most important independent Black churches; the A.M.E., A.M.E. Zion, and the Black Baptist Church. They did not, however, enjoy as many successes as they hoped for in converting Africans to Christianity. In the United States, Black missionaries became the most important disseminators of information about Africa. They kept the Africa interest alive. Black missionaries returned to the United States following service in Africa and told of their experiences. They sought continued and increased support for Africa missions. And while underscoring the racial, cultural, and political linkages between Africans and African-Americans, the missionaries did the most to persuade Black America that Africa deserved both their interest and consideration.[46]

Intellectual Interest

Who were the first Black intellectuals of the nineteenth century? The first Black colleges in the United States were not founded until after the Civil War. By 1900 there were approximately two thousand Black college graduates out of an estimated total Black population of eight million. If the intellectuals were journalists and educators who served as spokespersons for the race, then people like Frederick Douglass, George Washington Williams, Alexander Crummell, and Booker T. Washington figured prominently among them. Essentially, the Black intellectual's attitude toward Africa was little different from that of the masses of Blacks. By and large the general view of Africa was negative or indifferent, but there were Blacks at both extremes,—those who vehemently rejected any association with Africa at one end, and Blacks who espoused genuine pride in Africa and their African ancestry at the other end.[47] Frederick Douglass was the best-known Black leader up to his death in 1895, and it has been suggested that he held "a strong anti-African bias."[48] He flirted with support of the possibility of African-American emigration from the United States in the 1850s but it was removal to the Caribbean that he remotely considered. Africa was out of the question because to him it was merely a "foreign land." Always a staunch advocate of integration, he considered the United States to be the native land of Black Americans. However, Douglass has been partly misunderstood. He was not as much anti-Africa as he was anti-emigration or pro-United States. His position was that the Black struggle in the United States was paramount and that the removal of eight million Blacks from the United States to Africa was simply impractical. He felt that African-Americans owed no more to Africans than Africans owed to their brothers and sisters in the United States. There were needy millions in both locations. Finally, on one occasion at least, he identified the plight of Africans with that of African-Americans and noted in a Pan-African sense that "a blow struck successfully for the Negro in America, is a blow struck for the Negro in Africa."[49]

Alexander Crummell was not only an advocate of selective emigration and Christianization in Africa, as noted earlier, but, anticipating some twentieth century Black intellectuals, he was also a defender of Africa. His most important ideas in this regard are incorporated into his collection of sermons, speeches, and addresses, published as *The Future of Africa* and *Africa and America*. Crummell was especially vigorous in his support for Liberia, which he exclaimed was a "marvel of modern history . . . little short of a miracle."[50] Experiencing only pride in his unmixed African ancestry, Crummell was aware of the past greatness of his race, which he felt Europeans ignored, and he believed in its future greatness. In his "Hope for Africa,"[51]

Crummell recounted the brutality of the slave trade, stating that "from 1562, down to the commencement of this century, the dark and bloody history of Africa was lengthened out and prolonged. . . ."[52] However, during the first fifty years of the nineteenth century, Crummell claimed, "all this history is being reversed."[53] He appealed for recognition of the "civil and religious" improvements made in Africa and the "religious solicitude" Africans manifested. "All of this progress has taken place during the short period of fifty years."[54]

George Washington Williams, another late nineteenth century Black intellectual, was concerned about Africa, too. Williams was the first major Black American historian and has to his credit the two-volume *History of the Negro Race in America* (1883) and his *History of the Negro Troops in the War of the Rebellion*. In his first work, Williams showed contempt for Africa and explained Africa's "fall from a high state of civilization" as "forgetfulness of God."[55] Williams had earlier delivered the class oration at Newton Theological Seminary in Newton Center, Massachusetts, from which he graduated in 1874. His address was entitled "Early Christianity in Africa"[56] and was suggestive of his familiarity with an interest in Africa, that continued throughout his life. In 1890 Williams was commissioned by *McClure's* magazine to do a series of articles on Africa. Despite the protests of King Leopold and the Belgians, who feared his visiting the Congo would expose their wickedness toward Africans, he sailed for West Africa. He made stops in many colonies and locations in West Africa and was distressed with the selfishness and oppressive rule of Americo-Liberians. His next stop was the Congo, where he was very critical of what he observed. He publicly denounced King Leopold for the cruel exploitation of the Congolese, stating that, "All the crimes perpetrated in the Congo have been done in your [Leopold's] name. . . ."[57] Before he completed his African journey, that also took him to Angola, around the Cape of Good Hope, up the coast of East Africa, and to Zanzibar, Williams was exclaiming "Africa for the Africans" and advocating United States support for a Congo Free State, that he hoped would bring independence and self-respect to the people of the Congo.[58]

The most important and arguably most influential Black intellectual of the nineteenth century was not an African-American but West Indies (St. Thomas) born Edward Wilmot Blyden. Blyden was a prolific writer and erudite vindicator of the Black race, who spent most of his life in Liberia and Sierra Leone. As a litterateur, educator, theologian, politician, statesman, diplomat, and explorer, varying roles he crowded into his eighty-eight years, Edward Blyden made an impact on the world of ideas far greater than any of his nineteenth century Black contemporaries. He has been called, by the most competent student of his Pan-African ideas, "easily the most learned and articulate champion of Africans and the Negro race in his own time."[59] Blyden was a one of a handful of Blacks to command the attention of the English-speaking academic and literary world in the previous century. He influenced the ideas of Black America's leading intellectuals from Alexander Crummell and Frederick Douglass to George Washington Williams to Booker T. Washington to his twentieth century counterpart, W.E.B. DuBois. Race vindication was the basic intent of most of Blyden's writings and his themes usually included the glorification of the past achievements of the Black race, accentuating Black pride and the advocacy of a distinct "African personality," the preservation of African culture, and the salutary effect of Islam on Blacks compared with the retarding effect of Christianity. Much of the credit for exploding the myth of African backwardness and Black inferiority belongs directly to Blyden's writings or indirectly to his influence on Black and White thinkers alike.

Congress on Africa

The major conference on Africa in the nineteenth century was sponsored by the Stewart Foundation for Africa,[60] based in

Atlanta, Georgia. This Congress on Africa (1895)[61] was held in conjunction with the better-known Cotton States and International Exposition, at which Booker T. Washington delivered his "Atlanta Compromise" address. The Congress was depicted as "the most distinguished gathering of learned men of both colors that has ever assembled together within the history of the South"[62] and, to be sure, it had an impressive list of speakers, including several Africans and African-Americans: Orishetukeh Faduma from Sierra Leone; Etna Holderness from the Bassa peoples (Liberia); Alexander Crummell, presented in the program as, "Twenty Years Missionary in Africa"; the Honorable John H. Smythe, former Minister to Liberia; Bishop Henry M. Turner, representing the A.M.E. Church; and Timothy Thomas Fortune, activist, businessman, and editor of one of the leading Black newspapers in the United States at this time, the New York *Age*. Edward Wilmot Blyden, intellectual potentate of proto-Pan-African thought, was unable to attend because of failing health but sent his letter of "Greeting and Commendation."

The Congress was originally planned for April 22–30, 1896,[63] but was evidently moved up to December 1895 in order to take advantage of the large gathering expected for the Cotton States Exposition. The rationale for the Congress was to make available in the South, especially for Blacks, reliable information about Africa. African-Americans, it seems, were the worst victims of mis-conceptions and biased information regarding their ancestral homeland. This Congress on Africa intended, through the missionary impulse, to shed brand new light on the much maligned "dark continent." The upshot of this crude scenario was that most of the misinformation vis-à-vis Africa up to the 1890's can be traced to the same components exalted at the Congress as the new disseminators of fresh, accurate information about Africa. This included missionaries setting forth their prejudiced perceptions of African religious life, travelers–adventurers personally describing what they saw in Africa (or thought they saw) with no apparent constraint on hyperbole or exaggeration, and pseudo-scholars, with characteristic intellectual arrogance, proclaiming themselves as absolute authorities on Africa. Now enticed into joining this drama were the sons and daughters of Africa living in the United States, who some claimed—because of the "blessings" of their Western experience—were primed and ready to participate in, and even lead, the crusade for Africa's "emancipation from heathenism".

The Congress was held from Friday through Sunday, December 13–15, 1895, and the sessions were divided between the Lloyd Street Methodist Episcopal Church, Bethel A.M.E. Church, and Moody Tabernacle, all in Atlanta, Georgia. Rev. J.W.E. Bowen, who later became Vice President of Gammon Theological Seminary (and its first Black officer), was selected Secretary of the Congress. Although no record was found of the numbers in attendance, audiences were described by Rev. Bowen as "large," and "vast," and he states that the "vestibules, and even sidewalks . . .was banked with a mass of anxious humanity."[64] Each of the nine sessions (three per day) was devoted almost exclusively to the reading of papers on subjects dealing with Africa and African-Americans.

Some of the remarks made at the Congress were rather startling. Blyden, in his "Greeting and Commendation" noted that the Ashanti chiefs, whom he called "refractory," were recently admonished for eschewing "progress and development" and opposing "efforts for the amelioration of the condition of their people." He considered it the duty of a "superior" civilization to assist an "inferior" one and applauded the "Providential agencies" engaged in the magnificent work of Africa's regeneration.[65] Faduma, the Yale-trained Yoruba, indicated some "drawbacks" to missionary work in Africa but he appeared to subordinate these to the "successes," among which he listed exploration (including exploration in the Congo, where the pernicious Leopold was described as having a "broad heart"), commerce, and "a third tribute to missionary success. . . the partition of Africa among foreign nations."[66]

The Honorable J.H. Smythe, in his paper, "The African in America and the American in Africa" made frequent references to what now could easily be called the Pan-African idea. Smythe especially identified the racial commonality of Black people and their collective struggles which transcended geographical boundaries. Typical of the thought which pervaded his essay is this one excerpt,

> If I have . . . created in you a preference for your race before all other races; and this sentiment, if produced, will place you *en rapport* with the Negroes in Africa, who have no conception of any land, greater, more beautiful than their own; any men braver and manlier than themselves, any women better, lovlier, and handsomer than African women, then you will retire from this place with a feeling of stimulus rather than satiety, of unrest rather than repose; then shall I retire from my effort to interest you in Africa, and Africa in America with satisfied pride in having performed something of duty as a Negro—clear in his conviction of the high density in reserve for Africa and its races, and of your duty to be loyal to your race, since true allegiance will make us sharers in that glory which the sacred writing declares shall come when Ethiopia shall stretch forth her hand unto God.[67]

The Rev. M.C.B. Mason generated some enthusiasm among the Congress sponsors, the Stewart Foundation, by repeating a theme familiar to them and consonant with their own design for missionary work in Africa—that African-Americans, by virtue of their ability to resist the ravages of African fever, were best suited for evangelical work in Africa. Whites could not readily adapt to the unhealthy, deadly climate in Africa, notwithstanding their willingness to risk death for Africa's salvation. Consequently, Whites were less desirable than Africans and Black Americans. Mason made it clear that his plea was not for emigration to Africa and hastened to add that he did not believe in the divinity of slavery, declaring that "a system so cruel, so degrading, so inhuman, so barbarous was not God's, his hand never directed it, his eye never approved it."[68] Black people in America were obligated, he went on, to African evangelization: ". . . the obligation is by racial affinity, by providential preparation, which did not include slavery, by special adaptation and by divine command. . ."[69]

Bishop Turner, the complex A.M.E. militant-nationalist-emigrationist, was absent when his paper was scheduled to be delivered. However, the paper, entitled "The American Negro and His Fatherland," was read by the pastor of Bethel African Methodist Episcopal Church in Atlanta. Turner's remarks sidestepped his customary denunciation of the United States and suggested that African-Americans were brought to the United States by divine forces in order to "have direct contact with the mightiest race that ever trod the face of the globe."[70] In his own special brand of convoluted logic Turner argued that Europeans did not *steal* African-Americans from Africa, rather, Europeans *rescued* Africans, now in the United States, from brutal slavery still extant on the continent. Blacks remained in slavery in the South until they discovered that God was indeed supreme and could be found through faith in Jesus Christ. Emancipation came and the Black American was "thrown upon his own responsibility." Turner then switched back to more familiar terrain, "There is no manhood future in the United States for the Negro." Following this line was an even more familiar thesis.

He argued impatiently for African-American abandonment of the United States, which consumed, with caustic epithets, the remainder of his paper.

> . . . I believe that two or three million of us should return to the land of our ancestors, and establish our own nation, civilization, laws, customs, style of manufacture, and not only give the world, like other race varieties, the benefit of our individuality, but build up social conditions peculiarly our own, and cease to be grumblers, chronic complainers and a menace to the white man's country, or the country he claims to be bound to dominate.[71]

The 1895 Congress on Africa, more than anything else, was an intellectual exercise, with Africa's people, history, culture and potential, as the principal attraction. As such, there was little observable follow-up. Moreover, it is difficult to assess its ideological impact because the extent to which it fulfilled its purpose of "awakening a deeper interest among our students and people in [sic] behalf of the evangelization of the Dark Continent"[72] is hard to measure. However, more missionaries did join the "African field" after this Congress and it seems they were more knowledgeable about Africa.[73] In addition, the low-burning flame of interest in and interaction with Africa was kept alive, if only among a select group. The Congress also influenced the Africa work of most Protestant denominations in the United States that had foreign missions programs on the continent. These included mainly the Methodists, Baptists, and, to a lesser extent the Presbyterians.[74]

African-Americans' interest in Africa during the nineteenth century was selective but continuous. Africa had its champions and detractors. There were back-to-Africa zealots and stay-at-homes. When the twentieth century arrived, the degree of the Africa interest changed as well as the substance. One important manifestation of the early twentieth century interest was an immediate increase in the number of the African-American intellectuals who felt the need to come to Africa's aid.

NOTES

1. The term "African-American" as used in this study refers to people of African descent in the United States. This clarification is made necessary by the fact that many people of African descent from other parts of the Americas—Colombia, Venezuela, Brazil, and elsewhere—also identify themselves as African-Americans. The point is, there should be no presumption that "African-American" *always* refers to

Blacks from the United States. In addition, the term "race," except when quoted from other sources, is used by the author of this book in a broad social (not scientific) context and as a synonym for skin color purely for the sake of simplicity and convenience.

2. John Hope Franklin, "George Washington Williams and Africa," in *Africa and the Afro-American Experience* (Washington, D.C., 1973), history department, Howard University, 16; Floyd J. Miller, *The Search for a Black Nationality: Black Colonization and Emigration 1787–1863* (Urbana, Illinois, 1975), viii.

3. The Paul Cuffe Manuscripts are housed in the New Bedford, Massachusetts Public Library. A two-reel microfilm set of the Cuffe collection is available for a fee. An old but helpful biography of Cuffe is Henry Noble Sherwood, "Paul Cuffe," *Journal of Negro History* (April, 1923), 153–229. Two more recent biographies of Cuffe are George Salvador, *Paul Cuffe: The Black Yankee* (New Bedford, Mass., 1969) and Sheldon Harris, *Paul Cuffe: Black American and the Africa Return* (New York, 1972).

4. Henry Noble Sherwood, "Paul Cuffe and His Contribution to the American Colonization Society," *Proceedings of the Mississippi Valley Historical Association for the Year 1912–1913*, VI (1913), 370–402.

5. Louis Mehlinger, "Attitude of the Free Negro Toward African Colonization," *Journal of Negro History* (July, 1916), 271–301; Leon Litwack, *North of Slavery* (Chicago, 1961), 2–29, *passim*; Bill McAdoo, "Pre-Civil War Black Nationalism," *Progressive Labor* (June–July, 1966), 36–38.

6. An excellent study of the American Colonization Society is P.J. Staudenraus, *The African Colonization Movement, 1816–1865* (New York, 1961). Dated but useful is Early Lee Fox, *The American Colonization Society, 1817–1840* (Baltimore, 1919).

7. Staudenraus, *The African*, "Preface," vii.

8. Thomas C. Richards, *Samuel J. Mills, Missionary, Pathfinder, Pioneer and Promoter* (Boston, 1906), 190–191.

9. Quoted from Henry Noble Sherwood, "The Formation of the American Colonization Society," *Journal of Negro History* (July, 1917), 222.

10. Miller, *The Search*, 58.

11. For more detail on the activities of Coker and Cary in Liberia *Ibid.*, 54–57.

12. Russwurm was actually second, by two weeks, to Edward Jones who graduated from Amherst. See Benjamin Quarles, *Black Abolitionists* (New York, 1969), 113.

13. Carter G. Woodson, *The Mind of the Negro as Reflected in Letters Written During the Crisis, 1800–1860* (Washington, D.C., 1926), 160–161 ff. For an example of Russwurm's pre-1830 position, see his letter to R.R. Gurley of the American Colonization Society, dated February 26, 1827, Woodson, *The Mind*, 3.

14. Russwurm is often given credit for founding the *Liberia Herald*. This is unlikely. It is probably more likely that Russwurm "revived" rather than founded this Liberian newspaper. See Staudenraus, *The African*, 167–168, 191.

15. Several other auxiliaries of the ACS founded their own colonies in Africa including New York, Pennsylvania and Mississippi. Information on the latter three colonies in Africa can be found in the American Colonization Society papers housed at the Manuscripts Division of the Library of Congress. For the Maryland Colony, see the study by Penelope Campbell, *Maryland in Africa: The Maryland State Colonization Society, 1831–1857* (Urbana, Illinois, 1971).

16. For a short account of Russwurm's life, see William Brewer, "John B. Russwurm," *Journal of Negro History* (January, 1928), 36–52; see also Miller, *The Search*, 84–90.

17. The terms "emigration" and "colonization" are sometimes used interchangeably. For purposes of this study, colonization refers to a program of resettlement of Blacks in West Africa or elsewhere not initiated by Blacks, even though those resettled individuals might have gone voluntarily, particularly in reference to the activities of the ACS. Emigration refers to the efforts of Blacks to initiate voluntary settlement in West Africa or elsewhere, regardless of the sources of their support and motives for that support. These distinctions are discussed further in Howard Bell, *A Survey of the Negro Convention Movement 1830–1861* (New York, 1970).

18. *Ibid.*

19. "Minutes of the Fifth Annual Convention for the Improvement of the Free People of Colour in the United States," Howard Bell (ed.)

Minutes of the Proceedings of the National Negro Conventions, 1830–1864 (New York, 1969), 14–15.

20. *The Liberator* (April 23, 1831), (July 9, 1831), (July 20, 1831), (November 19, 1831).

21. Staudenraus, *The African*, 216–219.

22. American Colonization Society, *Fifty-Second Annual Report* (Washington, D.C., 1869), 53.

23. Benjamin Quarles, *Black Abolitionists* (New York, 1969), chapter 9.

24. Robert Weisbord, *Ebony Kinship: Africa, Africans and the Afro-American* (Westport, Connecticut, 1973), 19–20.

25. *Ibid.*, 20.

26. A.H.M. Kirk-Greene, "America in the Niger Valley: A Colonization Centenary," *Phylon* (Fall, 1962), 235.

27. Martin R. Delany, "Report of the Niger Valley Exploring Party" in Martin Delany and Robert Campbell, *Search for a Place: Black Separatism and Africa, 1860* (rprt. Ann Arbor, Michigan, 1969), 77–78.

28. For a discussion of African-American and "New World" Africa interest before the Civil War, see Hollis R. Lynch, "Pan-Negro Nationalism in the New World Before 1862," *Boston University Papers on Africa*, Vol. 2, *African History* (1966), 149–179, reprinted in several anthologies on African-American history.

29. For introductions to Crummell's life see W.E.B. DuBois, "Of Alexander Crummell," *The Souls of Black Folk* (rprt. New York, 1965), 157–165; Kathleen O'Mara Wahle, "Alexander Crummell: Black Evangelist and Pan-Negro Nationalist," *Phylon* (Winter, 1968), 388–395; William H. Ferris, *Alexander Crummell* (Washington, D.C., 1920); Wilson J. Moses, "Civilizing Missionary: A Study of Alexander Crummell," *Journal of Negro History* (April, 1975), 229–251.

30. "Emigration and Aid to the Evangelization of Africa," in Alexander Crummell, *Africa and America* (Springfield, Massachusetts, 1891), 406–428.

31. Alexander Crummell, *The Relations and Duties of the Free Colored Men in America to Africa* (Hartford, Connecticut, 1861), 27.

32. On Singleton, see Roy Garvin, "Benjamin or 'Pap' Singleton and His Followers," *Journal of Negro History* (January, 1948), 7–23;

Walter Fleming, "Pap Singleton, The Moses of the Colored Exodus," *American Journal of Sociology* (July, 1909), 61–82. The book on the Kansas migration is Nell Irvin Painter, *Exodusters: Black Migration to Kansas after Reconstruction* (Lawrence, Kansas, 1986).

33. George Tindall, *South Carolina Negroes* (Columbia, South Carolina, 1952), chapter 8.

34. *Ibid.*

35. Important discussions of Bishop Turner, for whom there is no major full-length biography, can be found in Mungo Ponton, *The Life and Times of Henry M. Turner* (Atlanta, 1917); Minton Batten, "Henry M. Turner, Negro Bishop Extraordinary," *Church History* (September, 1938), 231–246; E. Merton Coulter, "Henry M. Turner: Georgia Negro Preacher-Politician During the Reconstruction Era," *Georgia Historical Quarterly* (December, 1964), 371–410; Edwin Redkey, "Bishop Turner's African Dream," *Journal of American History* (September, 1967), 271–290; id., *Black Exodus* (New Haven, 1969); and Carol Page, "Henry McNeal Turner and the Ethiopian Movement in South Africa, 1896–1904," M.A. thesis, Roosevelt University, Chicago, Illinois, 1973.

36. Edwin Redkey (ed.), *Respect Black: The Writings and Speeches of Henry McNeal Turner* (New York, 1971), 124.

37. *African Repository* (July, 1876), 83.

38. Redkey, (ed.), *Respect Black*, 117.

39. *Ibid.*, 119.

40. *Voice of Missions* (January, 1894), 1–2.

41. Drake, "Negro Americans . . .," 668n.

42. Franklin, "George Washington Williams . . .," 18; for Daniel Coker, see the *Journal of Daniel Coker, a Descendent of Africa* (Baltimore, 1820).

43. Alexander Crummell, *The Relations and Duties of the Free Colored Men in America to Africa* (Hartford, Connecticut, 1861), 36.

44. See especially, "The Regeneration of Africa," in Alexander Crummell, *Africa and America*, 433–453.

45. *Ibid.*

46. Franklin, "George Washington Williams . . .," 18; Drake, "Negro Americans . . .," 670–671; Walter Williams, "The Rise of the African Missions Movement in Black American Churches, 1877–1900,"

paper presented at the Annual Meeting of the Organization of American Historians, April, 1975, 14–16.

47. August Meier and Elliot Rudwick, *From Plantation to Ghetto: An Interpretive History of American Negroes* (New York, 1966), 2–3; Walter Williams, "Black American Attitudes Toward Africa, 1877–1900," *Pan African Journal* (Spring, 1971), 189–190; Bernard Magubane, "The American Negro's Conception of Africa: A Study in the Ideology of Pride and Prejudice," Ph.D. dissertation, U.C.L.A., 1967, 66–71.

48. Williams, "Black American Attitudes . . .," 175.

49. Philip Foner (ed.), *The Life and Writings of Frederick Douglass* (New York, 1955), iv, 513; Nathan Irvin Huggins, *Slave and Citizen: The Life of Frederick Douglass* (Boston, 1980).

50. Crummell, *Africa and America*, vii.

51. In Alexander Crummell, *The Future of Africa* (New York, 1862), 285–323.

52. *Ibid.*, 307.

53. *Ibid.*, 308.

54. *Ibid.*, 306.

55. Williams, *History*, I, 24; also chapters 4 and 11. See also Walter Williams, "Black American Attitudes . . .," *Pan-African Journal*, 177–178.

56. Reprinted in Williams, *History*, I, 111–114.

57. Quoted in Franklin, "George Washington Williams . . . ," 26.

58. *Ibid.*, 28–29.

59. Hollis R. Lynch, *Edward Wilmot Blyden: Pan-Negro Patriot 1832–1912* (London, 1967), vii. Also on Blyden see Edith Holden, *Blyden of Liberia* (New York, 1966). Two useful essays on Blyden are Andrew Billingsley, "Edward Blyden: Apostle of Blackness," in Nathan Hare and Robert Christman (eds.), *Pan-Africanism* (New York, 1974), 154–167; Robert July, "The First African Personality: Edward W. Blyden," in July's *The Origins of Modern African Thought* (New York, 1967), 208–233. Some of Blyden's own works can be found in Hollis R. Lynch (ed.), *Black Spokesman: Selected Published Writings of Edward Wilmot Blyden* (London, 1971). A complete list of Blyden's works are in Lynch, *Edward Wilmot Blyden*, "Bibliography."

60. The Stewart Foundation is discussed in chapter 3.

61. A record of this Congress on Africa has been preserved in J.W.E. Bowen (ed.), *Africa and the American Negro: Addresses and Proceedings of the Congress on Africa* (1806 rprt. Miami, Florida, 1969).

62. Atlanta Constitution (n.d.), reprinted in *Quarterly Bulletin* (February, 1897) 7.

63. There is a discussion of the coming Congress, with its plans and motives, in the June 1895 issue of *Quarterly Bulletin*, 1–2.

64. "Minutes of the Congress on Africa," in Bowen (ed.), *Africa*, 234–235.

65. Edward Wilmot Blyden, "Letter of Greeting and Commendation," in Bowen (ed.), *Africa*, 16.

66. Orishetukeh Faduma, "Successes and Drawbacks of Missionary Work in Africa by an Eye-Witness," in Bowen (ed.), *Africa*, 126–136.

67. Bowen (ed.), *Africa*, 195.

68. M.C.B. Mason, "The Methodist Episcopal Church and Evangelization of Africa," in Bowen (ed.), *Africa*, 145, 146–147.

69. *Ibid.*

70. Bowen (ed.) *Africa*, 195.

71. *Ibid.*, 196.

72. R.S. Rust, "The Needs of Africans as Men," in Bowen (ed.) *Africa*, 211.

73. Indispensable for insight into the missionary impact in West Africa, although his discussion focuses on Nigeria and British missionaries is E.A. Ayandele, *The Missionary Impact on Modern Nigeria 1842–1914: A Political and Social Analysis* (New York, 1967), especially chapters 2, 3, 5, 7, 11. A good compliment to this is Ayandele's *Holy Johnson: Pioneer of African Nationalism 1836–1917* (New York, 1970) and Jacob Ajayi, *Christian Missions in Nigeria 1841–1891* (New York, 1972).

74. Rev. W.H. Sheppard was the most important Black Presbyterian with Africa service to his credit. For some of his views on Africa, see the *Tuskegee Student* (April 8, 1905), 1.

CHAPTER II

Africa Renascent: Black American Intellectual Interest in Africa

Black American intellectual interest in Africa, unlike the general interest among the rest of the Black population has been a *force vitale* throughout the twentieth century. The opportunity for intellectual expression by Blacks was severely hampered in the nineteenth century by slavery and its aftermath. Also, in the nineteenth century, as noted in Chapter 1, the Africa interest centered more often on emigration and the missionary programs than anything else. With the growth of the African-American intellectual community following Reconstruction, owing to the establishment of Black colleges and universities, expansion of the Black press, and the start of a rural to urban migration, Black intellectual expression on many issues became much more formidable and accessible to other Blacks. As in the past, identification with Africa seemed to turn on the plight of Blacks in the United States. The decades of the 1850s and 1890s, exceptional periods of heightened oppression for Black Americans, revealed the interplay between hard times and identification with or retreat to Africa. Back-to-Africa schemes proliferated. To be sure, there was no relief from persecution for Blacks by 1900 and the emigration passion continued to attract adherents.

However, the first two decades of the new century also witnessed a small but dedicated group of Black intellectuals marshalling an unprecedented amount of literature celebrating the African past. Their numbers were relatively small and many were not formally trained, but their impact was very important.

They took on the difficult task of countering the influence of Social Darwinism and pseudo-scientific racism—then prominent in American society—in their efforts to bring dignity and respect to the Black past and Black people. The efforts of these persistent Black intellectuals take on even greater significance in light of the fact that their campaign blossomed precisely at a time when Whites around the world, not only in the United States were engaged in the crude besmirching of Africans and their brothers and sisters overseas.

In many ways during the early decades of the twentieth century, the ideology of racism came to the fore and was a distinguishable feature of the general European and American milieu.[1] Atypical were the institutions in American life that did not foster the doctrines of Black inferiority. Permeating these racist assertions was the notion that Africa's people had contributed nothing to the forward march of civilization and human development. Science confirmed, as far as some White people were concerned, that Black people and Black culture were only deserving of the most impious, callous, out-of-hand rejection.

The so-called Negro History Movement, which included emphasis on the study of Africa, of the late nineteenth and early twentieth centuries, was a direct response, as an antidote, to the pervasiveness of race prejudice and discrimination.[2]

The juxtaposition of cultural and ideological concerns, interests, and expressions emphasizes the variations in this African-American intellectual interest in Africa. For some, the importance of rejoining Africa's traducers took first priority. For others, pointing with pride to Africa's culture and history, by itself, was not enough. They took uncomplicated ideological positions that, several scholars have already acknowledged, contributed immensely to the evolution of African nationalism[3] and "winds of change" that later engulfed Africa. Historian Sterling Stuckey has remarked that one expression of a growing early twentieth century interest in the African heritage "was a veritable proliferation of Negro history groups."[4] Among the most significant of these were the American Negro Academy, the Negro Society for Historical Research, and the Association for the Study of Negro Life and History (changed in 1973 to the Association for the Study of Afro-American Life and History). The individuals involved, their writings have confirmed, waxed most eloquent in describing the evidence they unearthed regarding the noble history of Africa. They were a determined group and prominent among them were W.E.B. DuBois, Carter G. Woodson, John E. Bruce, Arthur Schomburg and several others. That the corpus of knowledge and literature gathered by these crusaders had a profound influence on Africans has been argued by Nigeria's E.U. Essien-Udom of the University of Ibadan. Professor Essien-Udom numbers literary endeavors, Black missionary activities, the opening of Black educational institutions to Africans, the providing of technical assistance and African-American assistance in the development of the African national consciousness and Pan-Africanism, among Black American contributions to Africa. Consequently, he anoints African-Americans as "the vanguard of modern African nationalism."[5]

The total effect of the trauma of slavery and its by-products, for Africa and African-Americans, will never be completely appreciated. Every single level of interaction between Blacks and Whites in America since slavery has been blinded in some way by its cancerous prejudices. The revered Alain Locke had this to say about slavery and its impact on Africa: "The dark shadow of slavery has thrown Africa . . . into a sort of chilling and terrifying eclipse. . . ."[6] Whatever else might remain uncertain about the catastrophe of slavery for African-Americans, it is certain that the experience of slavery was devastating for the African-American psyche. Black Americans grew up in the United States with a very negative self-image that they also transferred to Africa, since that was the land of their origin.

Because the typical African-American's opinion of Africa was so derogatory, there was a need to arrest the psychological bogey about Africa and Africa's people. In the first quarter of the twentieth century this concern found a willing cadre of Black votaries determined to combat White calumnies on them and on Africa's behalf. Initially, in the Western world it was assumed that Christianity could be the saving grace for Africa and African-Americans. Christianity, it was further assumed, was superior to all other religions, and its doctrines and organization would help promote the cultural and technological modernization of Africa. This view was held by the Black intelligensia, albeit with some exceptions, at the beginning of the century and was often articulated by individuals like Alexander Walters, T. Thomas Fortune, and Booker T. Washington. However, even Christianity did not rid African-Americans of the debilitating effects of self-rejection imposed on them by the arrogance of White supremacists. It became the task of Black history, Black literature, and Black culture to repair the damaged group psyche and heal the wounds inflicted by racism.[7]

William Edward Burghart DuBois did as much as any other single individual to buoy the Africa consciousness among African-Americans.[8] He was Black-America's most prolific writer, a non-agenarian, and is considered by many to be the "father of Pan-Africanism." DuBois was an exponent both of a cultural and ideological/political interest in Africa. His writings, which spanned almost the entire ninety-five years of his life, blended strands of all these phenomena insofar as Africa was concerned. This is best illustrated by the almost simultaneous publication in 1915 of DuBois's "The African Roots of War" and his Home University volume, *The Negro*. The former is indicative of his ideological/political perspicacity in that he argued persuasively that there was a connection between the coming of World War I and the scramble for colonies in Africa. The latter stimulated the effort already under way of a modified cultural nationalism by outlining the glory of Africa's past. To say the least, DuBois was a most complex individual.[9] He is a prime example of the dualism in Black thought that has long interested students of African-American intellectual history and continues to do so. After ninety-two years as a "son of Africa" but a citizen of the United States, DuBois renounced his American citizenship and abandoned the United States for Ghana, returning, as it were, "home." Despite its shortcomings, Harold Issaac's *New World of Negro Americans* was accurate in its assessment of DuBois's impact as unparalleled in the rediscovery of Africa in the thought processes of African-Americans "or [in] an alteration in attitudes toward it."[10] It is not the intention here to review DuBois's life and the many activities he crowded into it but merely to use some aspects of his early life as an important illustration of this revolutionary Black intellectual interest in Africa.

In his second autobiography, *Dusk of Dawn*, DuBois traced his awareness of Africa through a melody sung by his great-grandmother. He pointed out that his cultural and racial patterns were more Dutch and New England than African and Africa and that his "African racial feeling was then purely a matter of my own later learning and reaction; my recoil from the assumptions of the Whites."[11] He felt himself "African by race" and an integral part of the African-American community. He was confused by what he considered the discomfort of being able to "feel" a tie with Africa better than he could explain it. Yet he considered Africa his fatherland and his "tie to Africa remained strong."[12]

It seems that DuBois, by temperament and by training, having earned his Harvard Ph.D., was prepared to do battle on Africa's behalf. Aside from his affiliation with the Pan-African conference of 1900, his early published writings signal his sensitivity for Africa. In 1903 he reviewed a book written by Joseph Tillinghast entitled *The Negro in Africa and America*. The book abounds with racism, but DuBois displayed some patience in his youth by finding value in the emphasis the book placed on the importance of Africa for African-American history.[13] The following year he essayed that improvements in British policies toward Africa would be instrumental in the realization by African-Americans of the benefits of American citizenship.[14] In

1906, it was Franz Boaz, the anthropologist, speaking at the Atlanta University commencement exercises, who brought African history to DuBois's attention. It was a subject in which he never again lost interest[15]

Throughout his lifetime, even during this early period, DuBois edited a variety of magazines and periodicals, the most important of which were *Moon: Illustrated Weekly* (1905–1906),[16] its successor *Horizon: A Journal of the Color Line* (1908–1910), and *Crisis: A Record of the Darker Races* (1910–1934). One issue of *Moon* can serve as an example of DuBois's political interest in Africa as expressed in that fugitive periodical. Under "Tidings of the Darker Millions," DuBois, as was to become his custom in *Horizon* and *Crisis*, reprinted stories taken from other periodicals dealing with the endeavors of South Africans to protect their lands from theft by Europeans. This same issue had an appeal from the Methodist Episcopal Church-South's Bishop Hartzell encouraging African-American emigration to Liberia, although DuBois was never a back-to-Africa enthusiast.[17]

The first issues of *Horizon* evinced a distinct sympathy for all of the slanders Africa suffered. And serious sentinel of Africa's traducement that DuBois was, he was often stimulated by culture, ideology, or politics. In fact, it might be said that during this period he was sometimes visceral and his romance with Africa reflected the kind of therapeutic cartharsis that may have soothed an entire Black population. DuBois selected for publication in *Horizon*, as part of his political propaganda effort, articles condemning the exploitation of West Africans, continued attacks on the sinister behavior of Whites in South Africa and the Congo, the work of the Aborigines Rights and Protection Society (ARPS), and his call for an active Pan-African movement in response to the Liberian crisis of 1908.[18] His calculation to encourage closer identification with Africa saw him frequently publishing articles written by Africans or reprinting worthy articles on Africa first published in other journals or newspapers such as the *African Mail* or the London *Times*.[19]

The pages of *Crisis* during its first five years of publication seem to have been deprived of the earlier and subsequent concern for Africa that DuBois felt. To be sure, there were references to Africa but they lack the later, better-known DuBois intensity. However, the DuBois intellectual militance began to surface through other mediums.

Easily, DuBois's most significant political/ideological action on behalf of Africa and Africa's peoples was the indispensable catalyst role he played at the Pan-African Congress of 1919.[20] There were the expected resolutions and position papers at the Congress, largely ignored by the White world meeting at Versailles. Impossible to ignore, however, was the recognition by the Black world, symbolized by these Pan-Africanists congregating in Paris, that the myth of White invincibility and invulnerability had exploded with Germany's World War I defeat.

DuBois's strongest political statement prior to 1920, which attempted to unravel the apparent conundrum of the coming of a world war, was his sagacious "The African Roots of War." The gist of DuBois's argument was that the recent outbreak of war in Europe was ignited by European greed for the spoils of Africa. During the nineteenth century Europe was transmogrified. Economic changes wrought by the ending of the slave trade and the replacement of commercial capitalism with industrial capitalism sent Europeans scurrying around the world searching for raw materials and new markets. The greatest prize in this building drama was Africa. It was earlier anticipated that the "peaceful" dissection of Africa at Berlin in 1884–1885 would preclude the coming of a world war. Europeans were bent on realizing their imperial designs and exploiting the wealth of the entire world, "but the ownership of materials and men in the darker world is the real prize that is setting the nations of Europe at each others' throats today," stated DuBois.[21] DuBois went on to prescribe a formula for avoiding war in the future. What he called the "primitive" peoples of the world and Africa needed land, modern civilization, and home rule. He argued that the non-White people of the world (today's Third World) would not always be so passive toward foreign domination. When their patience ran out they would fight "and the War of the Color Line will outdo in savage inhumanity any war this world has yet seen. For colored folks have much to remember and they will not forget."[22] Both George Shepperson and Immanuel Geis have identified the striking similarity between DuBois's "The African Roots of War" (1914) and Lenin's *Imperialism* (1917),[23] in which DuBois also analyzed what he called an "aristocracy of labor" (capitalists and workers), who, DuBois claimed, were determined to exploit the world's non-White people. The article ended with DuBois noting paternalistically that the ten million men and women of African descent in the United States were best qualified to lead the salvation of Africa.

Not far behind DuBois's essay on the coming of World War I, perhaps even surpassing it in influence and importance, was the 1914 publication of *The Negro*. It was unquestionably inspired by his combined cultural and political concerns. The book was on African-American and African history, and in many respects was the best treatment of the subject up to that time. In one small, modest volume, DuBois attempted to outline the entire African past, continental and diasporic. DuBois pointed out the limitations of disciplined research on Africa and hoped that the general public would be introduced to the accomplishments of this important but neglected division of the human race. He noted with undisguised elation that Africans were the world's first iron smelters. He also enjoyed reporting the sub-Saharan influence on Egypt, because Whites often celebrated the accomplishments of the Egyptians and separated this land from Africa. When DuBois revealed that the ancient African kingdoms were at the forefront of the economic, social, and cultural development of human civilization prior to the sixteenth century, and that the Arab invaders in the western Sudan did not create West African states but merely improved on what they found, White scholars were doubtful of his conclusions. Politically, DuBois was careful to describe the relationship among capitalism, imperialism, and the rape of Africa. He again illustrated his fancy for taking advantage of Europeans' vulnerability in his condemnation of them for instigating the transatlantic trade in African slaves. Moreover, *The Negro* stands as important affirmation of DuBois's Pan-Africanism during the period 1900–1919, when it was sometimes considered to be languishing.[24]

So it was W.E.B. DuBois who set the pace for the intellectual interest in Africa. Although Booker T. Washington was the "race leader," DuBois was the arrogant intellectual. Much of what DuBois wrote the other Black intellectuals read. When he wrote about Africa perhaps some did not agree with him and others did not believe him, but notwithstanding their dissent or incredulity, they were influenced, inspired, and provoked by him.

James Weldon Johnson was an African-American who also devoted some interest to Africa. Johnson was Field Secretary for the NAACP from 1916 to 1920. He came to New York in 1915 from Jacksonville, Florida, where he had been born. He attended Atlanta, Columbia, and Howard universities and held a B.A., an M.A., and a law degree. He linked the struggle for Black American justice and equality to that of Africans in Africa.[25] James Weldon Johnson's first public expression of his feeling for Africa came as a contributing editor to the New York *Age*. In a powerful editorial, Johnson voiced an eloquent appeal for "internationalization" (international supervision of the former German colonies in Africa) in Africa.[26] He opined that "internationalization" and the African question were one and the same, "because the consideration of internationalization is concerned almost entirely with the status of former German colonies in Africa." Johnson noted that the question concerning the plight of Black Americans would not be permitted to be brought before the peace table since it was regarded as a "domestic question" to be resolved by African-Americans and the United States Government. Therefore, he continued, African-Americans had concluded that the wisest step to take at that time was for Black people to "put the African question up to the Peace Conference so strongly that it would compel a consideration of the rights of Negro people everywhere."[27] Returning to the question of the former German colonies in Africa, Johnson indicated that they could only be disposed of in one of three possible ways: (1) return the colonies to Germany, (2) divide them up among the allies, or (3) internationalization, with Africans having a large and increasing share in their own governance. Then, demonstrating a full-blown expression of the Pan-African idea, James Weldon Johnson argued that internationalization for the former German colonies

> should eventually lead to the whole of Central Africa being ruled by native Africans, and that in turn should lead to an Africa for Africans. And an Africa for Africans would make a great change for the better in the status of people of Negro blood all over the world.[28]

Johnson's most definitive statement on the nexus between Africans and African-Americans appeared in a pamphlet entitled "Africa at the Peace Table and the Descendants of Africans in Our American Democracy."[29] Here Johnson warned against "tampering" with African institutions and attempts at "sudden conversion" of Africans with "religious propaganda." Over time the more "backward" aspects of African society would gradually be abandoned, but prudence dictated that the new Africa be would be built on the basis of "recognized established foundations rather than from entirely new and theoretical plans." Johnson's formula for modernizing Africa acknowledged the importance of schools, education, and groups of African students attending the great universities of the world.

In another section of this pamphlet James Weldon Johnson commented on the special qualifications of DuBois as a race spokesperson. There was no other individual, according to Johnson, as pre-eminently prepared to press the issue of internationalization of Africa. The experience DuBois had gained at the Universal Races Congress in London (1911) was invaluable, declared Johnson. Therefore, one of the reasons DuBois was sent to France in 1919 by the NAACP was to bring pressure on the peace delegates to recognize and ameliorate the subordinate condition of the world's Black people. One device to be employed was to call a Pan-African Congress to meet in Paris. Johnson surprised conservatives and delighted nationalists with what was tantamount to a political threat when he stated, on Africa's behalf, that, "Self-determination will be secured only by those who are in a position to *force* [emphasis added] it from their overlords. The internationalization of Central Africa holds the promise of being the quickest and least costly step by which the natives can reach that position."[30]

Encouraged perhaps by a small group of Blacks in the National office, the NAACP was supremely interested in Africa and had broad sympathies for all oppressed peoples; certainly that was Johnson's position. In fact, it would be lamentable, he observed, if American Blacks ever became so parochial, narrow-minded, and self-centered because of their own oppression, that they could spare no sympathy for the sufferings of others, "not even their blood brothers in Africa." Johnson even struck a cultural-psychological chord, suggesting that an increased knowledge of Africa would eliminate shame and make African-Americans proud of Africa. In Johnson's estimation Africa's history would give the background that would enable the Negro to "hold up his head among the peoples of the world."[31]

The second half of Johnson's pamphlet took up a theme that varied slightly from part one and which engaged the remainder of his statement. First and foremost, he claimed, the main interest of the NAACP was not in Africa and Africans but "in America and colored Americans." The problems of Black America were national, while those of Africa were international. It was unlikely, he felt, that Europe could do very much about discrimination in Georgia, Alabama, and Mississippi.

And then, notwithstanding James Weldon Johnson's previous reference to the blood brotherhood of Africans and African-Americans, he suggested that there was a difference between the struggles of these two members of the African race, and revealed some of his naïveté:

> ... the fight for democracy for native Africans and the fight for democracy for people of African descent in the United States are not on the same plane. . . . The Negro in the United States is not a subject race and does not accept the status of a subject race.[32]

Despite Johnson's intimation that Africans accepted their subordinate status, he continued to be one of Africa's cheerleaders. The acceleration of the nationalist movements in Africa after World War I, and Africans' demands for self-determination, indicate that Africans had reached the limits of their tolerance for White exploitation. Africa moved quickly to shed those more obvious elements of subaltern circumstance with which she had been weighted down for too long. For Black America, the mission was similar. In both instances, *a luta continua*.

Much more exclusively intellectual regarding Africa than DuBois or Johnson during the first two decades of the twentieth century was Carter G. Woodson. His approach was essentially a combination of the psychological boost for African-Americans and Africans by ferreting out the truth about Africa's ignored history and proud culture. There was heavy emphasis on scholarship and what Woodson was fond of referring to as "scientific objectivity." At the same time, he is considered to be a part of that group of "New World" Blacks who contributed to early Pan-African thought and who had ties with African intellectuals.[33] He had regular contact, through correspondence, with his African counterparts, especially those in West Africa; Casely-Hayford (Gold Coast), Kobina Sekyi (Gold Coast), Kodwo Nsarku (Gold Coast), Dada Adeshigibin (Nigeria), D.E. Carney (Sierra Leone), and Majola Agbebi (Nigeria). They were quite interested in his work in African history and culture and considered it an inspiration to their own endeavors. Woodson's value to the intellectual phase of African nationalism has been singled out by one of the leading students of nationalism in Africa:

> [b]y the 1920s, the ideological influence on emerging African nationalism of the writings and political activities of such militant Negro Americans as W.E.B. DuBois and Carter G. Woodson was making itself felt.[34]

Woodson was born in West Virginia in 1875 and died at seventy-five years of age in 1950.[35] He took degrees from Berea College (Kentucky), the University of Chicago, and Harvard, where he received his doctorate in 1912. Woodson taught Romance languages in the Philippines and history in West Virginia and Washington, and he served as the Dean at West Virginia State College and Howard University. He is best remembered for his pioneering efforts in and unfailing devotion to the serious study of Africa and Black America. It is no exaggeration to assert, as Rayford Logan has, that no one succeeded in popularizing interest in the African past—most notably among Black Americans—as much as did Carter G. Woodson.[36]

Woodson came early to recognize the general neglect of African and African-American history in academe. He observed that there were no courses and no interest in this aspect of history. The assumed state of backwardness and retrogression of Africans and their diasporic descendents justified for some these missing pages from the world's history. There was also little available for those with a general interest in Black people and "neither stimulus nor outlet for the scholar seriously interested in Africa . . . existed."[37] Woodson set out, along with DuBois and others, to demonstrate, through the application of science to history, the legitimacy and humanity of the African past. His own writings—*The Negro in Our History*, *The African Background Outlined*, and *African Heroes and Heroines*—reflect this effort. Indeed, it could be argued that these concerns, plus his determination to offset the psychological damage being done to African-Americans by racist propaganda, led Woodson to found

the Association for the Study of Negro Life and History
(ASNLH) in 1915 and to publish its *Journal of Negro History* in
1916.[38] The stated objective of the Association, according to its
constitution, was to commit itself to "the collection of
sociological and historical documents and the promotion of
studies bearing on the Negro."[39] In addition to the *Journal*, the
ASNLH promoted general and scholarly interest in Africa
through the encouragement of scholarly papers and research to
be presented at its annual meetings. These meetings, in fact,
became important vehicles for the dissemination of accurate
information on Africa. In 1921 the Associated Publishers was
established as an affiliate of the ASNLH to publish and market
books and monographs on Africa and Black America. In 1925 the
Association inaugurated its Negro History Week program,
which devoted attention to the African past of African-
Americans. Publication of the *Negro History Bulletin* began in
1937, and it also emphasized African life, civilization,
institutions, and important personalities.

The early issues of the *Journal* as well as subsequent
numbers contained much information about Africa. Of the four
articles and four reviews in the January 1916 issue (the first), two
of the articles and one of the reviews dealt with Africa.[40] Most of
the early contributors to the *Journal* were Black, but there was no
intention to close its pages to non-Blacks. The criterion by which
all articles were judged was "scientific objectivity." Probably
more important than anything else in the African context was the
fact that the *Journal* found its way into Africa, especially into the
hands of African intellectuals, on whom it had an important
influence. Some of them even sent articles to be published in the
Journal. Consequently, *The Journal of Negro History* was a vital
element in the commerce of ideas between "old Africa" and
"new Africa," and in the transformation of Pan-African thought
into a viable Pan-African movement.

Two other African-Americans germane to the intellectual
ferment over Africa at this time were John Edward Bruce and
Arthur Schomburg. Bruce, the journalist-activist, and Schomburg

the bibliophile, came together in 1911 to form the Negro Society for Historical Research (NSHR), which was a forerunner to the Association for the Study of Negro Life and History. The NSHR followed the precedent of the American Negro Historical Society of Philadelphia and the American Negro Academy (ANA), both founded in 1897. The Academy, the better known of these two precursers of the NSHR, was an organization of Black intellectuals "and those distinguished in other walks of life," and their interest in Africa was somewhat limited in spite of the fact that the founder of the Academy was Alexander Crummell.[41] The NSHR concentrated on the collection of materials and facts pertaining to what was then called "the Negro," a term that included Blacks in the United States, West Indians, African-Brazilians, and Africans. It is true that, like the ANA, most of the efforts of the Society were reserved for gathering information on Black Americans, but Africa was not overlooked altogether. The NSHR, therefore, joined the struggle to break down the existing barriers of intellectual discrimination and to rectify the scholarly sins of omission and commission, of which Black people, in Africa and the diaspora, were the major victims. Its periodic meetings and "Occasional Papers" along with the individual efforts of its members, were important for maintaining a lasting bond between the sons and daughters of Africa, and the effort to improve the continent's image in general. One of the qualifications for membership was that prospective members, were required to show evidence of having done some reading in "race literature," of having a knowledge of "race achievement" and of wishing to do research. An initial membership list of fifty-five contained several Africans, including two Pan-African giants, J.E. Casely-Hayford and Edward W. Blyden.[42]

John Edward Bruce's letter of introduction to Moses da Rocha in Lagos, James Dossen in Liberia, and Abayomi Cole in Sierra Leone,[43] for J.E.K. Aggrey, is an instructive barometer of Bruce's influence and multifaceted interest in Africa, which was cultural, psychological, ideological, political, and sentimental. (J.E.K. Aggrey, an African who was traveling under the auspices of the Phelps-Stokes Foundation, later became a well-known Pan-Africanist). Although born a slave, Bruce acquired a rudimentary education and developed an early interest in journalism.[44] John Edward Bruce "was not a profound man" and "was not highly trained," but he was very much "a ready man."[45] He was well informed on world affairs, especially Africa, and was a copious writer. Bruce produced not only editorials and newspaper columns, but more than a score of short stories, poems, essays, and plays. In many ways, he was one of Black America's first examples of a "Renaissance man." He often wrote under the *nom de plume* "Bruce Grit" or "Rising Sun."

Bruce had a long and obsessive interest in Africa. One manifestation of this interest is the correspondence he carried on with Africans, beginning with the first letter in his manuscript collection, from an African, dated April 10, 1891,[46] and continuing until his death in 1924. In addition, he wrote for the *West African Record*, the *South African Spectator*, and the *African Times and Orient Review*, as well as for dozens of newspapers in the United States. The African Society of London listed Bruce as a member, and he later became its Honorary Secretary. He was also a member of the Order of African Redemption (Liberia) and the African Methodist Episcopal Zion Church. Bruce appears to have been highly religious because he often made reference to Africa's salvation through God.

In 1913 Bruce organized, in New York City, the Loyal Order of the Sons of Africa, and the rationale for its establishment signals his Pan-African thought.[47] Bruce held that the Sons of Africa were bent on uniting the worlds Blacks and "Colored" people. He claimed that the best response to the oppression of Black people by Whites was universal race solidarity. Bruce often states, in connection with the formation of the Sons of Africa, that the psychological moment had arrived for Black people around the world to "touch elbows and exchange ideas" in order to provide for mutual protection. He advocated regular contact with Black people in the world who "thought Black," which he practiced throughout his lifetime. To Bruce, "the battle of the darker races was an intellectual one."[48] But he did not feel confined to supporting only intellectual action for relief. With no effort to camouflage what he considered the problems of and solution for Black people, he stated,

> . . . if the Negroes of any part of Africa, the West Indies or the United States are suddenly confronted with a problem which affects their political, social or industrial well-being—and lack means to defend their cause, all should make common cause and come to the rescue with their means and counsel, and stand by the injured party until justice is done.[49]

There is evidence that Bruce practiced what he preached. Numerous Africans visited him in New York in addition to and including those with whom he corresponded regularly, such as Edward Blyden, Casely-Hayford, Tengo Jabavu, Kirkland Soga, and Majola Agbebi and his son Akinbami. They all testified to the marked influence Bruce had on their own thinking and the psychological boost they got from him regarding their pride in Blackness. Hayford, for example, wrote to Bruce asking for multiple copies of Marcus Garvey's *Negro World*, which he considered an important propaganda instrument, and promised to send Bruce in return fifty copies of the Gold Coast *Leader*.[50] There is even some indication that Bruce served as unofficial agent for Hayford's classic work *Ethiopia Unbound*. He received a request for the book from Sarah J. Ware of Staunton, Virginia, in November of 1911, and from others.[51] Moreover, he received correspondence from C.M. Philips, a London publisher, that made reference to the marketing of *Ethiopia Unbound* and the various newspapers and journals in which advertisements for it were being carried, among them, *African World, United Empire, Journal of African Society*, New York *Independent, Freeman, African Times and Orient Review*, Jamaica *Times*, and *Morning Post*.[52] When Casely-Hayford wrote to Bruce on April 7, 1915, he made no mention of *Ethiopia Unbound*, but wanted to know the attitude of the United States toward the World War. He closed with the hope that their correspondence would continue.

Bruce also maintained a close relationship with Majola Agbebi, the militant Yoruba Baptist from Nigeria. So enthusiastic, in fact, was Bruce about Agbebi that he attempted to immortalize him by having a special day, October 11, set aside each year for observance by African-Americans as Majola Agbebi Day.[53]

Just at a time when Marcus Garvey[54] and the Universal Negro Improvement Association (UNIA) were capturing the imagination of Black people in the United States, Africa, the West Indies, and South America, Bruce joined the movement after having some earlier reservations both about Garvey and UNIA.[55] Prior to his joining the "Garveyites," Bruce referred to Garvey as an "empty orator whose rhetoric was a mixture of frenzy and oral gymnastics."[56] He continued that Garvey had no influence among Africans or African Americans.[57] Bruce was eventually persuaded that Garveyism and what he was fond of referring to as "Bruceism" were one and the same. He even intimated that Garvey had actually joined him. He was offered the presidency in the United States section of the Garvey movement, but declined in favor of a "younger, more active man." Later, Bruce accepted the honorary title of "Duke of Uganda" in UNIA.[58]

Soon after he joined Garvey, Bruce began writing for the *Negro World* and was a devout Garveyite until he died. His columns in the *Negro World* and elsewhere affirmed his belief that Garvey was the leading spirit in the struggle for African regeneration. He hailed Garvey as "Jesus" and noted regularly that Garveyism was a divinely inspired mass movement bent on rescuing Africa "from the plunderers and buccaneers of an alien race."[59]

In addition to those Black intellectuals already mentioned, others—with lower profiles—infused necessary energy into this redemptive effort by intellectuals. There was no better embodiment of those in the background than Arthur A.

Schomburg. Schomburg's interest in Africa was not as sharply political or ideological as some of the others. He was mainly interested in digging up the African past and demonstrating the gifts furnished by Africa and people of African descent for the progress of human civilization. He was a bibliophile without peer and essayist of some repute, who actually suffered from a mulatto superiority complex, and who on occasion was rather patronizing toward Africa.[60] Arthur Schomburg is probably best known by the New York Public Library collection that bears his name and that is one of the best of its kind in the world.

Schomburg was born in San Juan, Puerto Rico in 1874 and was educated there and in the West Indies. Very early in his life he developed an interest in Black history and literature, and meticulously set about the task of collecting information about the Black past. This knowledge came to serve him well in debates with his White classmates. In 1901, Schomburg arrived in New York and, after securing employment with several different firms, one of which was a law firm, he was hired by the Bankers Trust Company of Wall Street, where he remained for twenty-one years. Following his retirement from Bankers Trust he became curator of the Fisk University Library in Nashville, Tennessee.

All of Arthur Schomburg's spare time was devoted to gathering information, books, prints, rare manuscripts, and pictures on the Black past—especially the Black past of Spain and Latin America. But his interest in African-Americans and Africa was considerable indeed. He served as president of the American Negro Academy and was one of the founders of the Negro Society for Historical Research. In 1924, he made a research visit to Spain where he made some startling discoveries about Africa's involvement in Spanish history, especially its cultural history. For example, it was revealed that two of Spain's most celebrated painters, Juan Pareja and Sebastian Gomez, were Black. In 1926, the Carnegie Corporation of New York purchased his collection for $10,000. The collection was presented to the New York Public Library and eventually became the Schomburg

Collection, which virtually no student engaged in serious research into African or African-American life and history has been able to avoid.

Arthur Schomburg was an accomplished author who wrote both for newspapers and magazines. His main theme of dignifying the African past was designed to reverse the negative self-image African-Americans had of themselves and their history. In this sense he was more involved in the psycho-cultural crusade than anything else. Two of Schomburg's most disciplined essays, written before 1919 and which still continue to influence some Black intellectuals, were "Racial Integrity: A Plea for the Establishment of a Chair of Negro History in Our Schools and Colleges" and "The Negro Digs Up His Past."

Schomburg was one of the first to demand equal consideration for Black history with White history, presaging contemporary debates over multiculturalism and curriculums of inclusion. In "Racial Integrity," he addressed the importance of "inspirational" and "relevant" history for Black people. To him it was an unpardonable injustice that Black students were languishing in ignorance about their own history. Africa was not to be despised and denigrated; learned, knowledgeable Blacks must come to Africa's defense and secure its rightful place in the annals of human history. Schomburg's logic, in his demand for a chair in Black history, was disarming and his analogies were profound. He pleaded especially for a change in traditional history offerings in colleges, which would include the history of Black people:

> . . . books take their proper places when applied to the White people, but when applied or measured up to the Black people, they lack the substantial and the inspiring. They are like meat without salt, they bear no analogy to our own; and for this reason it would be a wise plan for us to lay down a course of study in Negro History and achievements. . .[61]

His appeal for a chair in Black history was equally eloquent:

We have chairs of almost everything, and believe we lack
nothing, but we sadly need a chair of Negro history. The
institutions have their chair of history; it is the history of
their people and whenever the Negro is mentioned in the
text books it dwindles down to a footnote.

* * * *

Where is our historian to give us, our view and our chair
of Negro History to teach our people, our own history?
We are at the mercy of the 'flotsam and jetsam' of the
White writers.[62]

In the "Negro Digs Up His Past," Schomburg was no less
specifically purposeful, even though more general. The
achievements of the African and African-American past, he
argued, were shrouded in a secrecy that was more the result of
White scholarly conspiracy than ignorance. It was the duty of
Black intellectuals to free the past from the "vagaries of rhetoric
and propaganda and become systematic and scientific. . ."[63] He
even suggested that Black history, scientifically and accurately
reported, could also restore what bondage had wiped out, and
would "repair and offset" the social damage caused by slavery.

Aggressive individuals like DuBois, Woodson, Bruce, and
Schomburg were the assault troops in this intellectual campaign
for mobilizing interest in Africa and building incipient Africa
consciousness. They were the intellectual elite, the *crème de la
crème*. But to leap to the conclusion that these celebrities waged
this struggle alone would be a gross error in fact and a
miscarriage of the truth. An *a perte de vue* support element
existed, without whose backing this campaign with words could
not possibly have been mounted. These second-line troops do
not enjoy historical reverence because of their relative lack of
renown. But, as the proverbial chain is only as strong as its
weakest link, this intellectual effort was no "one man show."
Writers, teachers, lawyers, professors, ideologues, missionaries,
propagandists, and probably some soap box orators were
centrally or peripherally associated with the organizations

already mentioned. In their various capacities, this support
contingent carried the attack to the doorstep of their adversaries.
Joel Rogers, Hubert Harrison, Monroe Work, Benjamin Brawley,
William Scarborough, William Leo Hansberry, John W.
Cromwell, Horace Mann Bond, William Ferris are but selected
examples of a battalion of the Black intelligensia who joined this
verbal war over a respectable image for Africa and Black
people.[64]

William Ferris is a good example of a fairly obscure
individual who made an important contribution to the African
campaign. Ferris was a graduate of Yale University and, in 1913,
published a two-volume study entitled *The African Abroad*, which
was considered quite respectable in many scholarly circles. In
one section of the book Ferris summarized the historical
evolution of Africans, African-Americans and West Indians—
elucidating his Pan-African views—under the title of "An
Epitome of Deeds, Achievements, and Progress of a Colored
Race in Africa, Europe, Hayti, the West Indies, and America."[65]
Ferris emphasized the Blackness of ancient Ethiopians and their
influence on Egypt. In another chapter entitled "Some
Distinguished Foreign Negroes," Ferris drew attention to the
likes of Duse Mohammed Ali, editor/publisher of the pro-
nationalist *African Times and Orient Review*, and Majola Agbebi
and Casely-Hayford, including photographs of the latter two.[66]
Later in the decade when the magnetic force of Garvey's call of
"Africa for the Africans" swept through the United States, Ferris
found a platform for his local Black nationalism and Pan-
Africanism again, as editor of *Negro World*.

Not as intellecutally gifted as Ferris but equally proud of
mother Africa's past achievements and its special culture was
George Washington Ellis. In what may very well have been the
first monograph written by a Black American on indigenous
African life and culture, Ellis published his *Negro Culture in West
Africa: A Social Study of a Negro Group of Vai-Speaking People*.[67]
Ellis's treatment was sympathetic. He served for some time as an
official at the American legation in Monrovia, Liberia, and

therefore observed first hand the traditions and culture of the Vai, and others, for his ethnographic study. Particularly significant was his revelation of the recorded alphabet and script inspired the genius of the Vai-speaking peoples.[68]

Joel Augustus Rogers (1880–1966), and William Leo Hansberry (1894–1965), who fall just slightly outside the time frame under consideration here, were also noteworthy contributors to the case for Africa's importance. Rogers was not a trained academician (that is, he held no advanced degrees), but he was a tireless and meticulous researcher who in his day brought respectability to the study of African and African-American history. Because of the controversy surrounding much of his writing, Rogers was forced to finance the publication of most of his work out of his own pocket.[69] Hansberry was primarily a teacher for most of his life, at Howard University. He was a pacesetter in the study of African history and civilization. Educated at Harvard, Hansberry is best remembered for his spellbinding and inspirational lectures in the history department at Howard. Symbolic of the impact William Hansberry had on his students is their repeated testimony of his genius and the fact that the University of Nsukka (Nigeria) named their Institute of African Studies after him.[70]

The best example of an African-American intellectual who settled in Africa, for a time at least, is the unsettled T. McCants Stewart. A consideration of Stewart might seem to be more appropriate in a discussion on emigration or Americo-Liberians. At the same time, Stewart was an intellectual of sorts, being a contributor to various newspapers and periodicals, and generally a remarkable individual.

Born in Charleston, South Carolina in December, 1854,[71] Stewart attended Howard University and was awarded his law degree from the University of South Carolina in 1875. Between 1882 and 1910, Mr. Stewart taught law at Liberia College in West Africa, preached the Gospel and practiced law in Brooklyn, New York, settled and practiced law in Honolulu, Hawaii, lectured in England and settled a second time in Liberia. In 1911 he became an associate justice of the Liberian Supreme Court, left in 1914, and served as commercial agent for Liberia in England before moving to St. Thomas, Virgin Islands, where he died in 1923.

Stewart qualifies for consideration as an African-American intellectual in the defense of Africa by virtue of his support for Liberia, although he was sometimes unhappy with his adopted home.[72] A sizeable portion of his writings are characterized by high-pitched encouragement for African-American emigration[73] and rejecting the claims made by the French, German, and English press that the Aborigines were exploited and mistreated by the ruling elite. He pointed to their right to vote and the frequency of marriage between indigenous Liberians and Americo-Liberians as evidence of concord between the two groups. He asserted that the callous charges of Europeans were part of a concerted effort to discredit Liberia. T. McCants Stewart was also much opposed to and outspoken about Whites owning land in Liberia. He called them "birds of passage" who "feed for a season then fly away."[74]

What has been the impact of the expanded writings and thought of the Black American literati on militant African thinking between the end of the nineteenth century and the World War I period? To what extent was there a corresponding interest in political-cultural-ideological ideas? Did these African-Americans have a direct, indirect, or significant influence on the political thought of the leading African intellectuals in the pre-War period (J.E. Casely-Hayford, E.W. Blyden, Mensah Sarbeh, Kobina Sekyi, and others)? Moreover, in what way was this exchange of ideas enhanced by African students studying at Black American colleges and universities in the United States? The weight of evidence seems to clearly suggest (1) that there was contact, direct and indirect, and that Africans were indeed influenced by African-American intellectuals despite Casely-Hayford's and Kobina Sekyi's occasional reservations about some of the ideas of Booker T. Washington and DuBois; and (2) that African students studying in the United States were stimulated by their United States experience, especially in political-nationalist ways. The published writings of contemporary African nationalists and the work done by a few students of the subject tend to support these conclusions. The debate continues over whether the influence was great, mediocre, or marginal.

African and African-American Mutual Influences

One account of the African student experience in the United States argues that African nationalism and African political leadership during the colonial period were significantly affected and influenced by American education. These late nineteenth and early twentieth century students were initially recruited by missionaries, but they were much influenced by the protest ethos they observed while studying at southern Black colleges, and some were transformed into revolutionary "types."[75] John Chilembwe (known in connection with the Nyasaland uprising of 1915)[76] is but one example (which also might include Isaka Seme, John Dube, D.D.T. Jabavu, and Sol Plaatje) of those African students whose proto-nationalist thought was derived from their student sojourn in the United States. The metamorphosis from religion to politics is not as discernable among the first wave of students as among subsequent ones. Finally, it is argued that the students who came to the United States were much more politicized by their experience than were those who studied in Europe.[77]

Casely-Hayford's missive to DuBois in June of 1904 is an indication of the mutual interest existing in Africa and Black-America. Hayford complimented DuBois for *The Souls of Black Folk* and noted that ". . . if leading thinkers of the African race in America had the opportunity of exchanging thoughts with thinkers of the race in West Africa, this century would be likely to see the race problem solved." Casely-Hayford was a bit anxious about the solution to the "race problem" but was aware of the potential of ideological and political contact within the

Pan-African world. He sent DuBois copies of his own *Gold Coast Institutions* and *Africa and the Africans*, both of which he said contained points of view that were new and would be of interest to DuBois. This is apparently the initial communication between what might be considered the leading nationalist in West Africa (or so he became after Mensah Sarbah's death)[78] and the top ideologue in the United States. The letter was addressed to DuBois in care of the publishers of *The Souls of Black Folk* (1903), A.C. McClurg in Chicago. In order that there would be no misunderstanding, Hayford appended the postscript, "I am of course an African."[79]

Joseph Ephriam Casely-Hayford has been called "the greatest nationalist leader in West Africa in his time."[80] He was born in 1866 in what was then the Gold Coast (now Ghana) and educated at Fourah Bay College in Sierra Leone. After a brief teaching stint in Cape Coast, he went to England to study law. Hayford was called to the Bar on November 17, 1896, after which he returned to the Gold Coast to practice law. Hayford has left a brilliant record of a nationalist's views to examine, on the African side, regarding this transatlantic exchange of ideas. Hayford also had a busy journalistic career serving as editor of the *Gold Coast Leader* and later as editor—with another journalist-nationalist, S.R.B. Solomon (Attoh Ahuma)—of the *Wesleyan Methodist Times*.

This was a time in West Africa when the press played a special role in politicizing literate West Africans. Western education had produced by 1900 a number of Africans who became the "watchdogs of colonial rule." More than anything else it was through the medium of the African press that the African elites articulated their protests against the abuses of colonial rule. It was also this militant West African press, despite its poverty and ephemeral character, that brought to the attention of Africans the issues and events of the Black world beyond the continent. And, as usual, the militant newspapers were the most short-lived and poorest, owing to the withdrawal of European advertisements if they were too critical of colonialism. Among the better known papers were the *Sierra Leone Weekly News*, the *Lagos Weekly Record*, and the *Gold Coast Independent* in West Africa and Kirkland Soga's *Izwi Labantu* in South Africa, to which African-American writers contributed.

It is ironic that Casely-Hayford later came to question, in *Ethiopia Unbound*, both Booker T. Washington and W.E.B. DuBois. Hayford further took the position that it was not so much "Afro-Americans that we want as Africans or Ethiopians."[81] His pleas and warnings were intended for all Black people, but he made frequent references to African-Americans. He appealed for cooperation between "Afric's sons" in the uplifting of Ethiopia (Africa) and setting her on her feet among the nations of the world. African-Americans, according to Hayford, were unfortunately out of touch with their past and were "helplessly and hopelessly" wandering around in the dark for an identity that was unnatural. He considered them, in many respects, counterfeit Whites for whom he had little patience. They were worse off than the Hebrews in Egypt. A formula for relief from this acute case of cultural deprivation could be provided by Africans from the "East," and African-Americans should not be adverse to advice from Africans because there was much each could learn from the other. Preservation of and appreciation for African institutions, and the adoption of African names and clothing, were examples of what African-Americans needed. The great Black centers of learning in the United States would do well to establish professorships in African history, civilization and culture. Casely-Hayford boldly proclaimed that there were few Blacks in the United States who would be unable to trace their ancestry to one of the great tribal families of West Africa, if they would only take the time and trouble to do so.[82] His prediction was that if this cultural revolution did not surface with the current generation, it certainly would with the next.[83] It is beyond dispute that Casely-Hayford's foresight was affirmed in Black America and throughout the Pan-African world during the 1960s and 1970s.

In another section his semi-fictitious, semi-autobiograph-
ical, Pan-African-nationalist treatise Casely-Hayford is lavish
with praise for Blyden, of whom he was a disciple, as the
quintessential Pan-Africanist. But he was again critical of the
councils of DuBois and Booker T. Washington, calling both
"exclusive and provincial." The Black school of thought in the
United States (represented by DuBois and Washington) he
argued, aspired to White models and struggled for progress
according to White standards, "intellectually and materially."
Blyden, on the other hand, taught the importance of Africans
discovering their true place in the world order along "natural
and national lines." In other words, Hayford's admonition was
for

> Afro-Americans [to] bring themselves into touch with
> some of the general traditions and institutions of their
> ancestors, and, though sojourning in a strange land,
> endeavour to conserve the characteristics of the race. Thus
> and only thus, like Israel of old, will they be able,
> metaphorically, to walk out of Egypt in the near future
> with a great and real spoil.[84]

Not as well known as the attorney Casely-Hayford,
although his equal as a theoretical nationalist, was the writer-
philosopher-lawyer William Essuman Gwira Sekyi, also of the
Gold Coast. He is considered by one student of Africa to be "an
example *par excellence* of the African intellectual in nationalist
politics."[85] Most of his writings are unpublished but have been
thoroughly mined by Professor J.A. Langley, whose findings are
an important contribution to existing knowledge regarding the
West African nationalist's reaction to African-American thought
in the pre-1919 period. Implicit, if not stated, in some of the
earlier studies of contact and communication between Africa and
Black America is the view that African intellectuals were
enthusiastic about the ideas of their counterparts in the United
States. There is no attempt here to suggest that there was a lack
of excitement for the ideas of DuBois, Woodson, Bruce, Booker T.

Washington, or Marcus Garvey. However, subordinated or unknown in the past has been the outspoken rejection of the diasporic assumption of intellectual supremacy in the Black world. In other words, there were some West African intellectuals who were not at all prepared to relinquish *carte blanche* the intellectual high ground in the Pan-African world to African-Americans. African intellectuals were always excited, without qualification or reservation, about the desirability of cooperation. But as Casely-Hayford indicated, some Africans felt there was much that African-Americans could learn from Africa.

Kobina Sekyi was stimulated most by Marcus Garvey, even though there were aspects of Garveyism about which he had reservations. He suggested that Whites feared Garvey most because he was most effective in advertising race unity.[86] On the other hand, Sekyi was quick to point out that, given the peculiar nature of African social and political institutions, the salvation of Africa could only be directed from "African Africa" and by "African Africans." Africa could be, and ought to be, materially assisted by Africans abroad, but because of their inherited Anglo-Saxon prejudices they were disqualified from leadership in Africa. Like other West African intellectuals, Sekyi appealed for technical, industrial, and economic advice and student exchanges. He acknowledged some cultural differences, but encouraged cultural cooperation between African-Americans and Africans. He was opposed to emigration and insisted repeatedly that the political presumptions and pretensions of "New World" Africans were useless for Africa.[87]

The direct line of communication, once opened, between Africans and African-Americans was a boon to cooperation in the Black world. Colonialism and race prejudice were being challenged, but the knockout blow was not imminent. However, these twin blights on the Black world began to face more formidable organization and opposition. In 1903, Kirkland Soga wrote to T. Thomas Fortune and Booker T. Washington, inviting both to organize a Pan-African conference in the United States the following year.[88] There was an exchange of correspondence between Blyden and DuBois about the proposed *Encyclopedia Africana*.[89] J.E. Kwegyir Aggrey requested permission, in a ten-page holograph, to come to New York and study under DuBois.[90] Letters, newspapers, periodicals, students, missionaries, and politicos crossed the Atlantic Ocean in this most important formative stage of Pan-African thought to share ideas. In the aggregate, they established a foundation for the Pan-African movement, which eventually gathered the momentum necessary for the realization of some of the Pan-African dreams of these pioneering the "Old World" and "New World" African intellectuals.

NOTES

1. There is no dearth of studies dealing with racism and pseudo-scientific ideas about race in the early twentieth century; see, for starters Thomas Gossett, *Race: The History of an Idea in America* (Dallas, Texas, 1963), chapters 4, 7, 8, 11, 14; I.A. Newby, *Jim Crow's Defense: Anti-Negro Thought in America, 1900–1930* (Baton Rouge, 1965); and George Frederickson, *The Black Image in the White Mind: The Debate on Afro-American Character and Destiny 1817–1914* (New York, 1971), chapters 8, 9, 10. See also William H. Bruening, "Racism: A Philosophical Analysis of a Concept," *Journal of Black Studies* (September, 1974), 3–17.

2. August Meier, *Negro Thought in America 1880–1915* (Ann Arbor, Michigan, 1966), 260–264.

3. George Shepperson is generally considered the groundbreaker here. See his important "Notes on Negro American Influences on the Emergence of African Nationalism," *Journal of African History* (1960), 299–312. See also E.U. Essien-Udom, "The Relationship of Afro-American to African Nationalism," *Freedomways* 2 (Fall, 1962), 391–407. Also worth seeing is an essay by Cornelius Ejimofor, "Black American Contribution to African Nationalism and African Influence on U.S. Civil Rights," *Journal of Afro-American Issues* (Fall, 1974).

4. Sterling Stuckey, "DuBois, Woodson and the Spell of Africa: Black Americans and Africa Consciousness," *Negro Digest* (February, 1967), 23.

5. Essien-Udom, "The Relationship . . .," 404.

6. Alain Locke, "Apropos of Africa," *Opportunity* (February, 1924), 37.

7. Racism is briefly defined here as a view, ideology, or belief that holds that an individual's race (used conveniently as a synonym for skin color) is the principal determinant of all other capacities and qualities and that the subordination of "inferior" races by "superior" ones is necessary for the preservation of the social order.

8. For a helpful indication of those Black intellectuals who predate Woodson, DuBois, et al., and some of their writings on Africa, see Dorothy Porter, "Early American Negro Writings: A Bibliographical Study," *Bibliographical Society of American Papers* (3Rd Quarter, 1945), 192–268. Worth seeing also is her "Organized Educational Activities of Negro Literary Societies, 1828–1846," *Journal of Negro Education* (1936), 556–576.

9. DuBois's autobiographies are *Darkwater: Voices from Within the Veil* (1920; rprt. New York, 1969); *Dusk of Dawn: An Essay Toward an Autobiography of Race Concept* (1940; rprt. New York 1968); *The Autobiography of W.E.B. DuBois* (New York, 1968). DuBois has commanded, thus far, more biographers than can be mentioned here. Among them are Francis L. Broderick, *W.E.B. DuBois: Negro Leader in a Time of Crisis* (Stanford, California, 1959) and Elliot Rudwick, *W.E.B. DuBois: Propagandist of the Negro Protest*, second edition (New York, 1968). See also Rayford Logan (ed.) *W.E.B. DuBois: A Profile* (New York, 1971); Julius Lester (ed.), *The Seventh Son: The Thought and Writings of W.E.B. DuBois* (New York, 1971), 2 volumes; Philip Foner (ed.), *W.E.B. DuBois Speaks: Speeches and Addresses 1890–1963* New York, 1970), 2 volumes; and Joseph de Marco, *The Social Thought of W.E.B. DuBois* (Lanham, Maryland, 1983).

10. Harold Isaacs, *New World of Negro Americans* (New York, 1964), 195.

11. W.E.B. DuBois, *Dusk of Dawn* (New York, 1968), 115.

12. *Ibid.*, 116–117.

13. *Political Science Quarterly* (December, 1903), 695–697. DuBois was nevertheless quick to admonish a White Cornell University professor for a favorable review. See Walter Wilcox to W.E.B. DuBois, March 13, 1904; W.E.B. DuBois to Walter Wilcox, March 29, 1904, in Herbert Aptheker (ed.), *The Correspondence of W.E.B. DuBois, 1877–1934* (Amherst, Massachusetts, 1973), 74–75. DuBois also advised Charles Francis Adams that his article in *Century Magazine* (May, 1906), 110–111, "Reflex Light from Africa," was "ill-considered" and "sensational in its villification of Africa." W.E.B. DuBois to Charles Francis Adams, December 15, 1898 *Ibid.*, 144.

14. W.E.B. DuBois, "The Future of the Negro Race in America," *East and the West* (January, 1904), 4–19, cited in Herbert Aptheker (ed.), *Annotated Bibliography of the Published Writings of W.E.B. DuBois* (Millwood, New York, 1973), 19.

15. Stuckey, "DuBois, Woodson. . . ," 65.

16. See Paul Parrington, "The Moon Illustrated Weekly: Precursor of the Crisis," *Journal of Negro History* (July, 1963), 206–216.

17. *Moon* (March 2, 1906), a copy of which is located in Moorland-Spingarn Research Center at Howard University. One of the errors in Immanuel Geiss, *The Pan-African Movement: A History of Pan-Africanism in America, Europe and Africa* (New York, 1974), 234, is his characterization of DuBois as fighter for the back-to-Africa ideal in his early life, which DuBois never was.

18. *Horizon* (February, 1907), 3; (April 1907), 3–5, 7–10; (June 1907), 3–10; (November/December, 1908), 8–9.

19. This is true for almost every published issue of *Horizon*.

20. Pertinent issues of *Crisis* that deal with the 1919 Congress are January, 1919, March 1919, April 1919, and May 1919. DuBois's role at the 1919 Congress has been well studied. See, for example, J.A. Langley, *Pan-Africanism and Nationalism in West Africa 1900–1945* (London, 1973), 62–68. Langley is not as mesmerized as others with DuBois's role in 1919. See also Immanuel Geiss, "Notes on the Development of Pan-Africanism," *Journal of the Historical Society of Nigeria*, 3, 719–740 and *The Pan-African Movement* (New York, 1974), chapter 12, which questions sole dependence on DuBois's accounts for most of our information on Pan-Africanism. Older studies include George Padmore *Pan-Africanism or Communism* (New York, 1971), chapter 7; and Colin Legum, *Pan-Africanism* (New York, 1962) chapter 2. Clarence Countee's doctoral

dissertation, "W.E.B. DuBois and African Nationalism, 1914–1945" (American University, 1969) is useful. See also Adekunle Ajala, *Pan-Africanism: Evolution, Progress and Prospects* (New York, 1973), 195–230; and Ben Rogers, "William E.B. DuBois, Marcus Garvey and Pan-Africa," *Journal of Negro History* (January, 1969), 48–62. DuBois also sought support from influential Whites in the United States for the Pan-African Congress movement, most notably Walter Lippman and Charles Evans Hughes: Walter Lippmann to W.E.B. DuBois, February 20, 1919; W.E.B. DuBois to Charles Evans Hughes: June 23, 1921; Charles Evans Hughes to W.E.B. DuBois, July 8, 1921, all in Aptheker (ed.) *The Correspondence*, 223, 250–251. This 1919 Congress is discussed in greater detail in chapter 8.

21. W.E.B. DuBois, "The African Roots of War," *Atlantic Monthly* (May, 1915), 711.

22. *Ibid.*, 714.

23. Shepperson, "Notes on Negro American Influences," *Journal of African History* (1960), 229–312; Immanuel Geiss, *The Pan-African Movement* (New York, 1974), 230.

24. George Shepperson, "Introduction," *The Negro* (rprt. New York, 1970) (xxii). Relevant here also is Vincent Harding, "W.E.B. DuBois and the Black Messianic Vision, *Freedomways* (1969), 44–54.

25. New York *Age* (December 7, 1918), 3 and February 8, 1919), 3. Johnson also wrote occasionally for *Crisis* and *Century*.

26. New York *Age* (February 8, 1919).

27. *Ibid.*

28. *Ibid.*

29. NAACP Annual Conference (1919), "Africa and the World," 13–20, reprinted in Adelaide Hill and Martin Kilson, *Appropos of Africa* (New York, 1971), 384–392.

30. *Ibid.*, 386.

31. *Ibid.*, 389.

32. *Ibid.*, 390.

33. *Ibid.*, 339.

34. Shepperson, "Notes . . .," 306; Hill and Kilson, *Apropos*, 339.

35. A brief biographical sketch of Woodson is provided by Rayford Logan in "Carter G. Woodson," *Phylon* (4th Quarter, 1945), 315–

321. Interesting is the article by Sister Anthony Scally "The Carter G. Woodson Letters in the Library of Congress," *Negro History Bulletin* (June/July, 1975), 419–421. The May 1950 issue of the *Negro History Bulletin* also has several articles on Woodson.

36. Rayford Logan, "The American Negro's View of Africa," in AMSAC (ed.), *Africa Seen by American Negro Scholars* (New York, 1963), 220.

37. Ulysses Lee, "The ASNLH, the Journal of Negro History and American Scholarly Interest in Africa," in AMSAC, *Africa*, 403.

38. *Ibid.*, Stuckey, "DuBois and Woodson...," 63; Hill and Kilson, *Apropos*, 339; John Bracey, Jr. et al., *Black Nationalism in America* (New York, 1970), 312–319. See also Kelly Miller, "An Estimate of Carter G. Woodson and His Work in Connection with the Association for the Study of Negro Life and History, Inc." (Washington, D.C., 1926). Jacqueline Goggin has recently written the "first full-scale biography" of Woodson entitled *Carter G. Woodson: A Life in Black History* (Baton Rouge, Louisiana, 1993).

39. *Journal of Negro History* (October, 1917), 445.

40. Woodson was even critical of DuBois on one occasion for devoting only 144 pages (out of 401) in his (DuBois's) *Black Folk Then and Now* (a revision of *The Negro*) to the history and culture of Africa. See Lee, "The ASNLH...," 410.

41. Meier, *Negro Thought*, 266–267; Kilson and Hill, *Apropos*, 195–197.

42. A copy of the Constitution and membership roll of the NSHR as prepared by John E. Bruce can be found in Kilson and Hill, *Apropos*, 202–205.

43. B. 4–52; John E. Bruce Papers, Schomburg Center, New York Public Library, all now on microfilm. My citations in the Bruce collection refer to the various folders in which materials were located, and the way they were labeled at the time that I saw the Bruce Papers. For example, this letter to Moses da Rocha was labeled "B. 4–52;" sometimes their organization appeared to lack logic. Since the Bruce Papers are now on microfilm, obtaining an index guide would appear to be the best way to proceed.

44. There is a brief autobiography of Bruce, written before he was twenty years old, in the John E. Bruce manuscript collection at the New

York Public Library, Schomburg Collection. See also Peter Gilbert *The Selected Writings of John Edward Bruce: Militant Black Journalist* (New York, 1971), 1–9; Kilson and Hill, *Apropos*, 146–147 and William A. Ferris, *The African Abroad* (New Haven, 1913), II, 862–863.

45. *Calendar of Manuscripts in the Schomburg Collection of Negro Literature* (New York, 1942), I, 162. This is an excellent guide to the Bruce Collection. It contains a brief synopsis of most of Bruce's correspondence, and volume III has a particularly useful index to the Bruce articles, editorials, essays, poems, newspaper columns, and correspondence.

46. Letter from "Hoodo Hoo, agent of the King of Dahomey, Africa," B. MS-120.

47. Bruce Collection, B. 6-63.

48. *Ibid.*, B. 6-74.

49. *Ibid.*, B. 6-63.

50. *Ibid.*, Caseley-Hayford to J.E. Bruce, November 24, 1923, B. 5.

51. *Ibid.*, B. MS-125; Shepperson, Notes . . .", 308.

52. Bruce Collection, B. Misc. 13-5.

53. T.L. Harrison of Lagos, Nigeria wrote to Bruce on April 9, 1907 thanking him for his proposal to have October 11 observed as "Agbebi Day in memory of Dr. Majola Agbebi," B. MS-167; also Shepperson, "Notes . . .", 309–310.

54. Marcus Garvey, a titanic force in Pan-Africanism, is not analyzed at length here because his major influence came after 1919, the year this study ends. In addition there has been an explosion of publications about Garvey and the movement he led making Garvey publishing virtually a growth industry. Two of the better-known students are Tony Martin and Robert Hill. By Tony Martin, see: *Race First: The Ideological and Organizational Struggles of Marcus Garvey and the Universal Negro Improvement Association* (Westport, Connecticut, 1976); *The Pan-African Connection: From Slavery to Garvey and Beyond* (Canton, Massachusetts, 1983); for younger readers, *Marcus Garvey, Hero: A First Biography* (Canton, Massachusetts, 1983); *Literary Garveyism: Garvey, Black Arts and the Harlem Renaissance* (Canton, Massachusetts, 1983). Compiled and edited by Martin are *African Fundamentalism: A Literary and Cultural Anthology of Garvey's Harlem Renaissance* (Canton, Massachusetts, 1991), and *The Poetical Works of Marcus Garvey* (Canton,

Massachusetts, 1983). Robert Hill and Barbara Bair have edited *The Marcus Garvey and Universal Negro Improvement Association Papers* (Berkeley, California, 1983–1990), 7 volumes, and Hill produced *Marcus Garvey: Life and Lessons, a Centennial Companion to the Marcus Garvey and Universal Negro Improvement Association Papers* (Berkeley, California, 1987) and edited *Pan African Biography* (Los Angeles, California, 1987).

An excellent revisionist essay that elucidates Garvey's contribution to African nationalism and destroys the myth, all too popular, that he was an eccentric, exclusive "back-to-Africanist," is J.A. Langley, "Garveyism and African Nationalism," *Race* (October, 1969), 157–171. See also Langley's "Pan Africanism in Paris 1924–1936," *Journal of Modern African Studies* (April, 1969), 69–94, and his *Pan-Africanism and Nationalism in West Africa* (London, 1973), 68–71, 97–98, *passim*. Garvey's Africa interest is also treated in Ben Rogers, "William E.B. DuBois, Marcus Garvey and Pan-Africa," *Journal of Negro History* (April, 1955), 154–166 and in a volume edited by John H. Clarke, *Marcus Garvey and the Vision of Africa* (New York, 1974). E.U. Essien-Udom's Introduction to *Philosophy and Opinions of Marcus Garvey* (London, 1967) is very good as is the volume with the same title edited by his wife, Amy Jacques Garvey, with a 1986 preface by Tony Martin.

55. "Mr. Marcus Garvey," in Gilbert (ed.), *Selected Writings*, 146.

56. *Calendar of Manuscripts*, I, 165.

57. *Ibid.*

58. *Ibid.*

59. *Ibid.*, B. 4-50.

60. This conclusion is based on a conversation the writer had with Schomburg's biographer, Mrs. Eleanor Sinnette (June 25, 1975). See Elinor Des Verney Sinnette, *Authur Alfonso Schomburg, Black Bibliophile and Collector: A Biography* (Detroit, Michigan, 1989). See also J.A. Rogers, *Worlds Great Men of Color* (rprt. New York, 1972), II, 448–543, which contains a brief biographical sketch. There are also scattered biographical materials in the Schomburg Collection of the New York Public Library.

61. It should be pointed out again that, at this time, when references were made to "Negro history" by Schomburg, DuBois, Woodson, and others, they included African and African-American history. There was no fine distinction between Africa's history and the

history of people of African descent in the diaspora. Diasporic history in this sense was merely an extension of African history.

62. Arthur A. Schomburg, "Racial Integrity: A Plea for the Establishment of a Chair of Negro History in Our Schools and Colleges," Occasional Paper Number 3, NSHR, 1913; copy in Schomburg Collection.

63. In Alain Locke (ed.), *The New Negro* (rprt. New York, 1969), 231–232.

64. An extensive list of African-American writings on Africa has been provided by Dorothy B. Porter, "A Biographical Checklist of American Negro Writers about Africa," In AMSAC (ed.), *Africa*, 379–399, which contains the writings of all of those discussed here.

65. William Ferris, *The African Abroad*, I, 429–522.

66. *Ibid.*, II, 822–852, photographs, 822.

67. (New York, 1914).

68. See Richard B. Moore, "Africa Conscious Harlem," *Freedomways* (1963), 415–334.

69. Most Relevant for Africa was his pamphlet, *One Hundred Amazing Facts about the Negro: With Complete Proof*, 23rd rev. ed. 1957; *Africa's Gift to America*, 2nd rev. ed. New York, 1961, and *The Worlds Great Men of Color* (1926; rprt. New York, 1972), 2 vols.

70. For some of Leo Hansberry's work, see Joseph Harris (ed.), *Pillars in Ethiopian History: The William Leo Hansberry African History Notebook*, vol. I (Washington, D.C., 1974) and *Africa and Africans as Seen By Classical Writers: The William Leo Hansberry African History Notebook*, (Washington, D.C., 1981), II. This author had an opportunity to visit Nsukka and the Hansberry Institute in 1989 and found it in a state of disrepair and undernourishment. See Milfred C. Fierce, *Africana Studies Outside the United States: Africa, Brazil and the Caribbean* (Ithaca, N.Y., 1990).

71. There is no published biography of Stewart, and there is disagreement over his date of birth. Some accounts give it at 1852 and others at 1854 and 1855; all agree on the month of December. 1854 is used here as a compromise date. This date is given in G.F. Richings, *Evidences of Progress Among Colored People* (Philadelphia, 1904), 291. Biographical information discussed in this brief account of his life comes

from scattered notes in the T. McCants Stewart Papers in the Moorland-Spingarn Research Center at Howard University.

72. See Judge McCants Stewart, "Conditions in Liberia," *A.M.E. Church Review* (July, 1915), 7–14.

73. See New York *Age* (May 23, 1907), 5; (July 21, 1910), 5.

74. See New York *Age* (August 15, 1907), 4.

75. Richard Ralston "A Second Middle Passage; African Student Sojourns in the United States During the Colonial Period and Their Influence Upon the Character of African Leadership," Ph.D. dissertation, U.C.L.A., 1972, 188–194. Relevant for a discussion of African students studying in the United States during the last quarter of the nineteenth century is Walter Williams, "Black American Attitudes Toward Africa; The Missionary Movement, 1877–1900" Ph.D. dissertation, University of North Carolina, Chapel Hill, 1974, chapter 9 and Appendix F; revised and published as *Black Americans and the Evangelization of Africa, 1877–1900* (Madison, Wisconsin, 1982).

76. The story of John Chilembwe is most comprehensively covered by George Shepperson and Thomas Price in *Independent African* (Edinburgh, 1958). An early, short version of this story by Shepperson is "The Story of John Chilembwe," *Negro History Bulletin* (January, 1952), 2–8.

77. Ralston, "A Second Middle Passage, chapters 4, 5, 6.

78. Contemporary nationalism in West Africa is discussed in Martin Kilson, "The Rise of Nationalist Organizations and Parties in British West Africa," in AMSAC (ed.), *Africa*, 34–69.

79. J.E. Casely-Hayford to W.E.B. DuBois, June 8, 1904, in Herbert Aptheker (ed.), *The Correspondence of W.E.B. DuBois 1877–1934*, 75–76. This exact letter was sent to Booker T. Washington. The date was the same and the only difference in the text was Hayford's reference to BTW's autobiography instead of DuBois's *Souls of Black Folk*. The point here is that Casely-Hayford, and other Africans as well, was eager for contact with "New World" Africans. There is no record of a response from DuBois, but Booker T. Washington in his reply, invited Casely-Hayford to Tuskegee Institute to observe the work being done there: Casely-Hayford to BTW, June 8, 1904; BTW to Casely-Hayford, July 6, 1904: (BTW Papers, Library of Congress, Box 289).

80. P. Nnabuenyi Ugonna, "Introduction," in J.E. Casely-Hayford, *Ethiopia Unbound*, rprt. London, 1969, vii.

81. Casely-Hayford, *Ethiopia Unbound*, 173.

82. Alex Haley's *Roots*, probably the best known genealogy study, is the story of one African-American who traced his ancestry back to West Africa (the Mandingo People of Sierra Leone, Liberia and Gambia).

83. Casely-Hayford, *Ethiopia Unbound*, chapter 17.

84. *Ibid.*, 165 and chapter 16. The other published book of Casely-Hayford's well worth seeing is *The Truth about the West African Land Question*, rprt. London, 1971. See also Robert July, "The Metamorphosis of Casely-Hayford," in *The Origins of Modern African Thought* (New York, 1967), chapter 21.

85. J.A. Langley, *Pan-Africanism*, 98.

86. *Ibid.*

87. *Ibid.*, 98–103.

88. A. Kirkland Soga to BTW, December 9, 1903 (BTW Papers, Box 294).

89. W.E.B. DuBois to E.W. Blyden, April 5, 1909, in Aptheker (ed.), *The Correspondence*, 145–146.

90. *Ibid.*, 182–184.

CHAPTER III

The Stewart Foundation for Africa: A Vehicle for African-American Missionary Interaction with West Africa

The Stewart Missionary Foundation for Africa at Gammon Theological Seminary, in Atlanta, Georgia, was founded in 1894 by William Fletcher Stewart. Stewart was a White Methodist minister from Ohio and an 1843 graduate of Augusta College in Kentucky.[1] A deep-rooted concern for Black people in the United States, and later in Africa, was a part of the Stewart family tradition. Both William Stewart's father, John Stewart, and his grandfather Daniel Stewart, were Methodist ministers who embodied an all-consuming concern for Black people. William Stewart's alma mater, in fact, was disbanded by the Kentucky legislature, which took away its endowment funds because of its reputed anti-slave character. The endowment funds and the college's possessions were subsequently divided between the Methodist Church Conferences of Ohio and Kentucky. Moreover, the Stewart home on an Illinois farm during the abolitionist era was seldom found without Blacks as guests. Stewart's sympathy for Blacks also included more than a desire for their happiness and a recognition of their need for human rights and justice. Although William Stewart oftentimes found Blacks ". . . ignorant and in poverty; he helped them learn and gave them an opportunity to earn."[2] The family was fully imbued with two basic ideals, "to help hasten the spread of the Kingdom of God through the world, and to help the Negroes to grow up to the fullness of men in Christ Jesus."[3] To William Stewart and his family, the enslavement of Africa's peoples—in

77

the United States and Africa—was wicked and cruel, but Blacks, through the Spirit of God and His Providence, could receive the knowledge of the Redeemer and have their lives and condition transformed by the power of the "true religion." Consequently, Stewart concluded that Blacks in the United States, having experienced "racial uplift" (presumably through contact with "true religion," their enslavement to the contrary notwithstanding), "might become the messengers of light and love to those behind in the darkness of Africa."[4] His involuted reasoning was quite characteristic of clerics—and others—of the period.

William Stewart's earliest correspondence regarding his plans for the establishment of the Foundation or some similar agency is dated November 19, 1893, and speaks of his intention to contribute the revenue from his property to missionary work for Africa.[5] At this time his conception of what became the Stewart Foundation was that of a missionary training school-farm to be located in central Illinois. Thoroughly saturated with benevolent sentiments, Stewart later wrote of his expectation that this missionary training school-farm would "become a center for the diffusion of missionary intelligence, the development of missionary enthusiasm, the increase of missionary offerings, and through sanctified and trained missionaries hasten obedience to . . . preach the gospel to every creature."[6] Still later he wrote of his plans to make the agency permanent.[7] Stewart's wealth, such as it was, was acquired through the combination of savings ($400) and a gift from his father ($600), which was subsequently invested in soldiers' land warrants in Wisconsin costing ninety cents per acre. He improved, tenanted, and eventually sold this land and reinvested the proceeds in unimproved land. This land and its revenue plus some additional land purchased from the Illinois Central Railroad constituted the endowment he provided for the foundation established in his name.[8]

William Fletcher Stewart's plan for a missionary foundation for the "redemption" of Africa was inspired first by the exploits of Melville B. Cox,[9] a free Black Methodist from

Marietta, Ohio. Cox had been an evangelist among the Native Americans of Ohio and was so successful that, in 1833, he was sent to do "God's work" in Liberia. The Methodist church was now positioned for African reclamation. In addition, the crusades of William Taylor, later Methodist Episcopal Church Missionary Bishop for Africa and an eminent African traveler, stirred the enthusiasm of the Methodist church with his evangelistic victories in India, South America, and Africa. Indeed, it was Taylor who conceived the idea in the Southern Methodist Church that Africa would be saved for Christ by African-Americans because they "would become the chosen messengers of the cross."[10] W.F. Stewart wrote to Bishop Taylor, outlining his plans for a missionary training school for those individuals who might consecrate themselves to the cause of African "regeneration" and invited him to organize and manage the enterprise. Owing to his demanding schedule, Bishop Taylor, while applauding the plan, declined to participate in it. Disappointed but determined, Rev. Stewart approached the Gammon Theological Seminary with his scheme for preparing men and women for missionary work in Africa.

Gammon Theological Seminary was established specifically to train Christian ministers for the Black race and, therefore, was particularly well suited to combine its efforts with another kindred institution.[11] The energetic William Stewart now wrote, unfolding his plan, to Wilbur Thirkield, president of Gammon, and to Edward L. Parks, leader of the faculty. The reception at Gammon was enthusiastic, as the president and faculty considered this plan an opportunity to expand Gammon's usefulness. Gammon requested only that Stewart underwrite whatever expenses were involved. Stewart was excited over this response. He wrote to Parks that, "I am well pleased, and herewith hand you my check for $200 the amount you estimate will cover the cost of prize books and expenses."[12] With this agreement sealed, according to Stewart's son Grant, the educational and missionary movement of the Stewart Missionary Foundation for Africa was now seen as the culmination of

... a life-long ambition to contribute a worthy part to help a people [African-Americans and Africans] who had sat in darkness and had suffered from the cruelty of all true followers of Jesus Christ in the deliverance of the lowly peoples of Africa from their bondage and helplessness, and at the same time help the humble people of America to rise to a holy adventure in the Kingdom of God.[13]

Stewart's vision for the Foundation was broad indeed. The immediate concern and earliest priority would be the proper training of missionaries for the purpose of rescuing "darkest" Africa for the church. Furthermore, this *raison d'être* would be supported by literary, oratorical, and prize hymn contests (all, of course, exalting African work) among students in Methodist-run schools, colleges, and seminaries. Singing Black crusaders organized into duets, quartets or choruses and "intent on redeeming Africa from the dominion of the devil,"[14] were also to be used. At Gammon it was generally felt that wonders might be accomplished through this medium. Not surprisingly Stewart believed, "The Negro has peculiar gift and enthusiasm in the department of song."[15] There would also be lectures and addresses by leading minds in the church. These activities were to be complimented by periodic reports from missionaries in the field and testimony from converts in the missions. Plans also called for "Friends of Africa" to be organized in the schools and "Bands" in the Methodist congregations in the South to aid the Foundation and accelerate Africa's salvation.[16] Stewart put it this way: "I would like to commence doing some work in Africa, and would like that it should be the work of the Foundation assisted by the Bands, Friends of Africa, etc. The work so arranged as to form a vital link between the helpers and the helped, so that the assistance from African-Americans and the reports from the native Africans should act and react from the encouragement of both."[17] Stewart felt the financial crunch that visited the United States in the mid-1890s, but was hopeful that the work of the Foundation would not suffer. He wrote,

> Failure of parties owing me and failure of the bank where I had funds deposited have made it necessary for me to make temporary loans for current expenses. But I shall not allow anything to interfere with my support of the work we have begun. Let us all pray as if all depended on prayer and work as if all depended on work.[18]

The Rev. William F. Stewart, who since 1853 had been a member of the Rock River Conference of the Methodist Church (Ohio) and was now a harbinger for Africa's spiritual rehabilitation, seemed to have a peculiar penchant for the missionary prize competition, which consumed no little portion of his interest and energy. He advanced the money for the first year's prizes and recommended a plan for the competition.[19] "I think that missionary fire once kindled in young souls, love for the work will be superior to prizes,"[20] he noted. Announcements were sent to the executive officers of all affiliated institutions, describing the details and conditions for the contests and the prizes, whose general features included, (1) three categories of prizes, academy, college, and a theological seminary series open to Black students of the Freedman's Aid and Southern Education Society of the Methodist Episcopal Church. Prizes would be given in each series for work on some topic concerned with Africa as a mission field or missionary work in Africa; (2) each series would hold local elimination contests under the direction of faculty and all winning productions were to be regarded as the property of the Stewart Foundation, which had the option to publish them or otherwise use them as the Foundation saw fit; (3) and an annual exhibition in Atlanta of all prize works, presented free-of-charge and open to the public.[21] The choice of topics for essays and orations was left to individual choice, but the February 1804 issue of the *Quarterly Bulletin*, the publication of the faculty of Gammon Theological Seminary, carried the following suggested topics:

> Africa as a Mission Field; The Lessons of Missionary Work in Africa; The Missionary Work of David Livingstone; The

Need of Missionary Work in Africa; Bishop Hannington the Martyr Missionary; Self Supporting Missions in Africa; Results of Missionary Labors in Liberia; The Rum Traffic as an Enemy to Missions in Africa; The Slave-trade as an Obstacle to Missions in Africa; Samuel Crowther, the Native African Bishop; The Congo Free State as a Mission Field; The Relation of the American Negro to the Evangelization of Africa; The Best Means of Inducing the American to Engage in Missionary Work for Africa; Obligation of the American Negro to the Heathen in Africa.[22]

The feeling was pervasive in this division of the Methodist church in the United States that any parallels between the experiences of Africans and African-Americans were best explained by the theory of Providential Design.[23] Accordingly, there was a providential relationship between the emancipation of Blacks in America and their missionary role in Africa. In other words, God was now providing an opportunity for Black Americans to vindicate their emancipation and permanently etch their name in Christian history by evangelizing among the "heathen" of Africa and retrieving the continent for Christ. Indeed, "the other missionary fields of the world are being occupied. Africa alone is left for missionary work by the colored people of America," according to one distinguished churchman.[24] Stewart himself believed that African-Americans were God's chosen instruments for the necessary missionary work in Africa. He stated, "It seemed plain to me as it has done all along that the Christian Negro population must first be aroused to a sense of responsibility and then enthused with the Christ spirit. . . . This will lead Christian Negroes to make all necessary sacrifices and devote themselves to the evangelization of Africa."[25] To some, the role that African-Americans would play in the Christian conversion of Africa was "the greatest missionary event set up to this time in connection with the Negro race in America and their relation to Africa—probably one of the greatest in the modern history of the church."[26] White missionaries, apparently, it was felt, were the victims of such strong prejudices, provoked by the inhumanity of foreign traders in Africa, that they could not be effective, or at least not as effective as indigenous Africans or their "kith and kin," African-Americans.[27]

The very first Black missionary sent to Africa by the Stewart Foundation was Rev. Alexander P. Camphor, four years before the nineteenth century ended. The Foundation proclaimed that it was instrumental in sending more Black missionaries to Africa than any other agency and that it was "the largest and best endowed missionary agency for the colored race in the world."[28] Rev. Camphor was accompanied to Liberia by his wife, and served there for twelve years before returning to Birmingham, Alabama, where he organized a school for Black youths. Camphor eventually returned to West Africa following his appointment as Bishop for Liberia.[29] He had graduated from New Orleans University and took a B.D. from Gammon in 1895. He evidently had no serious early interest in going to Africa but later fell under the influence of J.C. Hartzell, M.E. Church-South Bishop for Africa after Bishop Taylor, who persuaded him to consecrate himself for Africa.[30] Speaking optimistically of Camphor and his wife, Hartzell had this to say just before their departure from the United States: "I expect great things of them. They are the first to go from our schools—representing this renewed African people in America."[31]

Alexander Camphor, who won an award while a student at Gammon for an essay entitled, "Africa's Awakening and Redemption,"[32] sailed for Liberia on December 19, 1896. In a series of letters partially reprinted in the *Quarterly Bulletin* (February, 1897), he revealed his motives for going to Africa, all of which were inspired by the "call" from Providence:

> After much prayer and meditation with God, my wife and
> I have cheerfully consecrated ourselves for Africa. We
> believe the call to be from above, so we willingly go in the
> name of Him who has promised to be with us always,
> even to the end of the world.[33]

* * * *

As I turn my face to Africa it is with joy and hope. I praise God that I am in some little measure counted worthy to toil for the Master. The great thought of serving Christ, the Church and humanity has taken a deep hold on me. I am willing to follow Him wherever He leads me. . . . I decided to go not for money. I did not know a word about salary . . . I felt that if God called me [H]e would provide for me and He has.[34]

* * * *

I go [to Africa] because I believe we young men ought to let the world see that we love the cause of Christ better than comforts, and even better than life; that this love should know no clime nor country, for I believe . . . that the world is our parish. . . . Say to the boys at Gammon that to win prizes in the Stewart Foundation is not all; they must win Africa for Christ as well, and for this they will get the hands of the Lord and imperishable prize, that shall shine with incessant lustre and beauty throughout all eternity.[35]

The fortunes of Africa as a mission field waxed and waned depending on the vagaries of the resources of the Stewart Foundation and the vicissitudes of the prevailing world order— mainly during the era of the First World War, when it became hazardous to journey across the Atlantic Ocean. However, African-Americans from Stewart were indefatigable evangelists in Africa throughout the foundation's existence. Extremely important (and to the researchers delight), the Stewart Foundation for Africa maintained a valuable and almost uninterrupted chronicle of African-Americans evangelizing in Africa through their publication of *Quarterly Bulletin* and *The Foundation*. As a result of increasing costs and declining revenues for the Stewart Foundation, however, they ceased publication in the mid-1980s.[36]

The Foundation was the official organ of the Stewart Missionary Foundation for Africa. It began publication in Atlanta, Georgia with the January 1911 number and for a time it was jointly published by Gammon Seminary and the Stewart Foundation. Its first editor was Rev. D.D. Martin, and the first page of the first issue carried this message about Africa and African-Americans by Wilbur Thirkield, President of Gammon when the Stewart Foundation was born and also President of the Congress on Africa (1895):

> One of the vital and urgent problems before us is the relation of the American Negro to the civilization and redemption of his Fatherland. God's hand must be recognized in his presence in America. This is now the home and heritage of these Americans born of the colored race. Here he will stay. But the forefinger of that same hand that brought him hither points the way to Africa for the tens, the hundreds, and in future years, to the thousands who shall be agents of God in the redemption of the Dark Continent. It will appear that the call is not for the weak, the poor, the ignorant of the race. Such may only relapse into barbarism. But Africa now needs the best brain, and the best heart, the finest moral fiber, and the most skilled genius and power that the American Negro can furnish for her civilization and redemption.[37]

In addition to news about African-American missionaries in Africa, *The Foundation* contained items ranging from the testimony of African students studying in mission schools in Africa and colleges and universities in the United States, who affirmed the benevolence of Christianity,[38] to the appeal for aid and the advertising of fund-raising campaigns.[39] Missionaries were recruited through the pages of *The Foundation*,[40] students who opted for Africa services were limelighted, complete with striking front-page portraits and short biographies,[41] and reports from remote mission stations in Africa run by the Stewart Foundation were printed.[42] Generally, every kind of information imaginable regarding Black missionaries and Africa was paraded between the covers of *The Foundation*. There was a regular monthly column entitled "Points," which carried quips like, "The missionaries in Africa the heroes of the hour" or "Our workers in Africa were never more in need than during this war period."[43] The names of the officers of the "Friends of Africa" or "Bands" were oftentimes printed in *The Foundation* to publicize the organizations and to plead for resources and help.[44] Most interesting was the frequent printing of prize winning essays, hymns, and poems,[45] such as those criticizing Liberia's maintenance of women's slavery[46] or the lengthy thesis on Liberia in the October 1919 issue.[47]

Rev. J.F.B. Coleman and his wife Gertrude were elected for missionary service in West Africa and sailed from New York on May 25, 1911. Their destination was the Industrial Mission on the St. Paul River in Liberia, which was sponsored by the Stewart Foundation and which Rev. Coleman would now supervise. Both were graduates of Claflin University and Rev. Coleman, who eventually became president of the Stewart Foundation's College of West Africa, was a 1911 graduate of Gammon. Prior to their marriage in March 1911, Mrs. Coleman was an instructor at Samuel Houston College in Austin, Texas. Mr. and Mrs. Coleman were both well trained, especially for Black Americans in the first decade of the twentieth century, and they are representative of the kind of Black missionary who opted for Africa service. They were, to be sure, very much the exception in terms of education. Consequently, Africa, through the missionary enterprise, received some of the most talented Blacks in the United States at this time.[48]

Rev. Coleman was not a frequent correspondent while he was in Liberia. Moreover, letters from him did not begin to appear regularly in *The Foundation* until March 1915, when he took over the Presidency of the College of West Africa.[49] However, in 1914 he wrote to *The Foundation* regarding fifty-four Black emigrants from Florida who were swindled by a fast-talking Liberian in the United States and regarding the financial crisis in Liberia, which had been exacerbated by World War I.

The emigrants had paid exorbitant fees to this swindler, who had grossly exaggerated conditions in Liberia and what new settlers could expect there. The newcomers were described as "simple country folk" who were members of the A.M.E. Church and who had little formal schooling. The Liberian government was completely surprised by their arrival, but was attempting to accommodate them as as best they could, with little apparent success. Rev. Coleman closed with this example of frustration in the group: "[O]ne seriously disappointed brother ran off, leaving his wife and children here, and hasn't been heard from since."[50]

Regarding Liberia's precarious financial situation in 1914, Coleman was brief and to the point. Ninety percent of Liberia's commercial trade was with Germany and because of the war, was now cut off. In addition, "there are no internal developments worth mentioning, and agriculture is at its lowest ebb," the Reverend lamented.[51]

Another husband and wife team who elected to go to Liberia as missionaries were Dr. W.G. Alston and Mrs. Nellie Alston, who, like Mrs. Coleman, was a college graduate and trained school teacher. Rev. Alston was a graduate of Bennett College, Gammon Theological Seminary, and educated at "other schools." Dr. Alston was appointed principal of Cape Palmas district in the Methodist Episcopal Church. Both sailed for West Africa in December 1911.

In Liberia, Rev. Alston plunged right into the work of proselytizing among the indigenous peoples. He traveled periodically to the remote areas surrounding Cape Palmas in search of converts. In one of his early important letters to *The Foundation*, he wrote that two local kings, King Booker and King Davis, had donated land on which to build new churches and agreed to look after the church's interest in their areas. He also proudly stated, "my work is still growing. I have baptized nearly seven hundred happy native Christians in the past six months."[52] Bishop Scott, now Bishop for Liberia and a frequent letter writer to *The Foundation*, spared no hyperbole in this sterling tribute to Dr. and Mrs. Alston, the tireless, dedicated missionaries:

> Alston returns to his work simply wild with enthusiasm. He and his wife, Nellie Landry Alston, were certainly cast in the moulds of heroism. He traveled his district on foot and in canoes and open boats, while he was tottering on his legs weakened by repeated attacks of fever. She, when too weak to go about the house, would have her classes gather about her bedside so that she might continue the work of trying to train them for God and the salvation of Africa.[53]

Maintenance of the Cape Palmas Seminary was almost totally dependent on voluntary contributions, in addition to what the Foundation provided. The demand for supplies and resources always ran well ahead of those available. Therefore, the resilient missionary often resorted to the direct appeal approach for assistance. Mrs. Alston made just such a pitch in the spring of 1913. She wrote about the importance of assistance from "friends in the homeland" and how the resources of the Seminary were being severely taxed, with only a limited number of scholarships. Effectively moving from the general to the specific, she mentioned such needs as "a clock, four or five dozen of Shakey and Moody's song books, underwear for twenty girls, stockings and shoes, strong shirts for boys and trousers for those that come with just a cloth." She closed by noting that "this year we have some girls from bush country, and they need everything."[54] This plea was reinforced by "missionary" hope and faith that the appeal would be carefully read and that there would be some response to its needs.

Rev. F.A. Price went to Liberia in 1905 as a missionary and remained for eleven years. He was in charge of the Wissika Mission, a frontier station in Cape Palmas. Price was born in Jamaica, West Indies and received his formal education on the island of Barbados. He later migrated from the West Indies to Brooklyn, New York, where he was trained as a missionary. His wife, Lulu Jones, was a graduate of Boylan Home School in Jacksonville, Florida, and met her husband while also undergoing training for the African field in Brooklyn. They later married in Africa. In 1916, Rev. Price was appointed Superintendent of the Cape Palmas district. He was scheduled to leave for his new duties after having remained briefly in the United States, following his return from Africa, less than a year before.[55]

Not all Black missionaries in Liberia and West Africa were husband and wife teams. Single church women in particular devoted a substantial portion of their lives to missionary work in Africa. One case in point was Miss Annie Hall. Annie Hall was a graduate of Clark University in Atlanta and received tutoring for missionary work under a Miss Flora Mitchell at Clark, as well as "special training" in Boston, Massachusetts, before accepting "the call to Africa." She was assigned to Cape Palmas in Liberia and upon Miss Alice McAllister's return to the United States in 1908 from Liberia, where she had been overseeing mission stations, Miss Hall was placed in charge of the Carraway Mission, where she supervised four mission stations. There are several articles in *The Foundation* by or about Annie Hall's work at Carraway, as well as frequent letters from her. She did a yeoman's job as a thoroughly dedicated missionary—now treating the sick and suffering; now raising money in Liberia as well as through appeals to the United States for various mission stations; now supervising and assisting in the raising of crops such as rice, cassava, and vegetables, plus rounding up edible meats; now clearing new farmland and building churches; now making preparations for funerals and comforting mourners; now visiting all of the surrounding mission stations.[56] Actually, as a champion of "God's cause" and agent of the Stewart Foundation, Annie Hall was neither unprecedented nor unparalleled, but epitomizes the Black American missionary who was convinced, beyond any doubt, that conversion to Christianity was a prerequisite for Africa's regeneration. Once in the field, this Black descendent of former slaves in the United States had the best of intentions and was primarily concerned with doing "good works" and saving souls for Christ.

Like Annie Hall, Martha Drummer was educated at Clark University and was specially trained for missionary work by Flora Mitchell, Superintendent of the Thayer Home, located at Clark. Martha Drummer was assigned to Quessua in Melange, Angola, which was about 400 miles from Luanda the capital. Following five years of service in Africa, Miss Drummer returned to the United States for a rest and did not return to Africa.[57]

Diana Bralah (McNeil) was a native of the Grebo tribe (Liberia) who was brought to the United States by Bishop William Taylor in 1892. By 1909 she had graduated from the University of Southern California. After that she received special missionary training at the Chicago Training School. At first she was delayed in her efforts to return to Africa for missionary work among her own people because of a shortage of funds in the missionary treasury. However, the October 1912 issue of *The Foundation* announced that, in answer to the many prayers on her behalf, the funds had finally been raised to finance her return home. She spent the remainder of her life as a missionary in West Africa.

Charles T. Wardah is another example, along with Diana McNeil, of an African student who was able to study in the United States under missionary auspices and who later attested to the value of a Christian education.[58] Wardah was a prince from the Bassa tribe in Central Liberia. His father, in an effort to protect Charles from the perils of local wars, made it possible for him to attend the Methodist Seminary at Cape Palmas, where he was converted. Reportedly "eager for training that he might carry the gospel of hope and civilization to his people,"[59] Bishop I.B. Scott brought him to Tuskegee in 1911.[60] In his graduation address at Tuskegee entitled "What a Liberian Can Do for His Country," Prince Wardah glorified the Tuskegee idea and "the gospel of sanitation as well as the Gospel of Salvation."[61] He also recommended the things a Tuskegee-like trained Liberian could contribute to his country's "uplift" and development,[62] from teaching the indigenous people about the sacredness of their bodies, which should not be mutilated with marks from sharp knives, to teaching the children about "agriculture, domestic science, right habits in the kitchen, housekeeping, and many other useful laws and habits."[63] Wardah concluded that the Tuskegee spirit could provide a knowledge of the "physical, mental, industrial, political, moral, and religious needs of the people. A native Liberian can be a powerful factor in making Liberia a great center of influence and Christianizing the Dark Continent."[64]

The Stewart Foundation and the Black missionaries representing it in Africa saw Africa's salvation through the adoption of Christianity. Almost everything the church or its agents did was guided by this belief. The White church committed to Africa's "salvation" had a counterpart in the Black church. For all of the same reasons and with almost all of the same results, the independent Black denominations set out to do their part in the rescue of the "Dark Continent."

NOTES

1. Most of the information on the life of William Fletcher Stewart, for whom there is no major published biography, contained in this discussion comes from the Stewart Papers, now being organized, cataloged, and microfilmed by the General Commission on Archives and History of the United Methodist Church at Drew University in Madison, New Jersey, under the directorship of Dr. William Beal. When this process is completed, the Stewart Papers will be returned to the Atlanta University Center in Atlanta, Georgia and will be located in the Special Collections section of the Woodruff Library. Of particular importance is a pamphlet published by Stewart's son, G. Grant Stewart, entitled, "William Fletcher Stewart, Founder of the Stewart Missionary Foundation for Africa: A Brief Historical Sketch" (Los Angeles,

California, 1941). See, also, Edward L. Parks, "Rev. William Fletcher Stewart, M.M.; A Memorial Address," published as a Memorial Edition of the *Quarterly Bulletin* (April, 1901) by the faculty of the Gammon Theological Seminary; and *Quarterly Bulletin* (February, 1894), 3, which contains a short biography.

      Rev. G. Grant Stewart was one of William Stewart's sons and compiled his biography from family materials and the informative correspondence between Rev. William Stewart and the Gammon Theological Seminary, its faculty, and various officials and administrators, much of which can be found in the Stewart Collection that will be housed in the Special Collections division of the Woodruff Library on the campus of the Atlanta University Center.

    2. *Quarterly Bulletin* (April, 1901), 20.

    3. G. Grant Stewart, "William Fletcher Stewart. . . ," 2.

    4. *Ibid.*

    5. W.F. Stewart to Gammon Faculty, Stewart Papers, as is all other correspondence cited.

    6. *Quarterly Bulletin* (April, 1901) 16–17; G. Grant Stewart, "William Fletcher Stewart. . . ," 4.

    7. W.F. Stewart to E.L. Parks, January 29, 1894.

    8. St. Clair Drake "Negro Americans and the 'Africa Interest'", in *American Negro Reference Book* (Englewood, New Jersey, 1969), 670, evidently paraphrasing Horace Mann Bond, mentions that ". . . one enthusiastic White Methodist donated over $200,000 to establish the Stewart Foundation for Africa. . ." This comment could only refer to William Fletcher Stewart, and no record of any such donation could be found by this writer in the Stewart Papers.

    9. In 1917–1918 there was a movement to have a new building for the College of West Africa erected as a memorial to Melville Cox, "the first Missionary to Liberia, and the first Foreign Missionary of the Methodist Episcopal Church." The movement was supported by President J.F.B. Coleman and the Bishop for Liberia, Alexander Camphor, who, incidentally, was the first Black missionary sent to Liberia by the Stewart Foundation. If Cox's name was given to the new building, it was given after 1919, the year this study ends. For the quote and discussion of the movement see *The Foundation* (February, 1918), 1; see also *The Foundation* (October, 1917), 4.

10. G. Grant Stewart, "William Fletcher Stewart...," 2–3.

11. Unfortunately, there appears to be no recent history of Gammon Theological Seminary, which was founded in Atlanta, Georgia (1883) for the training of Black Methodist clergymen. There is, however, a 1948 New York University Ed.D. dissertation by Prince A. Taylor entitled "A History of Gammon Theological Seminary" that is useful. Almost as old but nevertheless worthwhile on Gammon's history is Alphonso A. McPheeters, "The Origin and Development of Clark University and Gammon Theological Seminary," Ed.D. dissertation, University of Cincinnati, 1944. In a book entitled *Two Centuries of Methodist Concern: Bondage, Freedom and Education of Black People* (New York, 1974), the author James P. Brawley discusses Gammon Seminary, 315–346, and the Stewart Missionary Foundation for Africa, 326–327.

12. W.F. Stewart to E.L. Parks, January 29, 1894.

13. G. Grant Stewart, "William Fletcher Stewart...," 4.

14. *Ibid.*

15. *Ibid.*

16. *Quarterly Bulletin* (November, 1894), 5–6.

17. W.F. Stewart to E.L. Parks, February 10, 1896. Examples of how "Friends" and "Bands" were organized can be seen in *Quarterly Bulletin* (February, 1897), 1.

18. W.F. Stewart to Gammon Faculty, October 3, 1895.

19. W.F. Stewart to Gammon Faculty, January 29, 1894.

20. W.F. Stewart to Gammon Faculty, January 10, 1894.

21. *Quarterly Bulletin* (February, 1894), 2–3.

22. *Ibid.*

23. The origins of the theory of Providential Design in the United States can be traced to the early nineteenth century when the White advocates of Black colonization were its most important proponents. See P.J. Staudenraus, *The African Colonization Movement 1816–1865* (New York, 1961), chapters 1 and 2, especially the footnotes. For a brief discussion of the continuation of this doctrine after the Civil War, consult Drake, "Negro Americans...," 667–673.

24. "Bishop Walden's Lecture on Africa," *Quarterly Bulletin* (February, 1895), 3.

25. W.F. Stewart to E.L. Parks, October 1, 1895.

26. *Quarterly Bulletin* (February, 1894), 2.

27. *Quarterly Bulletin* (February, 1895), 1; *Outlook* (Spring, 1894) 6; *The Foundation* (June, 1913), 7.

28. This claim appeared in the October 1912 issue of *The Foundation*, official organ of the Stewart Foundation. No mention was made of the specific number of missionaries sent into the African field here or elsewhere. My own estimate is that during the fifteen-year period 1900–1915, after which it was risky to attempt to cross the Atlantic Ocean because of the outbreak of World War I, the Foundation sent a total of about 150 Black missionaries to Africa, an average of ten per year.

29. *The Foundation* (July–August, 1916), 1.

30. *Quarterly Bulletin* (February, 1897), 5.

31. *Quarterly Bulletin* (February, 1897), 4–5.

32. In this essay Alexander Camphor discussed the importance of God and Christianity to Africa—which would be responsible for the continent's eschatological rehabilitation: "God means the redemption of [H]is people, who have waited in pagan night and in the shadow of death," *Quarterly Bulletin* (February, 1897), 4–5.

33. Alexander Camphor to Bishop Mallalieu, December 1, 1896.

34. Alexander Camphor to Bishop Mallalieu, December 18, 1896.

35. It is uncertain to whom this letter was addressed—probably the Gammon faculty again—but it was written to Camphor from sea (Madeira), January 8, 1897. Rev. Camphor's expanded views on Africa up to 1909 are presented in his *Missionary Sketches and Folklore* (Cincinnati, Ohio, 1909). See also *Colored American Magazine* (November, 1909), 300–301.

36. There is a possibility that another periodical was published by the Stewart Foundation entitled the *Stewart Foundation Bulletin*, prior to the launching of *The Foundation* in 1911. This suggestion is made in *The Foundation* (January, 1919) 1, and if true would bridge the gap between the *Quarterly Bulletin* and *The Foundation* as a record of Black missionary activities in Africa. If this publication existed at all, it is most likely to be in the Stewart Papers. I hasten to add that my own painstaking search failed to locate it, leading me to speculate that the reference made to the *Stewart Foundation Bulletin* might possibly have been meant for the *Quarterly Bulletin*. In any event, the best collection of extant copies of *The*

Foundation is held by Rev. Josephus Coan of the Interdenominational Theological Center (ITC), who graciously loaned some of them to me during my first research visit to Atlanta, thanks to Ms. Honor Davenport, then Archivist at ITC. This publication, like all other Stewart Foundation material, will be found in the Special Collections section of the Woodruff Library on the campus of Clark-Atlanta University in Atlanta, Georgia.

37. *The Foundation* (January, 1911), 1. For the full text of this speech by Thirkield, see J.W.E. Bowen (ed.), *Africa and the American Negro*, 13–14.

38. See below, notes 61 and 62. See also the following issues of *The Foundation:* (January, 1911), 6; (September, 1913), 5; (June, 1914), 3; (October, 1914), 1; and 7; (February, 1916), 5.

39. *The Foundation* (August–September, 1912), 4–5; (November, 1912), 6; (December, 1914), 3–4; (October, 1917), 4.

40. *The Foundation* (November, 1912), 6; (December, 1912), 7; (June, 1913), 7; (August, 1913), 3; (September, 1913), 8.

41. *The Foundation* The Camphors: (February, 1911), 1; Colemans: (May, 1911), 1; Alstons: (January, 1912), 1; Hall and Drummer: (March, 1912), 1; Prices: (May–June, 1916), 1.

42. On the College of West Africa, see *The Foundation* (February, 1918), 1; (September–October, 1918), 1; (November, 1918), 1; for reports generally from several different places see *The Foundation* (February, 1913), 8; (June, 1913), 8; (September, 1914), 4 and 8; (December, 1914), 5; (August, 1915), 1; (December, 1916), 7; (May–June, 1919), 11.

43. *The Foundaiton* (January, 1915), 3; (April, 1918), 3.

44. For 1912, only as an example, see *The Foundation* (February, 1912), 6; (March, 1912), 6; (December, 1912), 6.

45. Prize-winning hymns, poems, and several essays appeared in almost every single issue of *The Foundation*. Some of the more instructive ones are in the following issues: (March 1912), 7; (November, 1912), 7; (June, 1913), 7; (October, 1913), 7; (February, 1914), 7; (September, 1914), 6; (March, 1915), 2–3; (December, 1916), 7, particularly the front page article entitled "Africa"; (January, 1917); (October, 1917), 9.

46. Two examples only, mentioned here are the (November, 1914) issue p. 6; and the (July, 1915) issue p. 8.

47. Philip T. Davis, a native Liberian and a 1919 graduate of Morristown College in Tennessee, "Liberia: The Hope of Africa," 9–10. Note especially his comments regarding politics and the attitude of "Americo-Liberians" toward "Afro-Liberians."

48. Most Blacks who had aspirations for higher education often wound up in theological training because this field offered the best possibility for a college-level education. Most other fields were severely limited or closed altogether.

49. *The Foundation* (March, 1915), 3. See also the announcement of Coleman's plan to go to Africa in the first issue of *The Foundation* (January, 1911), 6.

50. Letter from J.F.B. Coleman printed in *The Foundation* (December, 1914), 4.

51. *Ibid.* In the April 1919 issue of *The Foundation* (p. 9), Rev. Coleman, in an article entitled "The Negro and the Peace Conference," discussed the problems and possibilities of Pan-Africanism and self-determination, especially for West Africa. The article continues with customary African-American paternalism but indicates a concern for the importance of political machinations regarding Africa's future and, therefore, falls under the rubric of Pan-African thought, which, in my estimation, was quite popular among missionaries.

52. W.G. Alston to *The Foundation* (November, 1912), 6.

53. "Letter from Bishop Scott," *The Foundation* (June, 1913), 5.

54. "Letter from Mrs. W.G. Alston," *The Foundation* (June, 1913), 6.

55. *The Foundation* (May–June, 1916), 1. All of the Black missionaries mentioned—Bishop Scott, the Colemans, the Alstons, the Prices and some others—were honored as "Our Missionaries in Africa" on the cover of *The Foundation* (June, 1913), with their photographs. For examples of their correspondence as it relates to their missionary work in Africa, see almost any issue of *The Foundation* between 1911 and 1919, which is only the period covered by this investigation.

56. For Annie Hall see at least, *The Foundation* (November, 1914), 1; (March, 1915), 2; (September–October, 1912), 2; (May–June, 1919), 11; (November, 1919), 8.

57. *The Foundation* (March, 1912), 1, 6.

58. Sammy Morris, *The Foundation* (June, 1913), 5, was a third example. An unidentified African student who wrote to *The Foundation* (October, 1914), 7 was a fourth.

59. *The Foundation* (April, 1912), 1; this front-page article about Charles Wardah also includes a photograph and the story and photograph about another African student, Charles W. Siddah, whose circumstances are similar to Wardah's.

60. While a student at Tuskegee, Charles T. Wardah and another Liberian student were the subject of some misunderstanding regarding responsibility for their support while at Tuskegee. Bishop Scott apparently worked out a suitable financial arrangement with Booker T. Washington, whereby Olivia and Caroline Phelps-Stokes (Phelps-Stokes Fund) were to put up some or all of the money necessary for maintaining the Liberian students while at Tuskegee. Several important administrators at Tuskegee had no knowledge of the financial arrangement, especially Logan, the Treasurer, and the funds eventually were exhausted. Wardah had no money and was prevented from making further charges to his account, which was $57 in arrears. Wardah apparently became desperate and wrote to Emmet Scott seeking a solution. His letter triggered the exchange of much correspondence between administrators unfamiliar with the support provisions for the Liberian students. The matter was further complicated by one of Booker T. Washington's customary, lengthy absences from Tuskegee. Finally, the Phelps-Stokes sisters had to advance additional monies for the students' support. This incident illustrates one of the many difficulties African students encountered studying in the United States—and perhaps still encounter. The incident certainly did not sour Wardah toward Tuskegee because he remained a loyal, devoted Tuskegean, always championing its ideal. Booker T. Washington Papers, Manuscripts Division, Library of Congress, Box #47, folder #1 is where this correspondence can be found. Of special importance is the Wardah letter to Emmett Scott. Although Wardah was struggling with his English, his point is unmistakably clear. It reads in part, "I do not know what arrangement that Bishop Scott made with Mr. Washington, or with the school about me. Bishop Scott simply told me that Dr. B.T. Washington was going to support me . . . But it seemed (*sic*) to me like the school is [does} not understand . . ." This small portion of the letter indicates Wardah's bewilderment.

61. *The Foundation* (April, 1914), 7.

62. Yet another illustration of the Tuskegee influence on African-American-African interaction, discussed in greater detail in chapter 7.

63. *The Foundation* (April, 1914), 7.

64. *Ibid.*

CHAPTER IV

The Independent Black Church in Africa

The term "Independent Black Church" refers to those Christian denominations that have, by and large, been under the control of Black people in the United States since their beginnings. The more important Black denominations, the ones that concern us here, trace their origin to the last quarter of the eighteenth century. Essentially these include the Black Baptist Church, the African Methodist Episcopal Church (A.M.E.), and the African Methodist Episcopal Zion (A.M.E. Zion) Church. The Black Baptist Church was first organized as the African Baptist Church in 1788. By the end of the nineteenth century, the National Baptist Convention, an association of Black Baptist churches in the United States, was claiming a larger membership than both the A.M.E. and the A.M.E. Zion churches, with 1,349,189 members.[1]

The free Black communities of the North provided the setting for the formation of these Black churches despite the fact that most Black people in the United States at this time (turn of the eighteenth century) could be found in southern slaveholding states. Following the collapse of the slavocracy, with defeat in the Civil War, these independent Black churches enjoyed a period of rapid expansion in the South. Even before 1900 the Black church had matured to the point where it could join the effort directed to Africa's "salvation." The motives of Black churches for evangelizing in Africa did not differ to any significant degree from those of the White denominations. Since the early Black churches were imitations of the White churches, from which they separated, this should come as no surprise. The idea of the Social Gospel, an interest in and concern for the less fortunate, between 1880 and the end of World War I, found anxious subscribers both in the independent Black churches and the White church. Africa, therefore, offered a major opportunity for converting "heathens" to Christianity.

The missionary interest in Africa grew out of a desire to win converts for Christianity and also to train African catechists and workers. For this kind of effort, education was indispensable. The work of spreading the gospel was to be the shared responsibility of the indigenous catechist, one who spoke the local dialects, and Black and White missionaries from the Christian world. Since the Protestant denominations. Unlike the Catholics, the Protestant denominations depended heavily on an individual's ability to understand and read the Bible, and this created a need for the establishment of educational institutions.[2]

In the United States, Tuskegee and Hampton Institutes were considered good models for missionary-sponsored education in Africa. The apparent success of these institutions with Black Americans, recently removed from slavery, and the commonly held belief, which took hold soon after emancipation that education for Blacks should focus on manual occupations or industrial-vocational training, affirmed the Tuskegee-Hampton idea. There was also the widespread view among Whites that Black Americans in the United States and Africans approximated one another in intellect and culture. Therefore, "if the vocational approach to education had proved successful with the former, making them independent and economically self-sufficient Christian citizens, many missionaries believed that a similar course of action would prove successful in Africa."[3] One result of this thinking was that the number of mission schools in Africa increased rapidly.

Because of the opportunities for interaction they provided, Black missionaries evangelizing in Africa and, more particularly the missions movement of the independent Black church were major influences in shaping Black American attitudes toward Africa. African-American missionaries, whether sponsored by

White or Black churches, were devout ideologists for Christianity. "They took literally the commandment to spread the gospel, and their sense of Christian duty was real,"[4] writes one student of the subject. These Black American missionaries had a direct line into the Black community in the United States, and upon their return from Africa they spread the word about their African experience. This they accomplished from the pulpit, through lectures, and by their writings in the various religious and secular journals.[5] Most of them were well educated, since the best opportunities for higher education existed through training for the ministry, and the missions movement contributed significantly to paving the way for an introduction to one aspect of the Pan-African idea—the awakening in African-Americans of an interest in Africa.[6] Black American missionaries genuinely hoped to aid their brethren and sisters in the homeland and to speed up the pace of Africa's "regeneration." In their estimation, the best way to do that was through the spread of Christianity.

Due primarily to declining White sponsorship of Black missionaries to Africa by the end of the nineteenth century and the simultaneous growth of Black churches, more and more African-Americans were sent out to Africa by the independent Black denominations. Among the earliest individual Black Baptists were Lott Cary and Thomas Johnson. They lacked organizational support but, nonetheless, went to Liberia and Cameroons, respectively, to do mission work. Cary worked primarily among Americo-Liberians along the Liberian coast during the 1820s.[7] Johnson, who like Cary hailed from Virginia, volunteered for Africa in 1877. Because of failing health, Johnson was forced to leave the Cameroons after a stay of only one year. Upon his return to the United States, he enthusiastically campaigned to spread the Africa missions idea among Black Baptists. Most significant in this campaign, which placed a premium on lectures and the organization of conferences, was the publication of Johnson's autobiography, *Africa for Christ*, in 1882.[8]

Black Baptists

The first Black Baptist missionary fully supported by the Black Baptist Church was Rev. Harrison Bouey, who was sent to Liberia in 1879 by the South Carolina Baptist Convention. He was engaged in missionary work in Monrovia until 1881, when he returned to the United States. He remained for twenty-one yearsm and then returned to Liberia as a missionary in 1902, where he died in 1909.[9]

Equally influential among Black Baptists in African mission work was William W. Colley. Colley was sent to Nigeria by the Southern Baptist Convention in 1875 where he worked for four years.[10] When Colley returned to the United States in 1879, he spearheaded the formation of the Baptist Foreign Mission Convention in 1880. This was an organization of Black Baptists whose *raison d'être* was to spread the African missions idea among Black Baptists. The Foreign Mission Convention immediately sent six missionaries to Liberia and they opened the first organized Baptist mission station in Africa after slavery's abolition in the United States. During the next fifteen years, a dozen Baptists served in Liberia. Because of disease and death among these volunteers—two died six months after their arrival and five others were forced to return to the United States due to ill health—by 1895 the mission station had to be abandoned.[11]

Up to 1895 the fragmentation in the southern Black Baptist Church limited the effectiveness of its foreign missions program. However, 1894 representatives of the Foreign Mission Convention met with delegates from two other Black Baptist organizations, namely the eight-year-old American National Baptist Convention and the two-year-old National Educational Baptist Convention, and decided on a merger. Atlanta, Georgia, in 1895, was the scene for the formal organization of the National Baptist Convention (N.B.C.). With its formation, many of the obstacles for mission work in Africa were soon removed.[12]

The first secretary of the Foreign Mission Board was Rev. L.M. Luke, who was born in Cado Parish, Louisiana. He had served as field agent for the Foreign Mission Board for two years before the founding of the N.B.C. In December of 1895, while on a speaking engagement in Louisville, Kentucky, he was fatally stricken and his five-month tenure as secretary ended.[13]

When Lewis Jordan was selected as Luke's successor to head the Foreign Mission Board of the National Baptist Convention in February 1896, it signaled a new era for foreign missions in the Black Baptist Church. Jordan was born in Meridian, Mississippi and was a graduate of Roger Williams University in Nashville, Tennessee. At the time of his election as Secretary of Foreign Misisons, Rev. Jordan was Pastor of the Union Baptist Church of Philadelphia. Jordan was considered an organizational genius and he headed the Foreign Missions Board for almost twenty-six years, until his resignation because of failing health in September, 1921. He visited Africa on four separate occasions and was directly responsible for the opening of seven mission stations in Africa, from Liberia to the Union of South Africa.[14]

Jordan was also the first historian of Baptist foreign missions, and one month after he became Secretary, in March 1896, he began the publication of the official organ of Baptist foreign missions, the *Mission Herald*, which has enjoyed uninterrupted publication since its inception. The first issue of the *Mission Herald* announced that there was but one mission station operating in Africa at the time, in Capetown, South Africa under the direction of Rev. R.A. Jackson and his wife, but that station was making good progress. The church there was opened eighteen months earlier with five members and now had sixty. The *Mission Herald* also explained why Baptists should be interested in Africa: "There are quite 300,000,000 people in that 'dark land' many of whom have never heard of Jesus. We have the light; but not to keep."[15]

Remembering his own health problems in Liberia during an earlier visit, Jordan turned Baptist interest in Africa to the South. Moreover, Bishop Henry McNeal Turner's work there in 1898 served as an inducement to Baptist expansion into South

Africa, since Turner was critical of what he considered limited Baptist activity in African missions.[16] When the nineteenth century closed, the National Baptist Convention was supporting nineteen missionaries in Africa, mainly Liberia and South Africa, even though it had only been in existence for five years.[17]

Despite two very serious incidents that threatened the future of the N.B.C., the Foreign Mission Board continued to send missionaries to Africa. In 1897 a group of Virginia and North Carolina church leaders, upset because Lewis Jordan had moved the headquarters of the Foreign Mission Board from Richmond, Virginia to Louisville, Kentucky (considered to be a more central location), decided to break with the N.B.C. and form their own Lott Cary Foreign Mission Convention. They began to send a limited number of missionaries to Africa independent of the N.B.C. In 1915 there was a second secession over the issue of control of Baptist publications, which led to the formation of the National Baptist Convention of America. Two Baptist historians called these rifts the most unusual ones in the history of religious groups because "not a single doctrinal question was involved."[18]

In any event, the larger N.B.C. sent more missionaries to Africa than either of the two splinter groups. In 1906, twenty-five missionaries were being supported by N.B.C. funds in the African field. They were divided among West, British Central and South Africa—which was further subdivided into Cape Colony, Orange River Colony, Natal, and Transvaal.[19] However, after 1906 no mention is made of the total number of missionaries serving in Africa, and extant copies of the *Missionary Herald* for the period 1906–1919 do not provide this information, either. Nevertheless, there are several short biographical sketches of Baptist missionaries serving in Africa during the first two decades of the twentieth century.

In 1970 the Foreign Mission Board celebrated its ninetieth anniversary, and the July–August issue of the *Mission Herald* carried an historical survey of the past ninety years of foreign mission work. Ten years later, the July–August and September–

October 1980 issues of *Mission Herald* further celebrated the long history of Africa work for Baptists and commemorated the centennial of N.B.C. Foreign Missions, especially in Africa. In its 110th year, the *Mission Herald* (which is still being published) in its January–February issue carried a large front-page photo of Nelson Mandela with the headline "Free At Last," illustrating the ongoing continuity of N.B.C. interest in and interaction with Africa, into the last decade of the twentieth century.

One of the first Baptists to head for Africa after 1900 was Emma B. Delaney. Miss Delaney was born in Fernandina, Florida and was trained at Spellman Seminary in Atlanta, Georgia. In 1901 she sailed for British East Central Africa (Chiradzulu, Nyasaland), where she worked as a missionary for five years. Along with Rev. L.N. Cheek, she founded the Providence Industrial Mission in what is now Malawi, even though she did not remain very long to run it. This mission was destroyed in 1915 but reopened in 1926.[20] From East Africa Emma Delaney returned to the United States. However, by 1912 she had returned to Africa, this time to Liberia, where she founded the Suehn Industrial Mission. She ran this mission station until 1919 when she returned to the land of her birth for good. Her successor at the Chiradzulu station was one of her earliest converts and students, Daniel S. Malekebu, whom she had earlier brought with her to the United States for medical training.[21]

A husband and wife team that served a tour of duty in Africa under the sponsorship of the N.B.C. was Daniel and Ora Horton. The Rev. Daniel Horton was a native of Jamaica, West Indies, where he was born in 1885. He later came to Atlanta, Georgia, joined the Reed Street Baptist Church, and graduated from Morehouse College. In Atlanta he met the future Mrs. Horton, who was a graduate of Spellman Seminary. On January 13, 1917, Rev. and Mrs. Horton sailed for Grand Bassa, Liberia. They worked in the Baptist Industrial Academy at Grand Bassa, which had been established in 1914. Mr. and Mrs. Horton ran the mission school and organized several churches among the Bassa people, the largest and most important being St. Simon Baptist Church. The work of the Hortons in Liberia, which also included instructing Africans on how to buy land and build houses, was characterized by the *Mission Herald* as "a life-long labor of love.[22]

Miss Delia Harris was the final missionary sent into the African field in 1919. She sailed on October 8, but soon returned to the United States in order to receive treatment for her eye problems and to raise funds for her mission school. She first worked at the Suehn Industrial Mission but later founded the Burrough's Industrial Mission, both in Liberia. Upon her return to Liberia in the late 1920s she continued to labor at Burrough's, where she spent the remainder of her life.[23]

A.M.E. Zion

In 1900 the A.M.E. Zion Church was the third largest independent Black denomination in the United States, behind the Baptists and the A.M.E. Church. Zion was founded in 1796 in New York City when White members of the John Street Methodist Church attempted to segregate its Black members. During the antebellum period the limited growth and expansion of the A.M.E. Zion Church was confined to the northern states among the free Black population there. Bishop James W. Hood (after whom the A.M.E. Zion Theological Seminary was later named) was most responsible for Zion's expansion into the South after the Civil War.[24] In 1880, at the annual General Conference of the A.M.E. Zion Church, the Ladies' Home and Foreign Missionary Society and the General Home and Foreign Missionary Board were organized. This was the first indication of Zion's interest in African missions. By the time of the General Conference of 1884, the African missions interest had increased and more than $1,000 had been raised, since 1880, for African missions. Eight years later, at the 1892 General Conference, the foreign mission interest had declined considerably. It was not until the appointment of the first supervisor for African missions in 1896 that the mission interest in Africa took a turn for the better.[25]

The A.M.E. Zion Church between 1900 and 1919, insofar as the foreign missions field was concerned, operated primarily in West Africa.[26] By 1900 this church was better established in Liberia and on the Gold Coast than anywhere else. The first A.M.E. Zion missionary in West Africa was Rev. Andrew Cartwright, who went to Liberia in 1876. Although he was first, Cartwright did not go to Liberia as an agent of his church. It was only after 1880 that Cartwright received financial support and authority to conduct annual conferences of the A.M.E. Zion Church; until that time he was self-supporting.

Rivalry with the sister A.M.E. Church, as much as anything else, inspired A.M.E. Zion interest in Africa. That is, the fear that their competition would outdistance Zion in the African missions field persuaded Zion to step up their foreign missions program in Africa. In 1896 the first A.M.E. Zion Bishop for Africa was appointed, a Rev. John Bryan Small. Rev. Small was born in Barbados, British West Indies in March of 1845. He received all of his early education in the West Indies, where he was trained for the ministry, and graduated with honors from Codrington College in 1862. Upon graduation, Small was sent to West Africa by his father. He spent the next four years there and visited every part of the West African coast between Sierra Leone and Nigeria. Rev. Small returned to the West Indies in 1866 but, after spending the next five years there and in parts of Central America, he stopped in the United States on his way to England in 1871. During his stopover he became interested in the A.M.E. Zion Church, joined it two weeks after his arrival, and twenty-five years later was selected to supervise the West African mission field.[27] One year after his appointment, in 1897, Bishop Small headed for West Africa. He arrived in Sierra Leone in July of 1897.

In 1900, when Bishop Small made his report to the General Conference of the A.M.E. Zion Church, it was clear that a new era had arrived for Zion missions in West Africa. Based on his experience and observations, Rev. Small made several recommendations to the General Conference: (1) to establish of a program to recruit and train indigenous Africans for Africa mission work at Livingstone College and Hood Theological Seminary, both in Salisbury, North Carolina; (2) to establish a sound financial program designed to maintain and increase support for Zion missionaries in Africa; and (3) to temporarily delay sending Bishops to Africa, until the mission stations were sufficiently developed to warrant their services.

William Hockman, J. Drybold Taylor, Frank Arthur Osam-Pinanke, and J.E.K. Aggrey were among the first Africans to come to the United States to study at Livingstone College and Hood Seminary, at the encouragement of Rev. Small and as a result of his first recommendation. The first three returned to Africa soon after completing their studies. Rev. Drybold Taylor became a teacher and minister at the Keta mission station in the Gold Coast and William Hockman became his assistant. Rev. Osam-Pinanke became Pastor of the Cape Coast A.M.E. Zion Church. Aggrey, the best known of the four, remained in the United States to the disappointment of Bishop Small. It was in fact more than twenty years before Aggrey was to return to Africa.[28]

Financial support for the missions continued to be a problem for Zion. After 1900, the missions were beginning to be supplied with dedicated, well-trained indigenous personnel but there was always a shortage of funds. The total budget for Zion foreign missions in 1900 was less than $3,000. During the remainder of John Bryan Small's administration, which ended in 1905, there was no significant increase. Because money was in short supply, many of the catechists and teachers had to seek other employment in order to meet their obligations. Consequently, the mission effort of Zion was routinely damaged by weak financial support.[29]

Even though Bishop Small was succeeded by Bishop Alexander Walters, who was followed by Bishop George C. Clement as A.M.E. Zion Bishop for Africa, during the period

1905–1919 there was still no resident Bishop representing the A.M.E. Zion Church in West Africa. Both Small and Walters made periodic visits to Africa and the mission stations, but most of the decisions regarding A.M.E. Zion mission activities in West Africa were made from the United States. This is partly explained by Zion's reluctance, following one of the Small recommendations, to spend money maintaining a Bishop in West Africa until the mission stations were satisfactorily organized. It is also partly explained by Zion's unwillingness to turn over the supervision of West Africa to an African Bishop.

Nevertheless, during the administration of Rev. John Bryan Small, several milestones were reached in the foreign missions program of the A.M.E. Zion Church. The first A.M.E. Zion mission station was established in 1896 (Gold Coast). The first Church School was organized in West Africa (Gold Coast) on October 25, 1903. The first Christian Endeavor Society, designed to supplement mission work was organized on September 27, 1904 (also Gold Coast). And, the first A.M.E. Zion Choral Union was established at Cape Coast in 1905.

When Bishop Small died in 1905 the African work was left to a home church that knew very little about it. The church searched for a suitable replacement, one who was knowledgeable about Africa. Selected was the Rev. Alexander Walters.

Alexander Walters was born in Bardstown, Kentucky, on August 5, 1858. All of his early life was spent in Bardstown and he was educated in the state of Indiana. Walters was elected a Bishop in the A.M.E. Zion Church in 1892. In addition to serving as president of the 1900 Pan-African Conference in London, Walters was president of the Afro-American Council. When Walters became Bishop of Africa, he set in motion his plan to organize a new department to aid foreign missions, the Department of Life Members. A donation of $20 was required to become a life member in the Foreign Missionary Society of the A.M.E. Zion Church. The new organization's main purpose was to secure additional funds to supplement the budget for African missions. By 1908 Bishop Walters indicated that he was pleased with the effort being undertaken in connection with the new department.[30]

Bishop Walters made his first visit to West Africa in 1910, five years after his appointment as Bishop for Africa. His special interest was Liberia since the mission program there had been a disappointment. He quickly reorganized the Liberia Annual Conference and traveled throughout the country in order to revive the mission stations. One problem he faced, especially at the Brewerville station, was that of superstition. Rev. H.T. Wright and his wife, who were African-Americans, were accused of taking part in "un-Christian" activities, which contributed to tension between the missionaries and native Liberians. The mysterious death of Mrs. Wright did not help matters any, and Rev. Wright had to be relieved of his duties.

Bishop Walters was not only well known but he was well liked in Liberia. He supported the idea of American assistance to Liberia during her economic and diplomatic crisis in the period 1908–1915.[31] He felt that the United States was morally obligated to help Liberia since the country was founded by Black United States citizens. If the United States would provide help during this time of need, Walters was convinced that Liberia's future was assured. For his efforts in this direction the Liberian government conferred upon Alexander Walters the Liberian Medal of Distinguished Service.[32]

From Liberia, Bishop Walters went to the Gold Coast during the same year, 1910. He visited the mission stations in east and west Gold Coast and commended the work being done by Africans. At the Keta mission station, Bishop Walters met Dr. W.E. Shaw, who had replaced J.J. Pearce, the first African-American missionary on the Gold Coast (1906). Pearce was transferred to the Liberia Conference in 1909. Dr. Shaw was a hard worker who had established a good relationship with the local people. One of Shaw's major complaints to Bishop Walters was the problem inherent in absentee supervision. He felt that one factor that was germane to the West Africa missions program was close and regular supervision of the Africa conferences. Shaw also felt that absentee supervision was "a real mission killer."[33] After Bishop Walter's visit to the Gold Coast in 1910, not a single Bishop of the A.M.E. Church visited the Gold Coast conferences for a period of fourteen years. The explanation that was most often given was a shortage of funds.[34]

The administration of Alexander Walters as Bishop for Africa came to an end in 1917. Because of a sudden illness he requested that Bishop George C. Clement relieve him of his African duties.[35] His twelve years work along the Guinea Coast was described as "a pageant of brilliance . . . but behind this curtain of brilliance was the shadow of heartbreak: Our church has not the funds to undertake so vast an endeavor."[36]

Bishop George Clinton Clement hailed from North Carolina, where he was born in 1871. A graduate of Livingstone College, Bishop Clement was ordained a minister in the A.M.E. Zion Church in 1893. He served as editor of Zion's publication, the *Star of Zion* from 1904–1916 and as manager of the A.M.E. Zion Publishing House, from 1914–1916. In May of 1916 Rev. Clement was elected Bishop. He later became president of the Board of Foreign Missions.

In 1917 Liberia entered World War I on the side of the Allies. The entire west coast of Africa was declared a war zone. Recognizing the need for immediate help, the Foreign Missionary Society organized for "African relief." The plan was to rush missionaries and supplies to West Africa, especially to Liberia, in order to administer to the needs of the Liberian people and Liberian soldiers returning from the war. A group of Zion missionaries that included Henrietta Peters (USA), I. Ishabalala (South Africa, a Zulu employed by Zion), Rev. Isaac Cole (USA), Rev. P.D. Ofosuhene (Gold Coast), Rev. Thomas E. Davis (USA), and Clement prepared to leave New York, and all of them departed for West Africa except Clement. He was denied a visa on the grounds that he was a threat to internal security.[37] Moreover, Clement was denied entry to West Africa throughout the period he served as Bishop for Africa.

Meanwhile, by January 1919, the Foreign Mission Society had raised $6,000 for their relief fund and was planning for a new drive to raise $8,000 more. Since Bishop Clement was unable to visit the African field even after the war ended, he proposed in 1920 that the sister institutions of Zion, the A.M.E., and the C.M.E. (Colored Methodist Episcopal) churches be allowed to supervise the work of Zion where possible.[38] There is no indication that his suggestion was acted on. However, Clement did appoint the Rev. Thomas E. Davis to take charge of the work in Liberia. There was no field supervision of the mission stations on the Gold Coast during this period notwithstanding the fact that the *Missionary Seer*, a Zion periodical, made several announcements that Bishop Clement would soon sail. Nevertheless, between 1917 and 1920 the war relief efforts of Zion to raise funds for West African missions were their most important accomplishments.[39] Because of the war and the absence of supervision, the Zion mission stations in Liberia and the Gold Coast were confused and disorganized until the appointment of a new Bishop in 1924, the first resident Zion Bishop in West Africa, Cameron Chesterfield Alleyne.[40]

A.M.E. Church

The ground was broken for A.M.E. mission work by one of the church's founding members, Daniel Coker. He was not an emissary of the A.M.E. Church but was one of the eighty-eight emigrants originally sent to West Africa by the American Colonization Society in 1820. Nevertheless, his main reason for going to Liberia and Sierra Leone was to win converts for Christianity, under the banner of the A.M.E. Church.[41]

The work begun by Coker collapsed after his death in 1846. His followers and converts became disillusioned and disorganized, and began to scatter. There was still no official A.M.E. envoy to Liberia or Sierra Leone, but the Church did appoint Americo-Liberians as their representatives, and individual A.M.E. congregations supported emigrants to Liberia.[42] The first official missionary to Africa fully supported by the A.M.E. Church was Rev. John Frederick who reached Sierra Leone in 1886. He re-established the A.M.E. Church in West Africa, and although he was satisfied with the initial financial aid he received from his church, he later lost hope and fought frustration. He was saddened that both the financial and moral support he was receiving left much to be desired. In 1899 he withdrew from the A.M.E. Church and joined the White sponsored Wesleyan Methodists.[43]

In 1900 the African Methodist Episcopal Church was the second largest in membership among independent Black churches but it was first in the Africa missions field. By the time the nineteenth century ended, the A.M.E. Church was sending evangelists to West Africa, to Central Africa, and to Southern Africa. In addition to maintaining mission stations in Africa, the A.M.E. Church was operating several colleges in the United States, that attracted African students. Outstanding among them were Wilberforce University, Allen University, Paul Quinn College, and Morris Brown College.

Bishop Henry McNeal Turner did more than any other individual to expand the mission work of the A.M.E. Church in Africa.[44] In the latter part of 1891, Turner visited Sierra Leone and organized the first Annual Conference of the A.M.E. Church there in November. From Sierra Leone, Turner traveled to Liberia, where he also organized its first Annual Conference. Bishop Turner's visit to South Africa with his son David in 1898 was, like his visits to West Africa, a bonanza for A.M.E. mission expansion. His purpose for visiting was to reorganize the conferences there, to obtain first-hand knowledge of the needs of the church's work, and to provide for supervision of A.M.E. churches in South Africa.[45] By the time he left South Africa, he had effected a formal consolidation between the "Ethiopian Church"[46] and the A.M.E. Church—a process that had actually begun, through correspondence, before Turner left the United States. He created a storm of controversy with his colleagues by consecrating the African Rev. James M. Dwane without consultation as Vicar-Bishop for the South African work. In addition he conducted mass ordinations of ministers and indiscriminately received members into the A.M.E. Church.[47] Nevertheless it was Bishop Turner who established the building blocks for the twentieth century mission work of the A.M.E. Church in South and West Africa.

Between 1900 and 1919, five resident Bishops were assigned to oversee A.M.E. Church activities in West Africa: C.T. Shaffer (1900–1904), W.D. Derrick (1904–1907), C.S. Smith (1907–1908), W.H. Heard (1908–1916), and I.N. Ross (1916–1920). The first concern under Shaffer was the inauguration of an industrial school. In 1902 he negotiated the purchase of 100 acres of land from the Liberian government in order to organize such a school for boys. The institution, Shaffer Boys High School, also received an appropriation of $2,500 from the Liberian government for its upkeep, and, before Bishop Shaffer was succeeded by W.D. Derrick in 1904, all of the school's outstanding debt had been paid. Bishop Heard was the first to be elected for an eight-year term, and through the purchase of a power driven boat he greatly improved the church's capacity to visit its churches and schools, all of which were close to the St. Paul River.[48] The tenure of Bishop I.N. Ross (1916–1920) seems to have been devoid of any meaningful work in the West African field, because two of the better-known accounts of A.M.E. mission work in Africa during this period make no mention of his activities.[49]

One A.M.E. missionary in Liberia, J. Dunmore Clark, was unhappy about the Church's lack of progress there and was willing to talk publicly about it. He complained that the mission stations were not self-supporting due to a lack of industry on the part of the missionaries. He called for sweeping reforms in the mission department, including a shift away from evangelizing among the "civilized" Americo-Liberians to recruiting converts from among the Aborigines who were found outside the "civilized" settlements. He pointed out that in the seven-year period between 1909 and 1916, membership in the Liberia

Conference only increased from 301 to 376. "Surely," he proclaimed, "we ought to awake from our long and satisfied ecclesiastical slumber, become also intelligently dissatisfied, work in the actual cause of missions, and justify the use of the money and means that are being sent to this field by our home Church, for the present condition of our missionary work here are [sic] barely without excuse."[50]

In four provinces of South Africa (Cape Province, Natal, Orange Free State, and Transvaal), five A.M.E. Bishops served between 1900 and 1919: L.J. Coppin (1900–1904), C.S. Smith (1904–1907), W.D. Derrick (1907–1908), J.A. Johnson (1908–1916), and W.W. Beckett (1916–1920). The A.M.E. Church also commenced mission efforts elsewhere in Southern Africa, in what later became the Central African Federation, Northern Rhodesia, Southern Rhodesia, Nyasaland (Now Zambia, Zimbabwe, and Malawi), Bechuanaland (now Botswana) in 1901, Basutoland (now Lesotho) in 1903, and Swaziland in 1904. Their essential work, in addition to winning converts for Christianity and members for the A.M.E. Church, was the complimentary and parallel charge of maintaining mission stations and operating mission schools.[51]

The most important work in South Africa was done by the first Bishop, Levi Jenkins Coppin. One month after Bishop Coppin arrived in South Africa, in March 1901, the British Colonial Government officially recognized the A.M.E. Church, and permitted its ministers to perform marriages, apply for church sites and have its activities legalized. In addition, during Rev. Coppin's watch, church membership reached a total of ten thousand. This was two thousand fewer members than was reported by Bishop Turner in 1898, but Turner's total was the result of disaffected groups joining the A.M.E. Church, while under Coppin the swelling A.M.E. membership rolls was the result of individual conversions. Under Coppin, there was also an increase in the ministry from 133 in 1900 to 200 by 1904. New geographical regions were reached by the church in South Africa under Coppin, the total value of church and school property increased substantially, to $178,000.[52]

One interesting example of the influence that studying at a Black American college had on an African student is the case of Charlotte Manye Maxeke.[53] Born in 1873 to Basuto and Shosa parents in Cape Colony, South Africa, Charlotte Maxeke was trained as a missionary and became a teacher in the Wesleyan Mission School in Kimberly. In 1894 she joined a singing group that was touring Great Britain and the United States. When the group disbanded in Cleveland, Ohio, some members returned to South Africa and others remained in the United States. Charlotte Maxeke, with the aid of the Missionary Department of the A.M.E. Church, entered Wilberforce University. There she was instrumental in putting the Ethiopian Church in South Africa in touch with the A.M.E. Church, which later led to their union. Along with her husband, Marshall Maxeke, and another African graduate of Wilberforce, James Tantsi, she returned to South Africa in 1901 and established the Wilberforce Institute. For more than fifty years the school provided educational opportunities for South African youth. Charlotte Maxeke went on to become an outspoken nationalist and supporter of women's rights. Wilberforce Institute was closed in 1953 by the South African Government because of its advocacy of African rights.[54]

During the first nineteen years of the twentieth century the thrust of mission work in Africa for each of the independent Black churches had some similarities. They all continued work begun in earnest in the late nineteenth century and all had their mission work interrupted by World War I. They established mission schools, organized churches, maintained mission stations, and sent African students to the United States for missionary training. There was never enough money for mission work in Africa, but the idea of foreign missions was never totally abandoned. The Baptists, whose Africa missions were not as centrally organized as Zion or the A.M.E. Church had a hard-working, dedicated secretary in Lewis Jordan, who made periodic visits to supervise the West African missions but never took up residence in Africa. Moreover, Jordan managed the foreign missions work of the National Baptist Convention, giving it important continuity, throughout 1900–1919. The A.M.E. Zion Church had able administrators in John Bryan Small and Alexander Walters, but there were periods during which the African mission work suffered because of absentee supervision, all decisions being made from outside Africa. Livingstone College and Hood Seminary provided good training for Africans, who—Zion felt—would carry the brunt of Africa mission work. The A.M.E. Church had well-organized, in residence supervision by the ten Bishops who served in West Africa and South Africa during these two crucial decades. In addition to the African-Americans who served as African missionaries, the colleges A.M.E. sponsored, especially Wilberforce University, provided an effective training ground for Africans.

The legacy of African-American missionary activities in Africa during this period was that, as much as any other Black organizations, institutions, or individuals, and more than most, they kept the Africa interest alive. There were more African-Americans in Africa between 1900 and 1919 representing the church than any other agency or group. Motives aside, theirs was the highest level of interaction. Many of them returned to the United States and provided first-hand accounts of Africa. Since these Black missionaries had greater contact with the Black population than did emigrationists, intellectuals, or anyone else with an African interest in the Black community, what they said about Africa made lasting impressions on African-Americans and substantially informed the reality for those who cared about Africa. The indispensable fact was that they had been in Africa and had lived there. Unfortunately, they were no match for the negative images circulating about the continent, and some even embellished the crimes. Nevertheless, during the early twentieth century the role played by Black missionaries in general and the independent Black denominations in particular was a *sans pareil* bulwark in the perpetuation of the Pan-African idea.

In the midst of this missionary interest in Africa, emigration interest was also carried over from the nineteenth century. The A.M.E. Church's Bishop Turner was still the leading back-to-Africanist at the turn of the twentieth century. However, almost simultaneous with Turner's death in 1915 was the emergence of Alfred Charles Sam, the newest champion of the back-to-Africa idea. "Chief Sam," as he was known, attracted the attention of many despairing Blacks with his bold attempt to carry contingents of African-Americans to Africa just before World War I. Therefore it is to "Chief Sam" and his movement that our attention now turns.

NOTES

1. The A.M.E. membership was 452,725 and the A.M.E. Zion membership was 349,788. See Walter Williams, "Black American Attitudes Toward Africa: The Missionary Movement, 1877–1900," (Ph.D. dissertation, University of North Carolina, Chapel Hill, 1974), chapter 9.

2. Edward H. Berman (ed.), *African Reactions to Missionary Education* (New York, 1975), chapter 1.

3. *Ibid.*, 11. See also Kenneth King, *Pan-Africanism and Education: A Study of the Race Philanthropy and Education in the Southern States of America and East Africa* (London, 1971). For more on the Tuskegee-Hampton idea and education in Africa, specifically for the Tuskegee impact, see Edward H. Berman, "Tuskegee in Africa," *Journal of Negro Education* (Spring, 1972), 99–112.

4. Williams, "Black American Attitudes. . . ," 265.

5. William Seraile, "Black American Missionaries in Africa, 1821–1925," *Social Studies* (October, 1972), 198–202.

6. Walter Williams, "The Rise of the Missions Movement in Black American Churches, 1877–1900," paper presented at the Annual Meeting of the Organization of American Historians, April, 1975.

7. See Miles Mark Fisher, "Lott Cary, The Colonizing Missionary," *Journal of Negro History* (October, 1922), 340–418.

8. Thomas Johnson, *Africa for Christ, or Twenty Eight Years a Slave,* 6th ed. (London, 1892), See also Williams, "Black American Attitudes. . . ," 27–32.

9. William J. Simmons, *Men of Mark* (1887 rprt. New York, 1968), 675–676; Lewis G. Jordan, *Up the Ladder in Foreign Missions* (Nashville, Tennessee, 1903), 122; Lewis G. Jordan, *In Our Stead* (Philadelphia, Pennsylvania, n.d.), 33.

10. Two interesting little pamphlets that outline the work of the Southern Baptist Convention in West Africa and rationalize their presence there are C.E. Smith, *Our Work in Africa* (Richmond, Virginia, n.d.) printed by the Foreign Missions Board, Southern Baptist Convention and M.W. Egerton, *Our Work in Africa* (Baltimore, Maryland, 1901). Copies of both of these pamphlets are in the author's possession.

11. *Mission Herald* (July–August, 1970), 5–6; Owen D. Pelt and Ralph Lee Smith, *The Story of The National Baptists* (New York, 1960), 79–96, 140, 151–154.

12. Williams, "Black American Attitudes. . . ," 39.

13. *Mission Herald* (July–August, 1970), 4–7.

14. *Ibid.* In addition to Jordan's words, already cited, see his *Negro Baptist History* (Nashville, Tennessee, 1930). Informative on Baptist foreign mission activity is a ninety-four-page pamphlet by C.C. Adams entitled, *Negro Baptists and Foreign Missions* (Philadelphia, Pennsylvania, 1944), *passim.*

15. *Mission Herald* (March, 1896), 2.

16. *Voice of Missions* (July, 1898), 3.

17. *Missionary Review of the World* (April, 1900), 305, cited in Williams, "Black American Attitudes . . . ," 45.

18. Pelt and Smith, *Story of the National Baptists,* 102.

19. The individuals were, West Africa—Rev. H.N. Bouey (Sierra Leone), Dr. and Mrs. H.C. Faulkner (Liberia), Rev. Majola Agbebi (Nigeria); British Central—Emma B. Delaney (Nyasaland), Rev. L.N. Cheek (Nyasaland), Rev. John Chilembwe (Nyasaland); Cape Colony— Rev. J.L. Buchanan (Middledrift), Rev. E.B.P. Koti (Queenstown), Rev. Funiselo Solani (Idutywa), Rev. P.T. Mngquibisa (Transkei), Rev. G.

George (Middledrift), Rev. A. Ntlahla (Eastban), Rev. J. Ntleki (Cancele), Rev. H. Vanqua (Mt. Arthur), Rev. H. Mdungela (Beaconfield); Orange River Colony—Rev. A. Rakmetsi (Basutoland), Rev. J. Petruss (Bloemfontein); Natal—Rev. S.P. Ndhlovu (Durban), Rev. H.B. Dubi (Merbank), Rev. J.J. Gumede (Durban), Rev. J. Mtembu (Richmond); Transvaal—Rev. W.M. Leshega (Bosxburg), Rev. J.S. Kenane (Middleburg) Rev. B. Block (Pretoria). There were also five missionaries in the West Indies and South America. See *Mission Herald* (July–August, 1970), 11–12.

20. The Missions's destruction in 1915 was the consequence of the now well-known Nyasaland uprising led by Rev. John Chilembwe. Chilembwe was brought to the United States in 1897 by a White missionary named Joseph Booth. He was greatly affected by Black Americans, who inflamed his nationalism. He was especially influenced by Lewis G. Jordan and attended the Baptist-run Virginia Theological Seminary in Lynchburg, Virginia. Chilembwe returned to Nyasaland in 1900 and later worked closely with Rev. L.N. Cheek and Emma Delaney at the Providence Industrial Mission. In 1906 Rev. Chilembwe was listed as one of the foreign missionaries supported by the N.B.C. See above, note 19. The story of John Chilembwe is told by George Shepperson and Thomas Price in *Independent African: John Chilembwe and the Nyasaland Rising 1915* (Edinburgh, Scotland, 1958). For Chilembwe's period in the United States and the founding of the Providence Mission, see pages 85–123 and 133–142.

21. *Mission Herald* (July–August, 1970), 11; Jordan, *In Our Stead*, 17.

22. *Mission Herald* (July–August, 1970), 13; also, Jordan, *In Our Stead*, 24.

23. *Mission Herald, ibid.* Additional biographical sketches of Baptist missionaries in Africa can be found in Jordan, *In Our Stead, passim.*

24. For background information on the A.M.E. Zion Church, see David Bradley, *A History of the A.M.E. Zion Church* (Nashville, Tennessee, 1970); James W. Hood, *One Hundred Years of the African Methodist Episcopal Zion Church* (New York, 1895); and Beverly Shaw, *The Negro in the History of Methodism* (Nashville, Tennessee, 1954).

25. Williams, "Black American Attitudes . . . ," 71–75.

26. Most important for an account of the A.M.E. Zion Church's mission program for West Africa is Walter L. Yates, "History of the African Methodist Episcopal Zion Church in West Africa, Liberia, Gold

Coast (Ghana) and Nigeria, 1900–1939," Ph.D. dissertation, Hartford Seminary, 1967. Yates also wrote an M.A. thesis at Hartford (1963) entitled "The History of the African Methodist Episcopal Zion Church in West Africa, Liberia and Gold Coast (Ghana), 1880–1900."

27. Hood, *One Hundred Years*, 233–236.

28. J.E.K. Aggrey became one of the best-known Africans of this period. He was born on the Gold Coast in 1875. Aggrey went to Livingstone in 1898 and earned his B.A. and M.A. there and his D.D. from Hood. He also received an M.A. from Columbia University and completed all of the course work for a Ph.D. Aggrey was ordained an Elder in the Zion Church and spent time on the faculty of Columbia. Twice Aggrey served on a Phelps-Stokes Educational Commission (1920, 1924) investigating the educational needs and interests of Africans. He was instrumental in the founding of Achimota College (Gold Coast) and was one of its staff members prior to its formal opening in 1927. For details on Aggrey's life, see Edwin W. Smith, *Aggrey of Africa: A Study in Black and White* (London, 1929), G.A. Gollock, *Lives of Eminent Africans* (London, 1928), 117–131; Josephine Kamm, *Men Who Served Africa* (London, 1957), 150–160; Robert M. Bartlett, *They Dared to Live* (New York, 1937), 115–120; M. Munston, *Aggrey of Achimota* (London, 1944); and W. McCartney, *Dr. Aggrey: Ambassador for Africa* (London, 1949).

29. G.L. Blackewell, *The Doctrine and Discipline of the A.M.E. Zion Church* (Charlotte, North Carolina, 1901), 530–535.

30. Walters, *My Life and Work*, 143–146.

31. See chapter 6 in this volume.

32. Walters, *My Life and Work*, 150–160; Hampton T. Medford, *Zion Methodism Abroad* (Washington, D.C., 1937), 116–117.

33. Yates, "History of the A.M.E. Zion Church," 126.

34. *Ibid.*, chapter 3.

35. *Who Was Who in America, 1897–1942* (Chicago, 1943), I, 230.

36. "Annual Conference Minutes" (1916), 167 in Yates "History of the A.M.E. Zion Church," 134.

37. Yates, "History of the A.M.E. Zion Church," 136.

38. Annual Conference Minutes (1920), 167 in Yates, "History of the A.M.E. Zion Church," 137.

39. *Ibid.*, 134–148.

40. Samuel M. Dudley, *The African Methodist Episcopal Zion Church Yearbook, 1924–1943* (Washington, D.C., 1943), 52. See also Bishop Alleyne's *Gold Coast at a Glance* (Norfolk, Virginia, 1936), especially for the period 1924–1928, when he resided in West Africa.

41. Floyd J. Miller, *The Search for a Black Nationality: Black Colonization and Emigration 1787–1863* (Urbana, Illinois, 1975), 58–59. The best record of Coker's experiences is the account he left; see Daniel Coker, *Journal of Daniel Coker, A Descendant of Africa* (Baltimore, Maryland, 1820).

42. Williams, "Black American Attitudes . . .," 139–140.

43. Artishia W. Jordan, *The African Methodist Episcopal Church in Africa* (New York, n.d.), 46–47; Daniel A. Payne, *History of the African Methodist Episcopal Church* (Nashville, Tennessee, 1891), 487–489; Williams, "Black American Attitudes . . . ," 141–145.

44. There is no suitable study of Bishop Turner's work in the expansion of A.M.E. missions in Africa. Two insightful unpublished studies dealing with Turner in South Africa are Josephus Coan, "The Expansion of Missions of the African Methodist Episcopal Church in South Africa, 1896–1908," (Ph.D. dissertation, Hartford Seminary, 1961); and Carol A. Page, "Henry McNeal Turner and the Ethiopian Movement in South Africa, 1896–1904," M.A. thesis, Roosevelt University, 1973. Useful is Edwin Redkey (ed.) *Respect Black: The Writings and Speeches of Henry McNeal Turner* (New York, 1971).

45. Coan, "Expansion of Missions . . .," chapter 7.

46. This church was formed by a group of dissident South African preachers and laypersons who broke away from the discriminatory English Wesleyan Church, thus forming South Africa's first independent African church. Through contacts made by South African students studying at the A.M.E. Church's Wilberforce University (Ohio), the rebels attempted to affiliate with the A.M.E. Church. This union was fully consummated with Turner's visit to South Africa in 1898. See George Shepperson, "Ethiopianism and African Nationalism," *Phylon* (1st Quarter, 1953), 9–18.

47. Coan, "Expansion of Missions. . . ," chapters 7 and 8; Page, "Henry McNeal Turner. . . ," 105–133; Williams, "Black American Attitudes. . . ," 217–224, *passim*; Jordan, *A.M.E. Church in Africa*, 60–61.

48. Jordan, *A.M.E. Church in Africa*, 34–37.

49. Jordan, *A.M.E. Church in Africa*, 27–51; R.R. Wright (ed.), *The Encyclopaedia of African Methodism* (Philadelphia, Pennsylvania, 1947), *passim*.

50. J. Dunmore Clark, "An Eye Opener—Based on Twelve Years' Experiences on the West Coast of Africa and Seven Years as a Missionary in the A.M.E. Church," *A.M.E. Church Review* (October, 1916), 66; 63–68.

51. Jordan, *A.M.E. Church in Africa*, 59–116; Clara E. Harris, *The Woman's Parent Mite Missionary Society of the African Methodist Episcopal Church* (n.p., 1935), 15–24, 117–118, 128–142 provides useful information on the A.M.E. church in West and South Africa.

52. Coan, "Expansion of Missions. . . ," chapter 10.

53. Other examples during this period can be found in Richard Ralston, "A Second Middle Passage: African Student Sojourns in the United States During the Colonial Period and Their Influence on the Character of African Leadership," Ph.D. dissertation, U.C.L.A., 1972, *passim*.

54. Coan, "Expansion of Missions . . . ," 99–101, 345–348; Williams, "Black American Attitudes. . . ," 213–214, 249–251; Jordan, *A.M.E. Church in Africa*, 59–60, 67–69; Lewellyn Berry, *A Century of Missions of the African Methodist Episcopal Church, 1840–1940* (New York, 1942), 157–159, 186; Harris, *The Woman's*, 23–24.

CHAPTER V

Chief Sam's Back-to-Africa Movement

The back-to-Africa movement of Alfred Charles (Chief) Sam followed a pattern irregularly set in the nineteenth century. His most immediate predecessors were Bishop Henry McNeal Turner,[1] Benjamin "Pap" Singleton,[2] and a medical doctor from Barbados, J. Albert Thorne.[3] However, between the height of the movement led by Bishop Turner in the last decade of the nineteenth century and the movement led by Marcus Garvey (more than a back-to-Africa crusade),[4] which did not begin to pick up steam until after World War I, Chief Sam was the outstanding back-to-Africa exponent.

Alfred Charles Sam,[5] who has been characterized as a self-styled "Gold Coast Chief,"[6] actually claimed to be the grandson of a chief of the Obosse and Appasu in West Akim, Gold Coast, West Africa. The precise date of Sam's birth is unknown but speculation places it at about 1881 in the Gold Coast. He was described by his followers as "low brown" and as "black," standing about five feet six, inches tall and weighing 160 pounds.[7] His early interests as a young man involved the collection of rubber in the Gold Coast for export to the United States. Pursuing this interest he engaged in the commercial enterprise of transporting African-made goods in the United States and manufactured goods from the United States to Africa. In July of 1911, Chief Sam founded the Akim Trading Company, capitalized at over $600,000. The company was incorporated under the laws of New York State and its headquarters were located in Brooklyn, New York. The directors of the corporation were all Black and boasted that the Akim Trading Company was "the first Negro Corporation ever conceived amongst the race."[8] Their intentions were to keep it exclusively Black. They anticipated no problems with financing and fixed the price of single shares of stock at £10.8.0 (about $5). However, to "African Negroes, as an inducement . . . the shares would be sold at half price."[9]

Even though the Akim Trading Company of New York had some early success, in the interest of expansion and in an attempt to get greater control, Sam formed a new company in 1913 called the Akim Trading Company Ltd. This new enterprise was chartered under the generous incorporation laws of South Dakota and was designed for emigration and commercial shipping. This company would hasten the realization of one of Sam's many dreams, since he always wanted to return his Black brothers and sisters to the African continent.[10] The voice of the Chief Sam movement, the *African Pioneer*, was founded in October 1913. The purpose of this newspaper was to advertise the movement's plans for emigration and to serve as a medium for defending its cause.

Sam's contact through correspondence with two of the leading African-Americans in Oklahoma, Dr. P.J. Dorman and Professor J.P. Liddell, both of whom had an interest in emigration, brought him back to the "sooner state" in 1913. In February of that year Sam purchased the vessel *Curityba* from the Munson Steamship Company. Chief Sam's plan was not at all complex. He would travel through Oklahoma, Texas, and Arkansas outlining his scheme, advertising the program of his company, peddling stock, and organizing clubs to generate interest in his idea and to campaign for supporters. The specific objective of the Akim Trading Company Ltd. was "to open up trade between West Africa on the one hand, and Europe and America on the other hand; to develop Africa industrially for Africa and the world; [and] encourage the emigration of the best Negro farmers and mechanics from the United States to different sections in West Africa."[11]

The state of Oklahoma, by the second decade of the twentieth century, was an area where restlessness was widespread among African-Americans. Therefore, it was fertile stalking ground to a schemer like Chief Sam. Blacks began their trek from the South to Oklahoma mainly during the economic and social upheaval following the Civil War. However, some slaves had come to Oklahoma, then "Indian territory," with the so called Five Civilized Indian Tribes in the 1830s and 1840s, after Native American expulsion from the South.[12] This late nineteenth century Black march to Oklahoma occurred mainly between 1890 and 1910. It was part of a larger social movement of westward expansion in the United States during a period when many Blacks and Whites in the South were dissatisfied with the Old South and were searching for a place where land was plentiful and free, and opportunities unlimited. Eventually, Oklahoma developed into two separate communities, one White and one Black. This worked out fine for a time, since Blacks and Whites were essentially intolerant of each other.[13]

There were about ten important all-Black communities that sprang up in Oklahoma as a result of migration, up to about 1910: Boley, Langston, Taft, Tatmus, Summit, Vernon, Redbird, Clearview, Rentiesville, and Wybark. The oldest of these communities, Langston, was incorporated in 1891 with a population of 541. The town was named after John Mercer Langston, a prominent Black congressman from Virginia who served in the fifty-first Congress during 1890–1891.

Edwin P. McCabe, a Black nationalist, proposed in 1890 that Oklahoma become an all-Black state. McCabe believed in the idea of separation of the races and campaigned vigorously for a Black utopia.[14] The McCabe Town Company was formed and its agents traveled into southern states advertising land lots for sale in Oklahoma. One stipulation was that title to the lots could never pass to Whites nor could Whites ever reside or conduct business on them. Wide-eyed Blacks began arriving, willing to undergo some hardships in order to secure some land and have some peace. The resistance of Whites, who were also flocking to

Oklahoma, and Native Americans, forced McCabe to abort his plan for a Black state. When tensions between Blacks and Whites intensified, Black leaders began organizing for "escape." One of the proposals included plans for returning to Africa.[15]

George W. Washington, a wealthy Black man from Muskogee, Oklahoma, was an early supporter of emigration to Africa. In December, 1907, he embarked on a nine month visit to Liberia in order to evaluate the possibilities for relocation there. He returned excited about what he saw. Attempting to carry out his objective, he scheduled a state-wide convention for Blacks in October 1908 to review the plans for departing from the United States. The convention presented a resolution to Oklahoma senator, Thomas Gore, who in turn presented it in Congress. The resolution requested federal assistance to transport interested Blacks to Liberia. Many congressmen feared that the most desirable Blacks would take advantage of the plan and leave while the least desirable ones would remain. Since Congress did not wish to be saddled with these "undesirables," they saw little merit in the proposal and appropriated no money for it.[16]

Although relations between Blacks and Whites in Oklahoma had always been strained, until 1907 there was some kind of peaceful co-existence. However, when Blacks began to express an interest and play a role in politics, as Oklahoma moved toward statehood, things changed. Blacks were frightened, frustrated, intimidated, and murdered.[17] Gerrymandering, grandfather clauses, and outright lynching occurred. Compounding the plight of Blacks was the economic decline that came in 1913. Farm prices dropped sharply and, for small farmers—which most of the Blacks were—the situation became desperate.[18] The racial climate in Oklahoma was now as bad as in the South. Once convinced that they could not expect equality in treatment and opportunity in a state and a country dominated by White men and racist beliefs, several Oklahoma Blacks decided, as risky as the venture seemed, to cast their lot with this "Gold Coast Chief" named Sam.

The steamship *Curityba* was renamed the *Liberia* shortly after its purchase.[19] It steamed out of Galveston, Texas on August 21, 1914 destined for the Gold Coast Colony in British West Africa. Sixty African-Americans were on board, but some five hundred were left standing on the dock unable to make the trip because of limited space.[20] The Blacks on board the ship were mostly small farmers described as "well to do,"[21] who sold their farms and many of their possessions when they opted for emigration. However, a former judge, a professor, and a medical doctor were also among those making the trip. Thirty-eight of the returnees were from Oklahoma and thirty-one of the passengers were males, ten of whom were married. There were thirty-five farmers, two cooks, one mechanic and one lumberman. All those on board were citizens of the United States except Sam and Rev. Orishatuke Faduma,[22] who were both British subjects. The cargo consisted of cement, flour, lumber, hardware, breadstuffs, arms and ammunition, and household goods.[23]

Some weeks prior to the departure there was an attempt by the British to prevent Chief Sam from sailing for the Gold Coast. From the very beginning, the movement was viewed with some skepticism, especially by British diplomats. They suspected that Chief Sam was a confidence agent out to dupe his charges. Accordingly, Cecil Spring-Rice, the British Ambassador to the United States, inquired about whether Sam held genuine leases to land in the Gold Coast. When the Colonial Governor of the Gold Coast replied that Sam held no registered leases, the stage was set for blocking departure. Following a round of talks and dispatches among the British Foreign Office, the Colonial Office, the Governor of Oklahoma, and the United States Government, it was decided that Sam had violated no U.S. statutes and he could not be prevented from leaving, nor could the passengers be prevented from emigrating.[24] Actually, Sam had persuaded at least one British official, J.B. Keating, the British Vice-Consul in Portland, Maine, that he would confine the movement initially to freighting and would use the ship only for cargo. Sam thereby eliminated some of his opposition in the United States. Temporarily set back in the move to block the departure of Sam and his "pioneers," the Gold Coast Colonial Government quickly passed an ordinance requiring immigrants to provide twenty-five British pounds sterling for security before they could settle. The money was put up, obstacles were finally removed, and the path was cleared for the sail.

Subsequent events duplicated the pattern of disappointment for the emigrants that began in the United States. Unanticipated delays took place owing to financial insolvency and the difficulties with the British. Moreover, there were some problems recruiting a suitable captain and crew and in getting the Liberia in shape for the transatlantic voyage. In addition, many in the movement, despite Sam's warnings and pleas, sold their farms and most of their belongings and began to wait for departure in "Gold Coast Camps," which were really "tent cities" in Weleetka, Oklahoma and Galveston, Texas. Through the fall and winter of 1913–1914, because of repeated delays, the camps became overcrowded and were breeding centers for despair and hopelessness. Supplies of food and clothing dwindled since the occupants did not expect to be in the camps as long as they were. Also, much of their capital had been invested in the movement. Those who were finally making the trip were oblivious to the hazards of crossing the Atlantic Ocean in 1914,[25] on a British vessel, and attempted to pass the time on their "racial island" with social events. There was some seasickness and inclement weather, which did not help morale, nor did the death of one passenger during the final days of the voyage. When the Liberia reached the Cape Verde Islands off the coast of West Africa, the euphoria of arrival overtook all passengers.

However, during the stopover at Cape Verde, the British boarded the Liberia and took it to Sierra Leone, where it was detained and inspected without an explanation. The ship was delayed for forty-five days in Freetown. Food and coal supplies were almost exhausted, and the experience conjured up visions

of the sufferings at Weleetka and Galveston. The ship was
eventually released, and on January 30, 1915, five months after
its departure from the United States, the *Liberia* reached its
destination—Saltpond, Gold Coast, West Africa. The reception
by Africans was friendly; they welcomed the American Blacks
with "open arms and open houses." The British Colonial
Government, however, was troublesome. In addition to the
twenty-five pounds security required for each passenger, the
Colonial Government now required a $125 tax for each emigrant
to enter the Gold Coast. In spite of their already drained
resources, the emigrants came up with the money and were
finally permitted to go ashore.[26]

The first two weeks in Saltpond were pleasant enough, but
soon the local chiefs began imposing restrictions on the pioneers.
Thieves stole their household goods and the group suffered
disease, sickness, and a few deaths. Chief Sam became irrational,
unpredictable, and scarce. He left the coast where the African-
Americans were temporarily billeted and began to travel
throughout the colony. One report had it that he was in Liberia
attempting to launch another trading company.[27] The settlers
grew impatient and appealed, without success, through friends
in Oklahoma, for assistance from the State Department of the
United States. Some of the emigrants eventually accumulated
sufficient funds from relatives and friends back home to return
to the United States. Others, unable to raise the funds to return,
or having no inclination to do so, settled down to farming and
attempted to make the best of the situation. Still others drifted to
other areas along the coast of West Africa, namely Liberia and
Nigeria.[28] Chief Sam did in fact become a cocoa merchant in
Liberia. He married one Lucille Garrett, who had come to West
Africa with him on the *Liberia*. All three of their children died
shortly after birth, and Lucille later returned to the United States.
The exact date and location of Sam's death remains a mystery.
Nevertheless, it is assumed to have been in West Africa, the land
of his African dream.[29]

Chief Sam and the Africa Idea

Where does the Chief Sam movement fit in the Pan-African scheme? Insofar as its activities helped bridge a gap between Africans and African-Americans, it contributed to the idea of Pan-Africanism. The essay by J.A. Langley devoted to this back-to-Africa movement declared that the movement was "a . . . commercial aspect of Pan-Africanism."[30] This analysis also revealed that the Chief Sam movement transformed interest among key memebers of the West African press, especially the *Gold Coast Leader*, that first opposed the movement but later supported it, applauding the determination of Black Americans to settle in West Africa. Rev. James (Holy) Johnson, a West African nationalist-clergyman and a Pan-Africanist of some standing, was also influenced by the movement.[31]

Rev. Johnson saw Chief Sam's promised land pilgrimage as having declared objectives that he supported all his life, "namely, patriotism, promotion and self-help by Negroes in industrial and commercial projects. . . ."[32] While it can hardly be claimed that the African movement triggered the African nationalism of James (Holy) Johnson, it cannot be overlooked that the African movement of Chief Sam breathed fresh life into some aspects of Johnson's Pan-African thought. When the ship *Liberia* arrived in Freetown, Sierra Leone carrying the emigrationists in December of 1914, and the local Anti-Slavery Aborigines Protection Society decided to extend a formal welcome, it was Holy Johnson who delivered the address, in the name both of American-born Blacks and Africans. Here, he articulated some of his most eloquent and prophetic Pan-African views:

> . . . Negro Americans would help missionaries and other workers in the upbuilding of our desolated and aboriginal homeland, the repeopling of it, the regeneration of West Africa religiously, intellectually, morally, socially and otherwise.

* * * *

> Whilst we rejoice over and are thankful for what European
> or White evangelization has done for us, we are persuaded
> that the main burden of the work rests upon Africans,
> Africa's children, especially us the exiled ones, who have
> learnt in exile many practical, and helpful lessons that the
> old homeland has long been waiting for.[33]

Rev. Orishatuke Faduma was an African repatriate who returned home with the Chief Sam movement. Faduma was an enthusiastic supporter of the movement who studied at London and Yale Universities, taught in Black schools in the United States for seventeen years, and attended the Atlanta Congress on Africa (1895). He was formerly known as James Davies. Rev. Faduma insisted that the movement had been misunderstood by most people and that it was only natural for Blacks in diaspora to want to return to the land of their ancestors, especially since they were deprived of all human dignity in the United States. He continued that the movement had historical antecedents in Jamaica, Trinidad, and Brazil, as well as in the United States. That is, Blacks in the "New World" always wanted to return to Africa. Prior to emancipation, the idea was encouraged by philanthropists and diasporic Blacks who found their way back to Sierra Leone, Liberia, and Nigeria, suggested Faduma. Finally, according to Faduma, this movement clearly provided the germ for Pan-Africanism:

> The three leading ideas of the African movement were
> Negro nationalism [which he called "race patriotism and
> individuality"], Negro American missionary enterprise in
> Africa, and Negro participation in and leadership of the
> industrialization of Africa by Negro technical know-how
> [Langley's addition.][34]

In some of the local West African press, the African movement had an ambivalent reception. The Lagos papers were unconcerned or critical while the Gold Coast and Sierra Leonean press both were enthusiastic about the movement and were exchanging ideas "on the possibility of launching a Pan-West African movement for political and other reforms."[35] The African-American press observed the Chief Sam movement with increasing skepticism. The leading Black newspapers, notably the New York *Age* and the Tulsa *Star*, were critical of, even bitter toward, Chief Sam.[36]

These publications directed unfriendly editorials and headlines at "the man who immodestly compared himself to Moses and promised to lead his people to a land of milk and honey."[37] *Crisis* magazine opined, citing the White-controlled Chicago *Post* and New York *Sun*, that the plan to colonize Black citizens of the United States in West Africa was a fake. The *Post* was understanding but considered the scheme a "tragedy of human folly," which "usually [was] confined to members of the White race.[38] This newspaper continued cynically that if Blacks were wealthy enough to be the victims of such a large-scale swindle, that was evidence of progress. The *Sun* warned the followers of Chief Sam that there was another side to his roseate description of West Africa, and "only the most daring of pioneers would care to wrestle with the problems of life there."[39] *Crisis* summed up its position on the matter with a reminder of how serious emigration was and that Africa needed "capital not labor." Blacks in Oklahoma were advised by *Crisis* to "fight out the battle . . . because there was no ship in New York building for the African trade," owned by Blacks. Chief Sam and his lieutenants were no more than common cheats who belonged in jail, concluded *Crisis*.[40]

The New York *Age* was also apprehensive about Chief Sam and the Africa return. It called him an imposter who was out to deceive his "ignorant" charges. It even suggested that Whites were behind the scheme in order to buy up cheaply the valuable Oklahoma land that Blacks would be selling.[41] The *Age* followed the movements of Sam very closely and those of his followers in the United States from Oklahoma to New York to Portland, Maine and back to Galveston, Texas.[42] The February

19, 1914, issue of the *Age* reported that an African Prince, from Unyora, Albert Lake, in British Africa, who was living in the United States, considered Sam an imposter. Prince Frederick Bouman appealed to local authorities for Sam's arrest, indicating that he "was not a real chief." Prince Bouman went on to report that he and Sam had an earlier dispute over the sale of some stock in the first Akim Trading Company, at which time Sam admitted "in the African tongue" that he was not a chief, "but [was] acting for the chiefs of the Gold Coast."[43]

When the steamship *Curityba* was undergoing repairs in Maine for the transatlantic voyage, the *Age* encouraged the rumor that the ship was to be added to the yacht club controlled by the ultra-mysterious "Holy Ghost and Us Society," headquartered in Maine. This was a racially mixed revivalist, fundamentalist religious sect that had recently provided for some excitement for otherwise dull Portland, Maine. The Society had embarked on a global gospel mission and, by 1914, owned possessions around the world valued in excess of $3 million. The sect's Maine temple alone, which was the center of its continental activities, was estimated to be worth $250,000. There were also model farms, shoe factories, printing concerns, a fleet of ships, and a substantial number of devoted followers.

The White leader of the group, Rev. Frank W. Sandford,[44] attempted to establish a colony in West Africa, thereby suggesting the alleged connection with Chief Sam. The effort was abandoned when the Society's fleet, without explanation, was wrecked near the Gold Coast. Meanwhile, Rev. Sanford was incarcerated on a conviction of using the mails to defraud, which led to the collapse of the Society.[45]

As Chief Sam's African movement reached its demise, Faduma defended it staunchly by comparing this back-to-Africa movement with the voyages of Columbus, Magellan, Sir Walter Raleigh, Balboa, and the pilgrims. He surmised that Africans and the descendants of Africa were merely experiencing in failure the inevitable consequences of a pioneer project, disappointment Europeans had met earlier in more terrible form. And, writing in the Sierra Leone *Weekly News*, on September 11, 1915, he demonstrated remarkable perception:

> It is certainly better for American Negroes to die of African fever in the effort to contribute to Africa's development than to be riddled by the bullets of the white mob who control the local governments of the United States. . . . It is better to live even among pagans, where the majority respect their laws and life is secure than to live in a country where only the minority are law keepers as in the southern states.[46]

It might not be too far-fetched to suggest that Marcus Garvey might have been inspired by the machinations and maneuvers of Chief Sam. Garvey was working in the London offices of the *African Times and Orient Review* at the time of the Chief Sam movement, and this newspaper followed the movement closely.[47] Therefore, it is unlikely that Garvey could have avoided knowing about Chief Sam's fledgling movement even though there is no significant reference to Sam in Garvey's published writings and speeches.[48] Duse Mohammed Ali, sometime nationalist, sometime Pan-Africanist, sometime journalist—half Sudanese, half Egyptian-editor/publisher of the *African Times*, was very cautious about Chief Sam. He considered the movement to be, in fact, nothing more than a hapless charade. He stated,

> The name of Alfred Sam as a chief is unknown to me. All of the lands in the British colony are tribal lands which can neither be sold nor given away by the chiefs, and there is no part of the colony where sixty-four acres will be available for each of 1,500 persons. The country is covered with dense forests. I'm sure that even if the British government allowed them to have their own towns, it would not permit them to set up a form of government. It would be disastrous if these people were induced to go to Africa and find themselves stranded.[49]

The parallels between the two movements, Garvey's and Chief Sam's, are close enough to provide further currency for the hypothesis that some of the organizational prowess and at least some of the maritime business acumen (or the lack of it), noticeable in the Universal Negro Improvement Association, can be traced to this defiant "Ashanti Chief" known as Sam. Sam's Ethiopian Steamship Line and Garvey's Black Star Line, and the manner in which funds were collected, offers some basis for comparison—even though the Black Star Line was a much more assiduous enterprise. The active, demanding recruiting-publicity campaign adopted by both is comparable, although it was also more ambitious in Garvey's case. Their newspapers—the *Negro World* (Garvey) and the *African Pioneer* (Sam)—offer similarities as propaganda organs for both movements. The handicap of crew, maintenance, repair, and sabotage difficulties with the ship or ships involved argues strongly for the prevailing hostility toward permitting Blacks to engage in the racially exclusive maritime industry. Harassment, the result of suspicion—Garvey in the Caribbean and Sam in West Africa—by British and United States government officials was, not surprisingly, consistent. Moreover both Garvey and Sam were charged with using the mails to defraud. Garvey was convicted and Sam was not. Finally, a noticeable degree of inhibition, pessimism, and even sarcasm emanated from the Black press, Black intellectuals-professionals, and elitist-conservative Blacks, who considered "Chief Sam" and Marcus Garvey to be agents with unrealistic programs designed to cheat the Black masses.[50]

As a social movement, the Chief Sam episode is indicative of the despair and frustration of Blacks in Oklahoma between 1900 and 1915. As such, it has implications for broader disappointment among Blacks throughout the United States at that time. However, unlike many Blacks who were unhappy with their lot between 1900 and 1915, the Oklahomans seized an opportunity that they felt held out the possibility for some relief from their difficulties. The decision to emigrate was not quick or easy, but one that was carefully rationalized—weighing its possibilities with the brutal realities of life in Oklahoma. Those who joined the movement believed in racial self-determination and were easily attracted to the charisma of a "Chief Sam." That their hopes and dreams were not realized is once again indicative of the complexities and hurdles involved in an Africa return.

NOTES

1. The best treatment of Bishop Turner as a supporter of the back-to-Africa idea is Edwin Redkey, "Bishop Turner's African Dream," *Journal of American History* (September, 1967), 271–290 and Redkey's *Black Exodus: Black Nationalist and Back-To-Africa Movements, 1890–1910* (New Haven, Connecticut, 1969). See also Edwin Redkey (ed.), *Respect Black: The Writings and Speeches of Henry McNeal Turner* (New York, 1971).

2. See Walter L. Fleming, "Pap Singleton, the Moses of the Colored Exodus," *American Journal of Sociology* (July, 1909), 61–81; John G. Van Dusen, "The Exodus of 1879," *Journal of Negro History* (April, 1936), 111–129; and Roy Garvin, "Benjamin 'Pap' Singleton and His Followers," *Journal of Negro History* (January, 1949), 7–23.

3. Dr. Albert Thorne, beginning in the 1890s, advocated the repatriation of exiled Blacks in the West Indies and the United States in order to "civilize" Africans. Not very much is known about him or his program which does not appear to have attracted much attention. See "African Colonization Schemes," New York *Age* (August 12, 1922), 3–4; Weisbord, *Ebony Kinship*, 41–45. Thorne's own ideas and thoughts are in J. Albert Thorne, "An Appeal Addressed to the Friends of the African Race" (1896), a copy of which can be found in the Schomburg Library.

4. The movement led by Marcus Garvey was not technically a back-to-Africa one. Rather, and more accurately, it was a Black nationalist or Pan-African nationalist movement that had a back-to-Africa component. The Garvey movement has been misunderstood by popular writers, some masquerading as scholars—too often Whites—

who have been content to simply repeat, and thereby perpetuate, a superficial interpretation of Garvey, UNIA, and this movement.

5. The major work on Chief Sam and his African movement is William E. Bittle and Gilbert Geis, *The Longest Way Home: Chief Alfred Sam's Back-To-Africa Movement* (Detroit, 1964). A condensed version of the Bittle and Geis study can be found by the same authors, entitled, "Alfred Charles Sam and an African Return: A Case Study in Negro Despair," *Phylon* (Summer, 1962), 178–194. The Bittle and Geis sources are almost entirely American. An essay that draws heavily on contemporary West African newspaper accounts and, therefore, offers a different appraisal, is J.A. Langley, "Chief Sam's Africa Movement and Race Consciousness in West Africa," *Phylon* (Summer, 1971), 164–178.

6. Robert G. Weisbord, "The Back-To-Africa Idea," *History Today* (January, 1968), 30–37.

7. Bittle and Geis, *The Longest*, 70.

8. *Ibid.*, 71.

9. *Ibid.*

10. "Chief Sam and the Negro Exodus," *Literary Digest* (March 21, 1914), 646–648; New York *Age* (January 29, 1914), 1.

11. Quoted from Langley "Chief Sam's . . .," 165.

12. An introduction to the Five Civilized Tribes should begin with Angie Debo, *And Still the Waters Run: The Betrayal of the Five Civilized Tribes* (Princeton, New Jersey, 1972); see also William T. Hagan, *American Indians* (Chicago, 1971), chapters 3, 4.

13. Mozell Hill, "The All-Negro Communities of Oklahoma: The Natural History of a Social Movement," *Journal of Negro History* (July, 1946), 254–268; also William E. Bittle and Gilbert Geis, "Racial Self-Fulfillment and the Rise of an All-Negro Community in Oklahoma," *Phylon* (3rd Quarter, 1957), 247–260.

14. Indianapolis *Freeman* (July 29, 1905), 1.

15. Hill, "All-Negro Communities," 260–264.

16. Bittle and Geis, *The Longest*, chapter 3; Hill, "All-Negro Communities," 263.

17. See J. Saunders Redding, *They Came in Chains: Americans From Africa* (Philadelphia, Pennsylvania, 1950), 200–202.

18. Weisbord, "The Back-To-Africa Idea," 35.

19. This was done over the objection of Ernest Lyon, Liberian Consul-General in the United States, who claimed the name would be misleading and would give the impression that there was some official affiliation between this ship, the Chief Sam movement, and the Liberian Government. See New York *Age* (February 19, 1914).

20. Bittle and Geis, "Alfred Charles Sam. . . ," 178.

21. Langley, "Chief Sam's. . . ," 169.

22. See discussion below and note 33.

23. Langley, "Chief Sam's. . . ," 170; Bittle and Geis, "Alfred Charles Sam. . . ," 140.

24. For the attempt by the British to stop Chief Sam and their appeal for assistance from the United States, see Bittle and Geis, *The Longest*, chapter 5 especially pp. 113–116; See also New York *Times* (February 26, 1914), 2–4; Brooklyn *Eagle* (February 27, 1914), 3.

25. Interestingly, the New York *Times* reported incorrectly that this group of Oklahoma emigrants was missing, six months after they arrived on the Gold Coast (June 12, 1915), 5.

26. Bittle and Geis, "Alfred Charles Sam. . . ," 190; Bittle and Geis, *The Longest*, chapter 9.

27. *Ibid.*, 192.

28. *Ibid.*, 191–192; New York *World* (July 16, 1917), 4–5.

29. Bittle and Geis, *The Longest*, 208.

30. Langley, "Chief Sam's. . . ," 168.

31. *Ibid.*, 171.

32. E.A. Ayandele, *Holy Johnson: Pioneer of African Nationalism 1836–1917* (New York, 1970), 352–353. For more on Holy Johnson see Ayandele, *The Missionary Impact on Modern Nigeria 1842–1914* (London, 1966) and the same author's "An Assessment of James Johnson and His Place in Nigerian History," *Journal of the Historical Society of Nigeria* (1964), 486–516.

33. James (Holy) Johnson, cited in Langley, "Chief Sam's. . . ," 173.

34. Orishatuke Faduma, "What the African Movement Stands For," *The African Mail* (September 25, 1914), 521–522; (October 2, 1914), 2–3 cited in Langley, "Chief Sam's . . . ," 172n.

35. *Ibid.*, 173.

36. For some examples of their criticism, see Bittle and Geis, *The Longest*, 76, 92, 99–100, *passim.*

37. Weisbord, "The Back-to-Africa Idea," 35.

38. *Crisis* (June, 1914), 75.

39. *Ibid.*

40. *Crisis* (February, 1914), 190.

41. New York *Age* (November 23, 1913), 1.

42. See the New York *Age* for the following dates: (November 27, 1913), 1; (January 22, 1914), 1; (January 29, 1914), 1–2; (February 12, 1914), 1; (February 19, 1914), 1; (March 12, 1914), 1; (April 2, 1914), 1; (July 16, 1914), 1; (September 14, 1914), 2.

43. New York *Age* (February 19, 1914), 1. See also New York *Times* (February 26, 1914), 2–4 for more on Chief Sam's admission to not being a chief.

44. For a brief account of Sanford's career, see *Harper's Weekly* (February 15, 1908), 10–12.

45. New York *Age* (March 12, 1914), 1; Bittle and Geis, *The Longest*, 128–139.

46. Langley, "Chief Sam's. . . ," 176.

47. Edmund D. Cronon, *Black Moses: The Story of Marcus Garvey and the Universal Negro Improvement Association* (Madison, Wisconsin, 1955), 16–18.

48. It is not altogether clear exactly what Garvey was doing in the offices of the *African Times and Orient Review*. Edmund D. Cronon, *Black Moses*, 15, reports that Garvey went to London to learn more about the treatment of Blacks in other parts of the British Empire: "Here, he became associated with . . . Duse Mohammed Ali." Amy J. Garvey (Garvey's second wife), *Garvey and Garveyism*, 9, reveals that Garvey "worked" on this monthly publication. J.A. Langley's account states that Garvey was an "office boy," Langley, "Chief Sam. . . ," 168.

49. New York *World* (February 5, 1914), 2–3.

50. To be sure, there were also important distinctions between the two movements. The massive numbers involved with Garvey, the variety of divisions within UNIA, the Akim Trading Co., vis-à-vis the Black Star Line as major commercial efforts, the grandiose international conventions of UNIA, Garvey's powerful impact on Africans and his

influence in the Caribbean, South America, the United States, and elsewhere in the world serve as examples of the differences. Most important, though is the legacy of Garvey, considered by consensus the leader of the largest mass movement among Blacks ever in the United States and inspiration for Malcolm X, Kwame Nhrumah, and generations of students, while Chief Sam is barely known beyond a handful of diligent researchers and scholars.

CHAPTER VI

African-Americans and Liberia

The foremost interest in Liberia by African-Americans up to 1900 had most often centered on the possibilities for emigration and resettlement. This was true from Liberia's founding in 1822 to the coming of independence in 1847—an eventuality that provoked a new wave of seduction for Black American settlement in Liberia. Because of the dominance of emigration interest when the twentieth century opened, the principal interaction between African-Americans and Liberia was still through repatriation. An almost continuous, heated debate, which showed no sign of abating, prevailed in the African-American community over the pros and cons of either a wholesale or limited-scale exodus to Liberia. The pro-emigration forces were led by the resilient A.M.E. Bishop Henry McNeal Turner. Those who opposed emigration countered with Booker T. Washington as chief spokesperson.

Meanwhile the American Colonization Society, peerless bulwark for Black resettlement in Liberia for three-quarters of a century, had undergone radical changes in 1892 and, consequently, it dramatically reduced the amount of assistance it was providing for emigration. In 1903 its propaganda organ, now the *Liberia Bulletin* (until publication ceased in 1909), was quietly announcing that it was having difficulty furnishing the requested aid for prospective emigrants because "this Society is no longer the recipient of large funds for the purpose of sending colonists to Africa."[1] The ACS also complained about its inability to attract "desirable types" although there were numerous applications for emigration. The motives of these would-be emigrants, to the dismay of the ACS, left much to be desired. "Frequently it is stated that they are not doing well here, and there is no reason to suppose that they would do any better if they were sent to a foreign country," groaned the society.[2] The February 1907 issue of the *Liberia Bulletin* flatly announced that the ACS was unable to assist any emigrants to Liberia in the previous year.[3]

Despite the paltry support from the American Colonization Society, small groups of Black Americans continued on their own to trek to Liberia, and periodically they went with support from ephemeral organizations. In 1900 the *Indianapolis Freeman* announced for the African Jubilee Emigration Society that individuals could obtain passage to Liberia for less than $20 and upon arrival would receive twenty-five acres of land. This company was not identified beyond the mention of its name and interested persons were requested to send ten cents in stamps for "full printed information" to a T.A. Dunlap (who was President of the company), at 801 Stevenson Avenue in Nashville, Tennessee.[4] One individual who had recently arrived in Liberia from Denver, Colorado, defended his new home and held great expectations for a new life in Africa.[5] The Liberian Emigration Society replaced the now-defunct International Migration Society with similar plans for resettling African-Americans in the Republic.

During these early years of the new century several emigration conventions were held in the United States that were reminiscent of the 1850s, which also witnessed large meetings centering on emigration allure. The conventions were held mainly in the South, and the most important one was the Nashville convention of October 1901, that combined the existing independent emigration groups into one federation entitled the Colored National Emigration and Commercial Association (CNECA). It was not surprising that the CNECA was also dominated by Bishop Turner. This latest emigration association hoped to raise $100,000 through the sale of stock in order to purchase a ship to ply between the United States and Africa, "especially the Republic of Liberia," carrying emigrants as well as commercial products. Stock in the new organization was available at $5 per share and there was no limit on how much an individual could purchase. A membership fee was set at $4 per year, later reduced to $3, to cover the cost of anticipated expenses. The enterprise was evidently not as attractive as the organizers expected it would be because by 1904 the CNECA had not yet raised $2,000. This disappointing beginning inspired another series of Bishop Turner's now customary harangues. He indicated that at the current rate it would take one hundred years to sell the desired amount of stock in order to purchase a first-class vessel. He expressed doubt and thereby questioned his own chauvinistic pride with public queries like, "Is it possible the American Negro can start and finish nothing?"[6] His dissatisfaction revealed itself further when he attempted to resurrect interest by appealing to Blacks to "wake up" and flood the organization with hundreds and thousands of dollars. Turner's most biting exhortations almost became predictable when he was most frustrated. He queried on one occasion, for example, "Had all of us rather remain in this country and be disfranchised, uncivilrighted, shot, hung, burnt and skinned alive, without judge or jury, than build up a nation of our own outside of this devil-ridden country?"[7]

Nine months later this coalition of emigration organizations flopped, and Bishop Turner—as Chancellor and Treasurer—was imploring all stockholders to return their stock certificates and obtain their money. The funds were on hand, contrary to idle rumors about misappropriation, and would be refunded. However, few minds had been changed in the CNECA about the desirability of going to Liberia. To exponents of emigration, that was still the best hope for the future of Black people in the United States.[8]

For better or for worse, the emigration controversy continued to command much attention in the African-American community as far as Liberia was concerned. Essentially the debate was shaped by the question of whether the better part of wisdom suggested that African-Americans should remain and struggle for dignity in the United States or whether they should pull up stakes and seek out a new future in West Africa. Was emigration practical or unrealistic? Punctuating this *guerre de plume* was the pragmatic concern for emigration. Bishop Turner and the limited number of emigration supporters for his enterprise could not avoid the vexing and embarrassing question of logistics and resources.[9] Selective emigrants faced the thorny question of a suitable method for selection. Moreover, it was well demonstrated by emigration's track record that the most desired individuals (the educated, the skilled, and successful business persons) were least likely to abandon all that was familiar to them in the United States. In comparison with their less fortunate and less resourceful brothers and sisters, these Blacks, although despised and rejected by Whites (who made few distinctions among classes of Blacks), enjoyed a privileged position. The Liberian government, for its part oscillated between encouragement and discouragement and was most often ambivalent about the entire matter. Between 1890 and 1910, about one thousand Black Americans sailed to Liberia.[10]

Black American commercial interests were an interesting aspect to emigration at this time. Virtually unknown but characteristically ambitious was the New York, and Liberia Steamship Company. The idea for this Black-owned and operated steamship company was ignited by the great fortunes being made by European companies operating in East and South Africa. It was advertised as an inducement to prospective stock purchasers that the New York, and Liberia Steamship Company would surpass the profits of Europeans. The Company was headquartered at 116 Broad Street in New York and was organized by James R. Spurgeon, "chief promoter," and Augustus Faulkner, "traveling representative." It was capitalized at $50,000 and, since company policy was to place the controlling share of stock in the hands of Blacks, African-Americans were coaxed to purchase $5 shares of stock in blocks of ten through fifty.

African-Americans participating in the development of West African trade could also be, it was suggested, catalysts in the return of Black sovereignty in Africa (when it came). Trade would not be limited to the United States and Liberia, but would also include the Cape Verde Islands, Senegal, Gambia, Sierra Leone, and the Gold Coast. It was advertised that this new company had secured promises of cargo from the American Tobacco Company (10,000 hogsheads of tobacco a year), would put missionaries in closer touch with their missions, expected to reduce traveling time to Liberia from thirty-five to fifteen days, and planned to reduce the cost of palm and coconut oils—items indispensable for European industry. The plan, like others before it and some still to come, was ambitious and impassioned. It was welcomed by African-Americans and received a bold endorsement from the president of Liberia, Edwin Barclay, and his entire cabinet. But perhaps, like its counterparts, the eagerness of the New York and Liberia Steamship Company signaled its failure. After 1904 it was not heard from again.[11]

Another Black-sponsored commercial enterprise in existence at this time that involved Liberia was the Ethiopian American Steamship Freight and Passenger Colonization Company, capitalized at $500,000, and chartered under the laws of the Territory of Arizona. The organizers requested endorsement from Booker T. Washington but never got it. The steamship company expected to carry freight, fast mail, and passengers between San Pedro, California and Monrovia, Liberia. The company's Prospectus announced that it also planned to build railroads and that 100,000 Ethiopians (African-Americans) were wanted in Liberia. Not unlike the New York and Liberia Steamship Company, the existence of the Ethiopian-American Steamship Company was, to say the least, short-lived.[12]

The African Union Company (AUC) was another commercial enterprise involving African-Americans and Africa. It was not known to have interests in Liberia specifically, since all references were to Africa generally. The AUC was organized in December 1913 and later incorporated (March 1914) under the laws of the State of New York and capitalized at $500,000. Shares of stock sold for $25 each in the United States and for its equivalent in Africa. The purpose of the AUC was to establish commercial operations for African products with the markets of the world, to establish an African industrial school, and to assist in the general development of Africa. It was announced that the Company had officers in Africa, including the President and General Manager C.W. Chappelle, and that an auxiliary Board of Directors in Africa consisted of indigenous peoples.

The AUC Prospectus reported holdings in mahogany, timber lands and palm oil plantations, plus gold mines, moving picture shows, photographic facilities, and equipment and land in fee simple for educational and agricultural use. The Prospectus did not mention specifically where in Africa these holdings were. It was suggested that an initial investment would return better than a 20 percent profit and the company boasted that several African kings and chiefs had purchased stock in the corporation. Again no mention was made of the names of these "kings" and "chiefs" or their location.

Not much else is known about the AUC, but a good possibility is that the coming of World War I, as was the case with transatlantic commercial shipping generally, interrupted their plans.[13] Because most of these commercial ventures were so short-lived it is tempting to suggest that they were fraudulent. That, however, has not been confirmed but neither has the altruism of their organizers' motives. The best statement that can be made conclusively is that various commercial enterprises did exist—in name if not in fact.

The economic and diplomatic crisis that erupted in Liberia in 1907 served as a new and different source of interest and interaction between African-Americans and the Republic. Relatively speaking, the emergency whipped up unparalleled Black support for Liberia, although it was still less than overwhelming. Through the unprecedented coverage of this crisis by some of the Black American press,[14] African-Americans under the leadership of Booker T. Washington and Fred Moore (editor of the New York *Age*) attempted to persuade the United States government to take steps to deliver Liberia from imminent prostration.

Booker T. Washington was the best-known Black American leader of the period and was often involved in Africa's affairs. The range of Washington's preoccupation with Africa spanned the entire African continent, from Liberia and Togo in the west to Anglo-Egyptian Sudan in the northeast to Congo in the center, and included all of southern Africa. He was sometimes Africa's champion but more often he succumbed to the ideology of the "White man's burden" and accepted the fact of colonialism and European imperialistic designs for the continent. In spite of his naïveté regarding Africa, which was not out of character for the times, the "sage of Tuskegee" was immensely helpful on occasion. The best example of this succor was his energetic, laudible efforts on behalf of the little Republic of Liberia, which from 1908 to 1913, faced possibly the most threatening series of crises in its young history. It suffered from internal distress, especially financial, and externally it was rapidly falling victim to European (English, French, German) land-grabbing designs prevalent in Africa. These developments suggested that Liberia's sovereignty would not be respected. In short, Liberia was on the brink of collapse. It was Booker T. Washington who helped sound the alarm and, for ill or for good, was most responsible for United States intervention in Liberian affairs.[15]

Liberia was founded in 1822 by the American Colonization Society as an entrepôt for freed slaves and free Blacks from the United States.[16] It was partially modeled after Sierra Leone, its contiguous neighbor, which was established for similar reasons, and settled by British subjects in 1787. When Liberia formally shed its stepchild status and declared its independence, in 1847, much of the outside world recognized the new nation immediately, but the United States withheld formal recognition until 1862. Throughout the second half of the nineteenth century,

Liberia experienced the growing pains peculiar to all new nations, aggravated by outside encroachment and internal discord. By 1900 the situation was desperate and the Liberian government began to step up its efforts to attract outside help.[17]

Liberia had a history of troubled finances. In 1871, in an effort to arrest the situation, a loan was floated in London that was both insufficient and burdensome.[18] When Arthur Barclay, a West Indian from Barbados, was elected President of the Liberian Republic in 1904, he hoped to set his house in order. He negotiated a second loan with England (1906–1907) in an attempt to develop agriculture and reinforce border security.[19] However, these loans were not sufficient to satisfy Liberia's debts and the terms were unmanageable. Moreover, Sir Harry Johnson, the well-known "African authority," was instrumental in getting the loan as head of the Liberian Development Company. It was subsequently discovered that the company had no funds except those it obtained through the loan and that British officers, under the pretext of reform, had taken over Liberia's customs revenues and had taken charge of what military forces there were in Liberia. The company eventually went bankrupt and the Liberian government was forced to repay a loan, the funds from which they never saw. The worsening plight of Liberia's finances permitted England to intrude on her internal affairs in order to safeguard British interests.[20]

The specific events that led to Booker T. Washington's and, through his efforts, United States involvement were (1) a bogus mutiny by unpaid frontier troops in Liberia under the command of British officers, (2) the failure of Liberia to control raids into British and French territory by indigenous Liberian people, resulting in "wonton plunder, destruction of property and loss of lives. . . ,"[21] which England and France insisted had to be stopped or Liberia's independence could no longer be guaranteed, and (3) the chaotic condition of Liberia's finances. By 1908 the Liberian Government decided to petition the United States for help. It was decided to send a special diplomatic commission, headed by Vice President James Dossen, abroad to request aid.

The deputation from Liberia included, in addition to James Dossen, the Honorable G.W. Gibson, former president of Liberia, and Charles B. Dunbar, a leading Liberian attorney. Charles R. Branch and T.J.R. Falkner served as secretaries to the commissioners, while Charles Hall Adams accompanied the party as "general advisor" regarding local conditions. After a brief stay in New York, the Liberians, thanks to the efforts of Booker T. Washington, who was their constant companion and escort without portfolio, proceeded to the nation's capital, Washington, D.C. Booker T. Washington wrote to Theodore Roosevelt revealing the personal interest he took in the visit of the Liberian envoys. He stated that this was the first time that any such

> . . . Commission, composed of Negroes, has visited this
> country and I am most anxious that they be treated with
> just as much courtesy as the custom by the United States
> will allow even if an exception has been made I think it
> will be a fine thing . . . Whatever is done, or is not done,
> will attract a good deal of attention and result in wide
> comment among the Colored people.[22]

The Liberians had conferences with Theodore Roosevelt, Secretary of State William Howard Taft (who became president six months later and continued the cautious interest in Liberia's affairs), Elihu Root (who later replaced Taft as Secretary of State), and several other prominent officials of the United States government. Dossen served as spokesperson for the visitors, and their objectives or purposes for coming to the United States were manifold.[23] One report, issued following a 9:30 P.M. meeting at the White House, stated that "the envoys' primary purpose in visiting the United States at this time is to invoke the good offices of the [United States] government to prevent certain threatened encroachments of England, France and Germany upon their [Liberia's] territory. . . ."[24] It was duly noted that the

United States had no legal grounds for intervention in Liberia and therefore the Liberian appeal was for "moral assistance" and for the United States to use its "international influence in inducing England, Germany and France to abandon their policy of aggression."[25] Additional concerns centered on endeavoring to attract United States capital investment for Liberian development.[26] The delegates argued that an "awakening" had come to Africa and that, "Europe is seeking a new outlet for her money and a new reservoir of production and we [Liberia] can attribute her menacing attitude to no other cause than that they covet this African El Dorado of ours."[27] Two other important issues were identified as the need for industrial education in Liberia[28] and the need to keep the country "intact for all Negroes in America who might, in the future, desire to go to the fatherland."[29] Colored American Magazine, which along with the New York Age firmly supported this "diplomatic and commercial mission" to the United States, editorialized bluntly that Liberia wished America to take over her public debt (described as not too large) so that fairness and justice to creditors and Liberia would be ensured. The editorial went on to note that Liberia wanted the United States to "supervise" her fiscal affairs, which would "assure and secure" her creditors and provide essential fiscal training for Liberian citizens. Third, the United States was petitioned by Liberia to reorganize, strengthen and modernize her "military, interior, postal, educational, agricultural and judicial departments." The editorial closed by indicating that Liberia wanted the United States to adjust her boundaries especially those sections in which England, France, and Germany were interested.[30]

When their Washington, D.C. meetings were completed the Liberians were invited to Tuskegee Institute and there they were entertained by Booker T. Washington before returning to Liberia.[31] There was cause for reserved optimism because the government officials who met the envoys all seemed to be genuinely concerned about Liberia's predicament. African-Americans in 1908 were, by and large, a rural population and uninformed about events in Liberia. They were more sensitive about the recent Atlanta riots (1906)[32] and the so-called Brownsville affair.[33] Those Blacks who were aware of Liberia's crisis fully supported the requests of the Liberian delegation to prevent absorption by European powers. Indeed, because Liberia traced its origins to Blacks from the United States, it was felt the U.S. government was obligated to provide a favorable response to Liberia's courageous appeal for help. For his part in hosting the visitors and personally presiding over the public reception given the commissioners while in Washington, D.C., Booker T. Washington was lavishly praised by the Liberians upon their return home. A grateful Liberian Government bestowed upon the Tuskegean the "Order of African Redemption." Washington was the first American to be honored with this coveted title, believed to be much sought after by Europeans.[34]

Apparently, Roosevelt, Root, and the other U.S. government officials who received the Liberian visitors decided that before committing to any specific course of action it would be prudent to send a group of commissioners to Liberia to investigate the situation first-hand and make recommendations. In line with this decision, Theodore Roosevelt and Elihu Root requested an appropriation of $20,000 from Congress to cover the expenses of these commissioners.[35] The first order of business was to decide on the composition of the group. It was widely believed that the most logical choice to head such a mission was none other than Booker T. Washington.

Washington was anxious to be a member of the delegation to Liberia and several times was prematurely announced as such.[36] The State Department also felt it was important to have Washington on the United States contingent.[37] But between February and March of 1909, Booker T. Washington apparently changed his mind about going to Liberia. There are several possible explanations for this. First, it was anticipated that the trip would take about six weeks. Although the Tuskegee Board of Trustees gave their approval, evidently they were lukewarm about Booker T. Washington being absent that long, particularly since the school year was ending. This is surprising because Washington was often away from Tuskegee for extended periods (however, remaining in the United States). Second, the new Taft administration felt it was essential for Booker T. Washington to be available in an advisory capacity—especially in the early months.[38] In any event, Washington was out and his hand-picked replacement and personal secretary, Emmet J. Scott,[39] became a member of the United States Commission.[40] Scott was joined by Robert Post Falkner, former Commissioner of Education in Puerto Rico, who served as chairman, and Dr. George Sale, Superintendent of Baptist Missionary Schools in Puerto Rico and Cuba.[41] They were accompanied by Frank S. Flower, Civil Attaché; George Finch, Secretary; and Major P.M. Ashburn and Sidney Coleman, military attachés.[42] Scott was the only African-American in the group.

The objects of this United States Commission to Liberia were to investigate the situation in Liberia and make recommendations regarding how the United States could come to her aid. The Commission sailed from New York on April 24, 1909, aboard the cruisers *Chester* and *Birmingham*. There was some suggestion that because Scott was the only Black member of the delegation he would be discriminated against on board ship. This "race issue," although "sensationalized" by several publicity-seeking newspapers, was subsequently denied and dismissed by Scott.[43] The American delegation arrived in Monrovia on May 8, 1909, and were afforded a "hearty welcome and were being treated with marked deference by the people of Monrovia."[44] The claim was made that "Monrovia went wild over the arrival of the Americans . . . the local military authorities announced the coming of the Commission by the long roll of a drum and the people of Monrovia hastened to commanding points to see the glad sight of the American flag in the harbor."[45] A holiday atmosphere prevailed in Monrovia as all work was suspended and all stores in the city were closed. The commissioners were met on board ship by Ernest Lyon, the American Minister resident and Consul-General in Liberia. They were also met by the mayor of Monrovia and several important councilmen. The honors and celebration accorded the visitors had heretofore been reserved exclusively for presidential inaugurations. All parties involved held the greatest expectations for these American ambassadors and May 8, 1909 was considered a milestone in Liberian history, analogous with their 1847 independence.[46] The only damper on the whole affair was the disappointing absence of Booker T. Washington from the Commission. Apparently, the news had been circulated that he was a member and "The whole country was 'on edge' to see this world famed man." His reputation, which preceded his anticipated arrival, had elevated the Liberians' perceptions of him almost to the height of a deity.[47]

The Commission set up headquarters in Monrovia and the first few days were spent observing the expected diplomatic courtesies commonplace for events such as this. Everybody who was anybody was received by the Commissioners from the United States, Liberian, English, French, and German officials.

The Commission explored many aspects of the Liberian situation while traveling extensively throughout the length and breadth of the country. On one or two occasions the commissioners split up to investigate different matters; they traveled by boat and foot to hamlets, villages, and small towns. They made on-sight inspections in areas where there were territorial or boundary tensions between the English, French, and Germans and the government of Liberia. The commissioners had conversations with Liberian officials that centered on agricultural, commercial, financial, and military issues. After almost two months of extensive examination of the Liberian situation, the work of the commissioners was completed.[48] Before they left, however, they received a list of "Suggestions Submitted to the American Commission by the Government of Liberia." This three-page, fourteen-point memorandum essentially requested that the United States Government intercede in all of Liberia's affairs, domestic and foreign. It was a series of requests that were hard to distinguish from a plea for almost complete adoption.[49]

The Commissioners to Liberia returned to the United States on July 1, 1909, landing at Newport, Rhode Island. They were greeted with an enthusiastic welcome from the mixed-race crowd, including city officials, businesspersons and other prominent individuals. The commissioners agreed to take a short vacation with their families before convening on July 13, 1909, to formulate their report. All of the commissioners, when interviewed, were tight-lipped about their recommendations, stating that it was improper to comment prematurely. They indicated that their full report would be available as soon as possible.[50]

It is difficult to ascertain what percentage of the African American community was aware of the Liberian situation, much less taken by it. If the leading Black newspaper, the New York *Age*, and one of the popular Black periodicals, *Colored American Magazine*, are reliable barometers of the sentiment among Blacks, Liberia had their spirited and unqualified support.[51] Both organs, from the very beginning, announced their championship of the West African nation. They editorialized on Liberia's behalf and often printed front-page stories that emphasized Liberia's positive qualities.[52] The *Age* covered the activities of the United States Commission from its inception, monitoring its movements between the departure for Liberia and the return to the United States. It was solicitous in encouraging a U.S. rescue of Liberia, arguing primarily that Liberia was more closely identified with the United States than with any other country (all of her institutions being modeled after the United States) and that it was by citizens of the United States that Liberia was founded in the first instance. One editorial that serves as an example of the fervor of the *Age* exclaimed, "Liberia makes a manly appeal for America's help. America should grant it."[53]

Liberia was encouraged to call on the United States because of an 1862 treaty negotiated during the presidency of Abraham Lincoln that extended to them the "right to call on the

United States whenever necessary."[54] Now, more than a year after the Liberian Commissioners visited the United States and three months after Messrs. Scott, Sale, and Falkner returned from their fact-finding mission to Liberia, the details of the Commission's recommendations were made public. The recommendations were addressed to the United States Government and received a favorable reception from President Taft and Secretary of State Knox. There were six suggestions for dealing with the grave situation in Liberia:

1. That the United States extend its aid to Liberia in the settlement of pending boundary disputes.
2. That the United States enable Liberia to refund its debt by assuming as a guarantee for the payment of obligations under such an arrangement the control and collection of the Liberian customs.
3. That the United States lend its assistance in the reform of internal finances.
4. That the United States lend its aid in organizing and drilling an adequate constabulary or frontier police force.
5. That the United States establish a research station in Liberia.
6. That the United States reopen the question of establishing a naval coaling station in Liberia.[55]

Liberia's outstanding debts attracted the most attention and was assigned earliest priority and, therefore, was acted on first. The debt was about $1,400,000 and approximately $1,000,000 of that indebtedness was held by Europeans.[56] The first important step taken toward easing the pressure of Liberia's financial burden at the suggestion of the United States, was the appointment of R.P. Falkner (formerly head of the American Commission to Liberia) as a special financial agent for Liberia in the United States and Europe. A second and more important effort, involved the attempt to float an international loan for Liberia that would erase the existing debts. Reports on the amount to be raised varied between $1,000,000, $1,500,000, $1,700,000, and $2,000,000.[57] As part of this effort, President Taft delivered a special March 25, 1910, message to Congress in support of providing financial assistance for Liberia. The lion's share of these debt-funding negotiations was guided by the New York banking house of Kuhn, Loeb and Company. National City Bank of New York was also involved. More specifically, Booker T. Washington seems to have substantially influenced the floating of this loan for Liberia. He petitioned Isaac Seligman, a New York banker-businessman-humanitarian, to explore the possibilities of some New York bankers advancing the loan to Liberia. Paul Warburg, at this time a member of the Tuskegee Institute Board of Trustees and a partner in Kuhn and Loeb, was probably the individual who was most instrumental in the final outcome of this loan.[58]

    In 1912 an international loan involving the United States, Great Britain, France, and Germany was made available to Liberia. Most evidence suggests that the amount of the loan was $1,700,000. Nevertheless, the threat of bankruptcy and financial ruin subsided.[59] The loan was secured by the appointment of Americans and Europeans as receivers of customs in Liberia who, in the process, essentially became directors of the Liberian economy. Revenues from imports and exports, from poll-taxes, and from duties on rubber were also pledged to reduce the debt.[60] Before this episode finally ran its course, Black Americans led by Lieutenant Benjamin O. Davis, and later Major Charles Young,[61] were advising and directing the Liberian frontier police force, and Liberia had become, in fact, an unofficial colony of the United States.[62] As part of the 1912 loan agreement Major Young replaced Lieutenant Davis as head of the Liberian Frontier Forces. Part of the limited coverage on Liberia provided by *Crisis* indicated that Major Young, in 1914 and 1915, in addition to heading the Frontier Forces, was conducting a military school in Liberia. Some of the Liberian students attending that school graduated as third lieutenants and eventually studied in the military department of Wilberforce University. In December of

1915, Major Young had returned to Wilberforce, Ohio, which was his home, and was succeeded by Major W.F. York, who was later replaced by Major Wilson Ballard.[63] Major Young, promoted to Colonel, returned to Monrovia in 1919 to reorganize the Liberian army. After this he went to Nigeria on a research expedition, where he died in 1922.[64]

Liberians expressed gratitude for being lifted from the clutches of European imperialism now victimizing all of Africa except Ethiopia.[65] By May of 1914, some ambiguity had arisen over the scope of the loan agreement.[66] Liberia felt it was being humiliated by some of the conditions imposed on her by representatives of the holders of the loan. Among other things, the disputed areas included whether the Liberian frontier guards would be paid out of customs duties. Liberia was contending that she should have the privilege of paying her own forces. In addition, it was claimed that attempts were being made to interfere in the political affairs of the country, which was outside the scope of the loan agreement. More important was the delicate question of whether decisions regarding Liberia's affairs—which provoked concerns over the more sensitive issue of sovereignty—would be made in Washington or Monrovia. To help clarify these pertinent matters, John L. Morris, Secretary of the Treasury for Liberia, came to the United States for a round of talks in New York and Washington, D.C. Very little was resolved and the confusion continued. Booker T. Washington lost no interest in Liberia and Liberia's affairs, but he died a year after Morris's visit, in 1915.[67] The air never really cleared about the conditions of the loan agreement and Liberia's shaky sovereignty remained in suspension. World War I merely exacerbated matters by cutting off most of Liberia's trade with the industrial world. Her customs duties were cut in half by the discontinuation of British and German shipping. Interest payments on the 1912 loan fell behind and piled up. To make matters worse the Kru tribe began to rebel in 1915 and it took the arrival of the U.S.S. *Chester* and the spilling of a good deal of Kru blood to suppress the rebellion.[68]

The coming of World War I had also essentially ended emigration to Liberia for the decade. It became too hazardous, with German U-boats patrolling the Atlantic Ocean, to permit passenger or cargo ships to traverse these waters unescorted. This danger did not, however, prevent Chief Alfred C. Sam from sending a boatload of pilgrims to West Africa during the same period.

With the death of Booker T. Washington in December of 1915, there was a noticeable decline in African-American interest in Liberia. Moreover, the level of Black American interaction with Liberia was reduced as well. It might be that the interest level peaked in 1912 as Liberia obtained the $1,700,000 international loan, and retreated thereafter as no dramatic issues were evident around which African-Americans could rally. This fading interest was partly observable in the pages of the New York *Age*. However, the *Age* continued to outdistance all other Black newspapers and periodicals covering events in Liberia and Africa generally.

The New York *Age* did not monitor events in Liberia between 1915 and 1919 to the same extent that it had up to Booker T. Washington's death. Nevertheless, one editorial in December 1918 insisted that Liberia, by virtue of her status as one of the belligerents, was entitled to a voice in any World War I peace deliberations. Liberia had claims by dint of her altered boundaries both with England and France, continued the editorial. The *Age* felt that Liberia could also serve as a "tutor" for some of Germany's former colonies. The *Age* even offered to furnish eloquent and willing African-Americans as spokespersons for Liberia if need be, but reminded its readers that Liberia had a plentiful supply of able people instanced by President Howard, Walter Walker (Secretary of the Treasury), or James Dossen, now Chief Justice of the Supreme Court.[69] At the same time, the *Age* kept its readers informed regarding some of Liberia's internal affairs. There was special treatment in the *Age* on president-elect C.D.B. King's expectation that Liberia would maintain its "racial identity." Liberia wanted outside help and considered itself the "interpreter of Africans in Africa," but was adamant in its refusal to be absorbed by outsiders—politically, socially, or culturally.[70] The *Age* also criticized the appointment of a White bishop for Liberia in the face of the availability of several capable Blacks. It also admonished the Wilson administration for filling employment opportunities in Liberia, in connection with a new $5 million assistance package from the United States (ten positions in all), paying $3,000 a year plus expenses, with White men.[71] The 1912 loan to Liberia, by 1918, clearly proved to be inadequate for undertaking any serious internal development. Therefore, before the year ended, Liberia requested and received a $5 million dollar line of credit from the United States.[72]

Liberia's management of her affairs through outside loans continued during the following decades. The threats of European encroachment on her land also continued. Despite the efforts of African-Americans to aid the young nation, during her grave crisis, the Republic of Liberia remained on a precarious path.

The next time that African-Americans demonstrated any significant degree of excitement over events in Liberia came with the attempt by Marcus Garvey's Universal Negro Improvement Association (UNIA) to secure land in Liberia. The land had actually been promised to UNIA but President King, in the final stages of the negotiations with UNIA, along with the Liberian legislature, reversed himself, and eventually the land earmarked for UNIA went to the Firestone Rubber Company. It was W.E.B. DuBois who went to Liberia as an envoy of President Calvin Coolidge to help dissuade Liberia from giving acreage to Garveyites. Ironically, it was also DuBois, along with Rayford Logan, who led the charges of exploitation by Firestone in Liberia in the mid-1920s.[73]

Before Booker T. Washington became interested in events in Liberia, he became involved in a German effort to grow cotton commercially in Togo, West Africa. The Togo experiment lasted from 1900 to 1909 and represents the first attempt by Europeans to use the agricultural expertise of the descendants of ex-slaves in the United States to grow cotton in West Africa.

NOTES

1. *Liberia Bulletin* (February, 1903), 1–2, (February, 1904), 2–3.

2. *Liberia Bulletin* (February, 1902), 1; (November, 1904), 71–72.

3. *Liberia Bulletin* (February, 1907), 1.

4. *Indianapolis Freeman* (October 6, 1900), 8.

5. *Liberia Bulletin* (February, 1906), 57–59.

6. *Liberia Bulletin* (February, 1904), 2.

7. *Ibid.*

8. *Liberia Bulletin* (November, 1904), 79–80. For information on emigration sentiments among African-Americans involving Liberia between 1900 and 1910, consult Redkey, *Black Exodus*, chapter 11. For emigration sentiment generally during this period see August Meier, *Negro Thought in America 1880–1915* (Ann Arbor, Michigan, 1969), chapter 4.

9. One unwelcome source of support for emigration might have come from Senator John T. Morgan of Alabama, who said he was influenced by African-American moral support for Liberia and that since he came to the Senate he had long been interested in "clearing the way for the voluntary emigration of the African race." *Liberia Bulletin* (February, 1903), 58, 59–61. For more on Morgan's views regarding Africa and emigration see Redkey, *Black Exodus*, 61–63, 270–271, *passim*.

10. For a sampling of the emigration debate as reflected in the Black media see *Colored American Magazine* (January, 1907), 17–25, 44–48; (March 1907), 176–177; (July 1909), 47–52; *A.M.E. Church Review* (January, 1907), 251–256; (July, 1907), 75–76; New York *Age* (January 24, 1907), 5; (January 31, 1907), 5; (July 18, 1907), 3; *Liberia Bulletin* (February, 1904), 87–88; (November, 1904), 71–72, 87–88, 90–93, 95–96; (February, 1906), 62–73; (November, 1906), 50–51, 70–71; New York *Herald* (May 28, 1905), 1–2. There is an interesting pamphlet discussion

on the idea of emigration by Charlie Cobb, "African Notebook: Views on Returning Home" (Chicago, 1972), 14 pages, which is reminiscent of this early twentieth century debate.

The figure of 1,000 emigrants sailing to Liberia is estimated by Redkey, *Black Exodus*, 291.

11. All of the discussion above comes from *Colored American Magazine* (December, 1904), 735–742 and *Liberia Bulletin* (February, 1905), 80–81. *Colored American Magazine* ran full-page advertisements on this company, promoting the sale of stock in their September, October, November, and December (1904) issues.

12. This information on the Ethiopian-American Steamship Company comes from the Booker T. Washington Papers (BTW) (375). On the request for endorsement and Washington's response, see J.E. Lewis to BTW, May 5, 1908 and Emmet J. Scott (for BTW) to J.E. Lewis, May 18, 1908 (375).

13. Adelaide Hill, and Martin Kilson (eds.), *Apropos*, 206–208. One well known member of the African Union Company Board of Directors was Emmet J. Scott of Tuskegee, Alabama.

14. A useful summary of the attitude of the Black press toward Africa at the end of the nineteenth century is available in Walter Williams's "Black Journalism's Opinion About Africa During the Late Nineteenth Century," *Phylon* (September, 1973), 224–235. See the same author's broader, "Black American Attitudes Toward Africa, 1877–1900," *Pan African Journal* (Spring, 1971), 173–194.

15. Louis Harlan, *Booker T. Washington: The Wizard of Tuskegee, 1901–1915* (New York, 1973), 271–273 summarizes Washington's involvement with Liberia and in Chapter 11, all of Africa, which, in addition to Liberia, included Togo (discussed below), the Belgian Congo and Southern Africa. Harlan concluded that Booker T. Washington's "experience in African affairs simply illuminated his essential conservatism, showing him as in a tailor's mirror, from new angles but in the usual stance." Nevertheless, according to Harlan, Washington "had an influence, all over Africa, through the translation of his writings, particularly his Biography," *ibid.*, 273, 287. See also volume I of Harlan's two-volume biography of Booker T. Washington, even though it covers years preceding this study. *Booker T. Washington: The Making of a Black Leader, 1856–1901* (New York, 1972).

16. For Liberia's founding by the American Colonization Society: See P.J. Staudenraus, *The African Colonization Movement* (New York, 1961); Early Lee Fox, *The American Colonization Society, 1817–1840* (Baltimore, 1919); Henry Noble Sherwood, "The Formation of the American Colonization Society," *Journal of Negro History* (July, 1917), 209–219 and his "Paul Cuffe and His Contribution to the American Colonization Society," *Proceedings of the Mississippi Valley Historical Association* (1913), IV, 370–402. The reaction of free Blacks to the Society is treated in Louis Mehlinger, "Attitude of the Free Negro Toward African Colonization," *Journal of Negro History* (July, 1916), 271–301; William L. Garrison, *Thoughts on African Colonization* (1832; rprt. New York, 1969); Leon Litwack, *North of Slavery: The Negro in the Free States 1790–1860* (Chicago, 1961), 23–38, *passim*; and Benjamin Quarles, *Black Abolitionists* (New York, 1969), *passim.*

17. Secondary discussions of Liberia's history can be found in Richard West, *Back to Africa: A History of Sierra Leone and Liberia* (New York, 1970); Harry Johnson, *Liberia*, (London, 1966), 2 vols; George Dalton, "History, Politics and Economic Development in Liberia," *Journal of Economic History* (December, 1965); George W. Brown, *The Economic History of Liberia* (Washington, D.C., 1941); and Raymond L. Buell, *Liberia: A Century of Survival 1847–1947* (Philadelphia, 1947). Liberia's foreign policy and relations with the United States are treated in Charles H. Huberich, *The Political and Legislative History of Liberia* (New York, 1947), 2 vols, especially I, 1960–1962, for references to other sources dealing with Liberia's foreign policy and the United States; see J. Gus Liebenow, *Liberia; The Evolution of Privilege* (Ithaca, New York, 1969); and his *Liberia: The Quest for Democracy* (Bloomington, Indiana, 1987); Nnamdi Azikwe, *Liberia in World Politics* (London, 1934); Raymond Bixler, *The Foreign Policy of the United States in Liberia* (New York, 1957) and *Liberia: A Report on the Relations between the United States and Liberia*, U.S. Government Printing Office (Washington, D.C., 1928).

18. Walter Walker, "The Grab for Liberia and Her Needs," *Colored American Magazine* (August, 1909), 118; Brown, *Economic History*, 143–144.

19. *Liberia Bulletin* (November, 1906), 66–69.

20. Basil Mathews, *Booker T. Washington: Educator and Interracial Interpreter* (Cambridge, Massachusetts, 1948), 242–243; Louis Harlan, "Booker T. Washington and the White Man's Burden" in Odon E. Uya (ed.), *Black Brotherhood: Afro-Americans and Africa* (New York, 1971), 140–

141; Walter Walker, "The Liberian Crisis," *Colored American Magazine* (April, 1909), 209–211; New York *Age* (March 21, 1907), 1; Raymond Leslie Buell, *Liberia: A Century of Survival, 1847–1947* (Philadelphia, Pennsylvania, 1947), chapters 1–2; J.H. Mower, "The Republic of Liberia," *Journal of Negro History* (July, 1947), 272–273; Benjamin Brawley, *A Social History of the American Negro* (New York, 1921), 200–202; Report of the American Commission of 1910, "Affairs in Liberia," Senate Document no. 457, 61st Congress, 2nd Session (1910), 19–23.

21. Walker, "The Liberian Crisis," 209.

22. Booker T. Washington (BTW) to Theodore Roosevelt, March 21, 1908 (7).

23. New York *Age* (June 4, 1908), 1; (June 18, 1908), 3; (October 29, 1908), 9; *The Tuskegee Student* (June 20, 1908), 1; *Colored American Magazine* (September, 1909), 174–175, 222–223; BTW to Theodore Roosevelt, March 21, 1908 (7); Charles R. Branch to BTW, April 27, 1908 (368); BTW to Ernest Lyon, May 25, 26; June 15, 1908 (368).

24. New York *Age* (June 18, 1908), 3.

25. *Ibid.*

26. New York *Age* (June 4, 1908), 1.

27. There are three enlightening discussions of the possibilities for investment in Liberia provided by an African-American emigrant in Liberia from Tennessee by the name of Benjamin J. Gant. See *Colored American Magazine* (February, 1905), 90–92; (March, 1905), 153–154; (January, 1906), 25–26.

28. Booker T. Washington wrote and spoke frequently about his proposals for industrial education in Africa. Essentially, he promoted the Tuskegee model, which was well received. See Booker T. Washington, "Industrial Education in Africa," *Independent* (March 15, 1906), 616–619 typescript in BTW Papers (394); also New York *Age* (March 22, 1906), 2 and *The Tuskegee Student* (March 24, 1906), 1–3. Booker T. Washington consulted regularly with Olivia and Caroline Phelps-Stokes (Phelps-Stokes Fund) regarding industrial education in Liberia; the correspondence is too voluminous to cite here, but much of it, especially for 1908–1912, can be found in BTW Papers (47) and (53).

29. *The Tuskegee Student* (June 20, 1908), 1.

30. *Colored American Magazine* (September, 1909), 222–223.

31. Upon his return to Liberia, Vice President Dossen had great praise for the warm welcome his delegation received in the United States. He also declared that 600,000 of the "best trained" Black Americans could be the solution to Liberia's problems. New York *Age* (November 12, 1908), 1 (dateline Monrovia).

32. New York *Age* (September 27, 1096), 1, 3–4.

33. The "Brownsville affair" made news in the early 1970s because, after sixty-six years, Congress—in 1972—restored the Black soldiers involved (all of whom were dead except one) to good standing in the U.S. Army. A well-done account of this incident is John D. Weaver, *The Brownsville Raid* (New York, 1970). See also Anne J. Lane, *The Brownsville Affair: National Crisis and Black Reaction* (Port Washington, N.Y., 1971) and Jack D. Foner, *Blacks and the Military in American History* (New York, 1974).

34. New York *Age* (October 29, 1908), 9.

35. Liebenow, *Liberia*, 6–7; Theodore Roosevelt, "Message from the President of the United States" (to Congress), January 19, 1909, 60th Congress, Second Session, Document 666; also included here is Root's letter to Theodore Roosevelt, January 18, 1909, and several other letters and memos concerning "conditions in Liberia." Also, on the $20,000 appropriation request, see New York *Age* (January 28, 1909), 1.

36. *The Tuskegee Student* (March 6, 1909), 2; (March 13, 1909), 1.

37. BTW to Seth Low, February 16, 1909 (45).

38. BTW to Seth Low, January 22, 1909 (45); Seth Low to BTW, January 20, 1909; February 18, 1909 (45); BTW to Robert Ogden, March 4, 1909 (895).

39. Seth Low to BTW, March 19, 1909 (45); *The Tuskegee Student* (March 6, 1909), 2; (March 27, 1909), 2; (April 3, 1909), 2–3; New York *Age* (April 29, 1909), 1.

40. There is simply too much correspondence on the composition of this Commission to be cited individually. Most of it is between Booker T. Washington and people like Ralph Tyler, Robert Ogden, General Leonard Wood, James Dossen, President Barclay, Ernest Lyon, and others. See especially container (895), folder marked "Liberia." See, in addition, containers (6), (7), (8).

41. Booker T. Washington asked that his name not be used in making inquiries and recommendations regarding a "White man of

high character and strong executive ability who has had experience in reorganizing and rebuilding governments in the Philippines, Cuba, Puerto Rico or Panama in recent years. Of course he should be a man in sympathy with the race. Telegraph me at my expense names and addresses of such persons if you can find them." This is one possible explanation for the selection of Falkner and Sale, both of whom had experience in the Caribbean. BTW to Ralph Tyler, December 23, 1908 (7).

42. *The Tuskegee Student* (April 17, 1909), 3; New York *Age* (April 29, 1909), 1 (plus photograph); *Colored American Magazine* (May, 1909), 315–316.

43. Emmet J. Scott, "The American Commissioners in Liberia" (typescript), BTW Papers (394), also rprt. *Colored American Magazine* (September, 1909), 204–210; Emmet J. Scott to BTW, May 2, 1909 (587); New York *Times* (April 17, 1909); New York *Tribune*, (April 18, 1909), BTW Papers (1089).

44. New York *Age* (May 20, 1909), 1. See also *A.M.E. Church Review* (July, 1909), 78–79 for the hoopla and excitement over the arrival of the U.S. Commissioners.

45. *A.M.E. Church Review* (July, 1909), 78–79.

46. *Ibid.*; New York *Age* (June 17, 1909), 1, 3 (Editorial); *The Tuskegee Student* (May 22, 1909), 2; *Colored American Magazine* (September, 1909), 206–207.

47. *The Tuskegee Student* (June 18, 1909), 1, 3–4; (July 3, 1909), 2. Also on the disappointing absence of Booker T. Washington from the Commission, James Dossen to BTW, June 11, 1909 (394). Dossen claimed that one Liberian wrote him that, "I am exceedingly sorry that Dr. Washington did not find it possible to serve on the Commission: a report to Congress on Liberia over his signature would have carried more weight than of any White or Black American of whom I can think."

48. Most of the details of the work in Liberia can be found in Emmet J. Scott, "The American Commissioners in Liberia," BTW Papers (394). Emmet Scott also wrote an interesting account of his views regarding what he considered the value of African students being educated at Tuskegee, "The African in Africa and the African at Tuskegee," BTW Papers (335).

49. BTW Papers (394).

50. *The Tuskegee Student* (July 17, 1909), 1, 3; New York *Age* (July 8, 1909), 1.

51. An interesting example of Black American support for Liberia came from Denver, Colorado, where a group of Black citizens met and passed resolutions to give moral as well as financial aid to Liberia: New York *Age* (June 9, 1910), 1. Another example was Blacks in Pittsburgh, Pennsylvania, who also agreed to raise funds to aid Liberia. New York *Age* (June 23, 1910), 3.

52. From time to time stories were printed that were considered damaging to Liberia. In May and June of 1909, and perhaps at other times, this was the case, and it ignited a mild controversy over the identity of the author which the *Age* did not reveal. The correspondence regarding these controversial articles is too voluminous to detail here. In any event, see especially Ernest Lyon to BTW and Ernest Lyon to Emmet Scott, June 16, 1909, BTW to Ernest Lyon, July 15, 1909, Walter Walker to Emmet Scott, June 16, 1909 who claimed there was a "nigger in the woodpile" who was "adding fuel to the fire," all in BTW Papers (394). The *Age* printed an apology for publishing material damaging to Liberia and insisted that their intention was to help, not hurt, Liberia See New York *Age* (July 22, 1909), 4.

53. New York *Age* (July 8, 1909), 3. See also the editorial in the March 31, 1910 issue. The *Age* editorial (December 7, 1911) claimed that ten million U.S. Blacks had a sentimental interest in Africa. The total Black population in the United States at this time was estimated to be twelve million.

54. New York *Age* (February 3, 1910), 1; (April 21, 1910), 4; J.H. Mower, "The Republic of Liberia," *Journal of Negro History* (July, 1947), 269.

55. New York *Age* (March 31, 1910), 1; the February 3, 1910 issue discusses the Commission and its deliberations. Also useful is the October 14, 1909 issue and *The Tuskegee Student* (October 16, 1909), 1–2. Vice President Dossen of Liberia did some special transatlantic lobbying with Booker T. Washington on behalf of points 1 and 3; the boundary problems and internal finances. He requested that Washington use his influence in getting the United States to send warships to Liberia in order to "tighten control" over coastal tribes who were constantly in rebellion and were now resorting to smuggling. Dossen, moreover, claimed that "foreigners of certain nationality . . . [were] breeding

discontent among our natives" evidently these were the Germans, French, or British, or all three, even though Dossen mentioned no names. Dossen also accused Sir Harry Johnson of being a party to a financial scheme that manipulated a previous Liberian loan through the Liberian Development Company to the disadvantage of Liberia. Furthermore, and especially relevant, Dossen conjured up visions of the old Fanti Confederation with the following statement, which exudes Pan-West Africanism: "Liberia is destined to be Capital of the United States of West Africa [sic], an event which is the trend of thought amongst intelligent Negroes everywhere in West Africa and is bound to take place. . . . Neither you nor I will probably live to see that end but we can be in our day valuable contributors toward it." James Dossen to BTW, June 11, 1909; also March 24, 1910 and December 12, 1912 (394). See, in addition, Emmet J. Scott, "Is Liberia Worth Saving?" *Journal of Race Development* (1911), 280–287 and Roland P. Falkner, "The United States and Liberia," *American Journal of International Law* (July, 1910), 188–229.

56. New York *Age* (August 11, 1910), 1.

57. *The Tuskegee Student* (February 4, 1911), 1; New York *Age* (August 11, 1910), 1; *The Tuskegee Student* (December 17, 1910), 4.

58. BTW to Isaac Seligman, September 5, 1909 (394); Isaac Seligman to BTW, September 10, 1909 and September 20, 1909 (898); Emmet Scott to Paul Warburg, September 25, 1909 (898). *The Tuskegee Student* (February 5, 1910), 1 (rprt. from Washington *Post*).

59. All discussants mentioned above confirm the $1,700,000 figure, while Louis Harlan, "Booker T. Washington. . ." in Uya (ed.), *Black Brotherhood* , 144 indicates that the figure was $1,500,000.

60. *Ibid*; Richard West, *Back-to-Africa* (New York, 1970), 253–260.

61. New York *Age* (March 31, 1910), 4; (April 29, 1915), 1; *Crisis* (November, 1914), 16; (December, 1914), 63; Brown, *Economic History*, 168.

62. A worse fate yet awaited Liberia in the 1920s when she became a "colony" of the Firestone Rubber Company of the United States. Interesting but biased in favor of Firestone is *Liberia and Firestone* (Harbel, Liberia, 1956, no author listed). See also Nnamdi Azikwe, "In Defense of Liberia," *Journal of Negro History* (January, 1932), 5, 30–50 and *The Tuskegee Student* (April 9, 1910), 1–4, (September 24, 1910), 1.

63. *Crisis* (December, 1914), 63; (October, 1915), 271; (December, 1915), 65.

64. Edgar A. Toppin, *A Biographical History of Blacks in America Since 1528* (New York, 1969), 479–481.

65. Ethiopia is another African country in which African-Americans have demonstrated a continuing interest. The height of that interest came in the mid-1930s when Italy's fascist government invaded and raped that East African country. A doctoral dissertation that analyzes the historical relationship between African-Americans and Ethiopia is William R. Scott, "A Study of Afro-American and Ethiopian Relations: 1896–1941," Princeton University, 1971, especially chapters 3 and 5. Scott's revised dissertation is now published as *The Sons of Sheba's Race: African-Americans and the Italo-Ethiopian War, 1935–1941* (Bloomington, Indiana, 1992). A second Ph.D. dissertation that treats the African-American Ethiopia theme, although it is not the central focus of his thesis, is Bernard Magubane, "The American Negro's Conception of Africa: A Study in the Ideology of Pride and Prejudice," U.C.L.A., 1967, especially chapter 7, "Ethiopia—Its Significance in American Negroes' Consciousness of Africa," 288–316. See also Robert Weisbord, *Ebony Kinship* (New York, 1973), chapter 3, "Black America and the Italian-Ethiopian Crisis: An Episode in Pan-Negroism," 89–110.

66. New York *Age* (May 14, 1914), 1; (June 11, 1914), 1.

67. In what appears to be one of his final attempts to assist Liberia Booker T. Washington, in July, 1915 was making a major effort to get National City Bank to declare a moratorium on the Liberian loan because of the European war. New York *Age* (July 8, 1915), 2.

68. Liebenow, *Liberia*, 7, 191.

69. New York *Age* (December 7, 1918), 4.

70. New York *Age* (July 5, 1919), 1.

71. New York *Age* (October 25, 1919), 1; (December 14, 1919), 1.

72. George Ellis, "Liberia in the New Partition of West Africa," *Journal of Race Development* (January, 1919), 265.

73. W.E.B. DuBois, "Liberia and Rubber," *New Republic* (November 18, 1925), 328; Rayford Logan, "Liberia's Dilemma," *Southern Workman* (September, 1933), 362.

CHAPTER VII

Booker T. Washington, Tuskegee Institute, and the Togo Experiment

The idea for cotton growing in West Africa, at the instigation of non-Africans, can be traced at least as far back as the period that witnessed the decline of the Atlantic slave trade. Cotton was considered one possible substitute for slave trading and it was hoped that this staple could take on the character of legitimate commerce. During the first quarter of the nineteenth century, the French experimented with tropical agriculture in Senegal, setting up a model farm to grow, among other things, cotton and indigo. The French plan was to grow on this farm, with the use of African labor, many of the items cultivated on slave plantations in the U.S. South. New methods of irrigation and ploughing were employed, but in vain. By the early 1830s, owing to limited capital, unfamiliarity with conditions in the tropics and poor management, this ambitious undertaking was a failure.[1]

When the Civil War in the United States (1861–1865) interrupted cotton production, affecting the international demand for "king cotton," a wave of cotton-growing experiments emerged in West Africa. The French persisted in Senegal but they repeated many of their early mistakes and they again met with failure. Moreover, local Senegalese farmers considered groundnuts more profitable and therefore were unenthusiastic about cotton. British interest in cotton growing in West Africa dates from 1794, in their newly established colony of Sierra Leone. This initial effort also failed but a lack of success did not preclude other attempts to grow cotton in the same colony in 1808, 1825, and the 1830s. One of these early British efforts centered on Nigeria and the Gold Coast, where the Basel Mission attempted to grow cotton.[2] All these endeavors, however, were unsuccessful.[3]

In 1900 the United States did not produce the supply of cotton for the world market anticipated by the British and their textile industry. The deadly boll weevil and a series of devastating droughts in areas of the cotton-growing South partly explains the shortage. Consequently with the supply down and demand up, prices rose sharply. In Great Britain, "excitement reached fever pitch and something approaching a panic prevailed."[4] The time was now propitious for new cotton growing undertakings by the British in West Africa.

Between 1902 and the end of World War I, Great Britain attempted to grow (saleable) cotton in the Gambia, Sierra Leone, the Gold Coast, and Nigeria. Most of the work was organized under the British Cotton Growing Association and later by the Empire Cotton Growing Corporation. The British also brought in cotton-growing experts from the southern part of the United States for advice and counsel with their project. How many of these specialists were African-Americans, if any, which is doubtful, is unknown. However, at least two were West Indians and both were professors at the Lincoln Agricultural Institute in Jefferson, Missouri. Despite the enthusiasm of the initial phase of this cotton-growing attempt in West Africa, the program became essentially irrelevant and had to be abandoned because of difficulties with logistics and the limitation in markets brought about by the outbreak of a world war. In sum, Great Britain's plan to grow cotton for export in West Africa during this period "has been largely an account of naïve optimism and disappointing failure."[5] Since World War II, only in Nigeria have British cotton-growing efforts in West Africa begun to fulfill the ambitious early predictions of West Africa's cotton-growing potential.[6]

These French and British disappointments did not prevent the Germans from trying their hand at cotton growing in Togo at the start of the twentieth century. Unlike the British and French in West Africa, the Germans drew on the expertise of the former slave population of the United States.

The German colony of Togo in West Africa would not, at first, appear to be a likely place to find African-Americans growing cotton in the first decade of the twentieth century. The idea of Black Americans, Tuskegee graduates, going to Togo originated with a request from the German Embassy in Washington, D.C. sometime in late 1899 or early 1900.[7] A conversation later ensued between Booker T. Washington and one Baron Herman, representing the Kolonial Writschfliches Komitee, a German firm headquartered in Berlin. In August of 1900, at a meeting in Roslindale, Massachusetts, Baron Herman submitted a proposal to Professor Booker T. Washington and Tuskegee, suggesting that Tuskegee send to Togo two cotton planters and one mechanic, to provide instruction for Africans in what by the Germans characterized as rational and scientific cotton planting and harvesting.[8]

In his proposal to Booker T. Washington, Baron Herman was very explicit about the Kolonial Komitee's plans and expectations for this cotton-planting experiment in Togo. The Baron suggested that the Kolonial Komitee preferred three unmarried men but would accept one married man (among the three) and would underwrite costs for round trip transportation for all. Provision would be made for the Tuskegeans to leave on October 27, 1900, from New York, with a stopover in Hamburg and continuing on to Togo. Salaries for the team, it was proposed, would be $100 per month, or a little less if they were to share a percentage (50 percent) of the first year's cotton harvest. This was described as an inducement "to plant and raise as much and as good a [*sic*] cotton as possible." All three men were to have one-year contracts with a proviso for extensions if the first year's work and behavior were satisfactory. However, if the first year was unsatisfactory, the Kolonial Komitee would be under no obligation to uphold the contract, and, in fact could return the individual, or individuals, to the United States at the individual's own expense. Baron Herman also indicated that the Tuskegee team would have to bring most, if not all, of the supplies, tools, and implements necessary for "plantation-work" in Togo. Furthermore, the Kolonial Komitee would be perfectly willing to permit some diversified farming for the personal use of the Tuskegeans or for the local market (corn, sweet potatoes, bananas, peanuts), but not at the expense of cotton cultivation. In the interest of stimulating healthy competition, with a view toward producing the best possible grade of cotton, two plantations were proposed, fairly close to each other in location and with different varieties of soil in order "to give each planter the whole responsibility of the work and the result of his plantation." Finally, Baron Herman and the Kolonial Komitee expressed some concern over the difficulties the Tuskegee team might have exercising authority over the indigenous population and, more important, whether the Tuskegeans could be counted on to have the "necessary respect" toward the officials of the German government, who would, of course, be attempting to assist them in their work. They wanted Booker T. Washington's assurance that their concerns were unfounded, and therefore suggested the possibility that a man of the "highest education" be sent along to supervise the entire project.[9]

Booker T. Washington's response to the Kolonial Komitee's proposition was favorable and was most responsible for the enthusiasm now generated at Tuskegee and in Berlin on behalf of this Togo expedition.[10] Washington notified Baron Herman that the three men requested had already been selected, in addition to James Nathan Calloway, who was Washington's recommendation to lead the group. Calloway was a forty-year-old college graduate who had studied some German and who was currently managing one of Tuskegee's eight-hundred-acre farms. It was noted that he understood farming "both in a practical and scientific manner." Calloway's salary was to be $200 per month, and if he were acceptable to the Kolonial Komitee, he would be granted a twelve-month leave of absence from Tuskegee. Calloway's motives for going to Togo, like those his compatriots, were nonideological, and Booker T. Washington reported that, "He volunteers to go in a perfectly disinterested spirit, his only ambition being to have the young men who go out from here succeed."[11] In his response, the Principal of Tuskegee also allayed the fears of the Germans regarding the question of respect for German officials, stating, "I do not think . . . that there will be much, if any, difficulty in the men who go from here treating the German officials with proper respect. They are all kindly disposed, respectful gentlemen."[12] He also indicated that the group would quickly earn the respect of the Africans and cautioned the Germans about stultifying the progress of Black Americans by confining them to raising cotton, a practice then prevalent in the United States South.

On October 6, 1900, the Kolonial Komitee cabled Washington accepting the engagement of Calloway as well as "2 planters, 1 mechanic and also [the] proposed implements and seeds."[13] The cablegram was followed by a formal letter accepting all of the conditions set forth by Booker T. Washington in his letters to the Komitee of September 18 and 20, 1900, and outlining the plans for travel to Togo, which now called for the group to leave New York on the steamer *Waldersee* on November 3, 1900.[14]

Booker T. Washington's perceptions and views of Africa at this time (1900) could be the subject of much conjecture. Louis Harlan suggests that Washington, "early in his care," accepted White stereotypes about Africa, which were later modified as he became more enlightened.[15] In his "Atlanta Compromise," address (1895), Booker T. Washington commented on emigration and revealed his antipathy for any kind of Black exodus from the United States, including one to Africa.[16] In 1900 he continued this anti-emigration position in a speech before the A.M.E. church conference.[17] Later in the decade, Washington indicated that one of his ambitions as a student at Hampton Institute decades earlier was "to go out some day to Africa as a missionary."[18] Moreover, in 1909, Booker T. Washington was suggesting the possibility of establishing an "International Council of the Friends of Africa."[19] In short, these concerns as well as several others regarding Africa, irrespective of their ideological character, clearly demonstrate that Washington was very much conscious of Africa and possibly is the Black American individual with the most substantial record of active involvement, during this period, with Africa and Africans. Besides Togo, Booker T. Washington was consulted on the situation in South Africa,[20] the Congo,[21] Liberia,[22] and Anglo-Egyptian Sudan.[23] He never set foot on African soil, although invited on several occasions, yet he visited Europe several times. Nevertheless, he was responsible for other African-Americans visiting and working in Africa. To be sure, his Africa interest was always incidental and subordinate to his domestic concerns and the plight of Black people in the United States.

Before the details and conditions of the agreement between Tuskegee and the Germans were confirmed, probably even before receiving the September 3, 1900 letter from Baron Herman, Washington was lining up prospective candidates for this curious adventure. He wrote simultaneously to E.D. Whitehead, John Robinson, and Shepherd Harris, inviting each of them to participate. He said, in part,

> We have just had a call from the German Government for three of our students to go to a German colony in Africa for the purpose of conducting something like a model farm which can be used as an object lesson for the native Africans. Cotton, as I understand it, is to be the principal product, the colony is a healthy one, being on a high land on the West Coast of Africa.[24]

Robinson and Harris responded favorably, accepting the invitation and conditions. Whitehead was replaced by Allan L. Burks owing to the reservations of Whitehead's family regarding the potential hazards of such an expedition. The initial contingent of James Nathan Calloway (Faculty Advisor), John Winfrey Robinson (class of 1897), Lincoln Shepherd Harris (class of 1899), and Allan Lynn Burks (class of 1900) settled up their affairs in the United States and prepared for departure, while

Booker T. Washington worked out the finer details of their contracts with Baron Herman and the Kolonial Komitee.[25] There is some uncertainty over whether eight or nine African-Americans from Tuskegee went to Togo, but it seems quite certain that four died there and the venture, although carefully planned, never met the expectations of the Germans or the Tuskegeans.[26]

It was with a great deal of anxiety, and comparatively good press coverage, that Calloway, Robinson, Harris, and Burks left New York on November 3, 1900.[27] After a brief stop in Europe they pressed on to West Africa, reaching the Portuguese settlement of Bissau (formerly a slave trading post) on December 10. The party made frequent stops along the West African coast before stopping for one full day at Monrovia, Liberia. While in Monrovia they visited the Liberian senate, which was in session, and they had many kind words for the young nation. The Tuskegeans arrived at Lome, Togo on December 30, 1900.[28] However, they had not yet reached their destination, which was about one hundred miles in the hinterland; this additional journey took them about four days and was made on foot.[29]

The first task of these "pioneers" was to clear the land and locate a suitable place for their experimental cotton plantation. This they accomplished efficiently and expeditiously. With the assistance of local people they "made a desperate attack upon the mighty African forest" and established headquarters at a place called Misshoa.

The area selected for the experimental plantation was an estate of about 350 acres. Through direct local negotiations, James Calloway was able to recruit a work force. By the middle of January 1901, when the work was fully underway, approximately two hundred Africans were employed on the farm. Some men were paid by the day to cut brushwood and clear the land with pickaxes. Others, who came primarily from the coast, were paid 75 pfennigs (pf.) per day to "fell the trees and tear up the roots."[30] Women and children gathered and burned the roots and were paid 35pf. and 20pf., respectively.

Africans were also engaged in building dwelling houses, outhouses, and storehouses. Later, Africans were employed as general laborers around the plantations, took part in the planting and harvesting of the cotton crop, and drew ploughs and carts when horses or oxen were not available. Initially, twenty horses and twenty oxen were brought into Togo from the Sudan in order to pull the carts and ploughs. But the tsetse fly appeared and the animals perished, which meant that most of that work had to be done by Africans. Their rates of pay remained approximately the same.[31]

The soil of the Missahoa district was composed primarily of red gravel covered by a thin layer of humus. Light soil was selected for cultures that were subject to heavy rains in order to enable the water to run off quickly, which would, in turn, allow the air to reach the roots of the cotton plant. The most serious problems with the soils of the West African coast generally, which were considered imperfect, were the absence of lime, the limited amount of potash in the soil, and the difficulties of nitrification. This made the introduction of new plants or the improvement of indigenous species very difficult, if not impossible, to accomplish if the soil was not modified. When local flora appeared exuberant, it was because the plants of the region had, over time, adapted themselves perfectly to the soil. Therefore, the coastal areas had an advantage over the interior, where it was more expensive to send chemically treated manure.[32] The manure brought in and used by the expedition consisted of phosphoric acid and potash.[33]

The climate along the Guinea coast "is as different as are the races which inhabit it."[34] The yearly rainfall on the Gold Coast, in Togo, and in Dahomey averages between one meter twenty centimeters, and two meters. It falls almost entirely between the months of April and October, with the heaviest rainfall in July. On the whole, the climate of West Africa is suitable for growing cotton. Because of the warm temperature and the long dry season, the crop can be gathered without fear of rain. In addition, in Togo, if cotton is planted at the end of the rainy season, there is sufficient moisture for the plants to grow throughout the dry season. On the other hand, if cotton is planted in March, April, or May, the heavy July rains might destroy the first plants. Moreover, the heavy rains are often followed by fogs and cold nights. Therefore, the cotton plant is covered with mildew and the pods become moldy before opening.[35]

During the first six months of their stay at Missahoa, the Tuskegeans grappled with the problems of rain shortages but persevered. They complained about locusts and grasshoppers which appeared in "great clouds" and "jiggers" (chiggers) which bury themselves in your flesh and make a very large sore."[36] There were also complaints about the ants, which Alan Burks claimed were so plentiful that "if strung in a single file they would span the whole of Africa."[37] At the same time, John W. Robinson articulated the spirit of the "Tuskegee idea," in sometimes poetic fashion:

> . . . with the old Tuskegee idea of perseverance, thoroughness and mastery in one's undertakings we have plodded on, and today, away to [sic] the interior of Africa—a little to the North east of the highest point of the Gulf of Guinea nestled near the foot of the Argus Mountains upon the banks of the Argus River we have succeeded in transforming some 75 acres of this teaming [sic] forest and tangled jungle in varied fields of cotton and still continue to fell the forest primeval.[38]

All through 1901 the team worked diligently on the production of a cotton crop, and produced twenty-five bales of cotton.[39] They were cautioned by the Kolonial Komitee not to discuss the experiment with Germans or other Europeans who were now passing through Togo periodically.[40] The Kolonial Komitee did not want to encourage competition in the event that the experiment was a success.

Essentially, the Tuskegeans were made welcome by their African hosts. Calloway saw little distinction on one occasion between Africans and African-Americans or between Alabama and Africa. He stated, "The natives do not differ very much from the uneducated Negroes of the 'black belt' in the South. I believe the Africans have a better disposition. Color is about the same. If I did not know I am in Africa I could easily believe myself in Alabama."[41] Sometimes the local workers were described as "very kind [and they] showed a great deal of native intelligence." At other times they were considered "much like our American Negro, they talk more about pay than work." With the exception of Allan Burks, who had periodic chills and who was described as "our sick man most of the time now" the others seemed to fare reasonably well in the first year—even though all had fevers from time to time.[42] However, by November of 1901 signs of disillusionment began to surface. Shepherd Harris wrote to Booker T. Washington that, "We have harvested only two bales of cotton from the whole crop. The experiment so far has been a complete failure."[43]

James Calloway left Togo on January 6, 1902, for a month's vacation in the United States. Robinson was left in charge of the project and was determined that it should not suffer. In a letter to Booker T. Washington, he apologized for being brief and irregular in his writing but explained that since Calloway's departure he had been "very closely engaged." He continued that most of the month was spent traveling to locate experimental farms, "the other 5 or 6 days I am very busy with paying the laborers, going through with necessary correspondence and preparing reports for the 'Komitee' in Berlin." After a nostalgic reference to an old hymn sung at Tuskegee and before closing, with his determination to prove himself worthy, Robinson again expressed the Tuskegee ideal: "I am happiest when busiest. Hard work and I are friends of long standing. . . ."[44] Calloway's first letter from Togo, in May of 1902, following his return from vacation, which was combined with some efforts to recruit additional farmers for Togo cotton growing, announced the first tragedy to befall the experiment.[45] Two of the four new recruits, Simpson and Drake, were drowned when the rowboat carrying them ashore, upon arrival in Togo, capsized.[46] This was a severe blow to the morale of the Togo party, and Booker T. Washington remarked that "this news is shocking."[47] Nevertheless, there was no suggestion that the program should be abandoned. In the same letter that notified Booker T. Washington of the misfortune, Calloway requested more farmers immediately, at the behest of the Kolonial Komitee, in order to minimize losses. By July 1902, the Kolonial Komitee was appealing directly to Booker T. Washington for help. They wrote, "We are sorry that it has been impossible for you to secure young men as cotton farmers in this season, but we hope that you may be able to send us in [the] beginning of next year."[48] Later in 1902, the Kolonial Komitee lamented the fact that the two replacements missed their boat, the *Bluechar*, and did not sail for Togo as promised. They further complained about losing more money and pleaded with Booker T. Washington to try and recover the money spent for the tickets.[49] The Komitee continued to press Tuskegee for more cotton farmers for Togo, and (indicative of their broader designs) revealed plans for cotton growing in German East Africa.[50] Throughout late 1902 and all of 1903, evidence of what took place in Togo is much more fragmentary and many of the details remain foggy. Certain it is, however, that Shepherd Harris, in August 1902, succumbed to African fever and died. Moreover, sometime in 1903, both Calloway and Burks left the project and returned to the United States. Therefore, John W. Robinson wrote to Booker T. Washington in January 1904 that he was "in charge" of the enterprise and was the only remaining member in Togo of the original group.[51] He had, however, been joined by two replacements from Tuskegee, Horace Griffin and Walter Bryant. Bryant soon proved "unreliable" and "worthless" and was quickly dismissed by the Kolonial Komitee for inefficiency.[52] Griffin, to the delight of some and abhorrence of others, returned to the United States in 1905 and was outspoken and excoriating toward Africa and Africans. He fanned the flames of prevailing stereotypes about Africa, reporting that, "If a stranger goes among them [Africans] fat and well appearing, they will kill and eat him if they can. They devour their enemies captured in battle." Griffin went on with the convoluted line that slavery was a blessing for African-Americans because they "have been redeemed . . . from hell and degradation, and it may be that God has been preparing them to redeem the 'Dark Continent.'"[53]

Robinson kept his nose to the grindstone and worked in earnest to prevent the collapse of the experiment. *The Tuskegee Student* indicated that he was enjoying his work and was determined to prove that good quality cotton could be grown in Togo.[54] In May of 1904, Robinson summarized the work being done in Togo. Included in his discussion was the attempt "to develop a plant that will yield 1,000 lbs. of seed cotton to the acre . . . equal in quality to fully good 'middling'. . . ." He noted his establishment of "A Cotton School and Plant Breeding Station." At this time there were forty-five students, and the stated objective of the school was "to train young men for agricultural purposes." Robinson also emphasized the fact that the project had finally won the confidence of the local people, which, despite the common denominator of Blackness, took some doing due to their apprehensiveness toward strangers.[55] Because Robinson kept so busy with his work, with which he was apparently well satisfied, he subjected himself to a most exacting schedule. He also repeatedly expressed his loneliness and his interest in returning to the United States and Tuskegee.[56] In March 1906, John W. Robinson, the only remaining Tuskegean in Togo returned to the United States to participate in the twenty-fifth anniversary celebration of Tuskegee Institute. His return, that of unlike Burks and Calloway, was not permanent, and he went back to Togo later in 1906 with renewed vigor to make the project more successful than he already considered it.

The Tuskegee Normal and Industrial Institute was founded in the spring of 1881.[57] The principals in its founding were Blacks, the government of Alabama, southern Whites and northern philanthropists. Its first principal, the choice of General Samuel Chapman Armstrong—a former Union General,

Superintendent of the Freedman's Bureau, and Founder of Hampton Institute (1868)—was Booker Taliferro Washington, Armstrong's prize pupil at Hampton. In April of 1906, when Tuskegee celebrated its twenty-fifth anniversary, and the ceremonies attracted an august gathering indeed: Charles Eliot (president of Harvard), Andrew Carnegie, Lyman Abbott, and J.G. Phelps-Stokes among others. Making the 4,000-mile trek from West Africa to join the festivities was John Robinson, a member of Tuskegee's sixteenth graduating class and a celebrity in his own right. Robinson was given a prominent place on the four-day program and organized an African exhibit reflecting the customs, practices, and culture of several West African peoples.

Robinson's address to the gathering, delivered on Thursday, April 5, 1905, was a thorough synoptic history of the Togo expedition.[58] He first summarized the involvement of the Kolonial Wirtschafliches Komitee and the German government in the whole scheme. Second, Robinson surveyed the details of departure and arrival in Togo. He then outlined the participation of Calloway, Burks, Harris, Simpson, Drake, Griffin, and Bryant in addition his own role. He also made an effort to discuss what he considered the achievements of their work. The cotton produced increased from 25 bales in 1901 to 122 bales in 1903. The Kolonial Komitee was so pleased with Robinson's work that they increased his salary 25 percent by 1903 and gave him a 5 percent commission on all the cotton sent to Germany in 1903. His share in dollars and cents amounted to about $200.[59] In 1906, Robinson was reporting earnings of $2,000 from the Germans.[60]

When John Robinson returned to Togo in the middle of April, 1906, he was accompanied by his new bride, the former Miss Danella Foote, like him an 1897 graduate of Tuskegee and later a teacher there. Upon arrival, Robinson found things "topsy-turvy," with very little work having been done during his absence. Robinson worked hard to get things back into shape, and by July he had 125 acres of cotton planted. The following September a good crop was ready and being harvested. To say the least, Robinson had his hands full attempting to supervise the work of the plantation, run the school he earlier established (which now had one hundred students), and teach individual classes in modern methods of agriculture. He entertained visitors and took care of all the administrative details for everything. Despite his complaints, he continued to exude euphoria and spoke about "evidences of progress."[61] However, by 1908, Robinson's letters reflected fatigue and impatience. His health began to fade under the pressure of his burdensome schedule; he lost his enthusiasm and decided to remain only two more years.[62] It was probably with John Robinson's anticipated return in mind that Mrs. Robinson went back to the United States before her husband.

In September 1909, Booker T. Washington received a letter from the Kolonial Komitee, which stated, "To our great sorrow we are compelled to convey to you today the sad news that Mr. John Robinson has fallen victim to an accident in Togo. On the twenty-third of July we received the following telegram from the Governor of Togo: 'Robinson apparently drowned in the Mono' [River]."[63] Before notifying Booker T. Washington of Robinson's [accidental] death, the Kolonial Komitee had awaited "definite news by letter." This partially explains the time lapse between the reported date of Robinson's death and the date Booker T. Washington was notified—some fifty-two days difference. Robinson, the Komitee reported, was out with some of his African companions when his canoe overturned, and he was never seen again. His companions managed to get to land and report the incident. In their letter the Kolonial Komitee lauded Robinson's work and since Mrs. Robinson had not yet been informed of her husband's death, they prevailed upon Booker T. Washington to perform that unpleasant task. The Komitee promised to "look after the remains of Robinson and send along further information as it became available. The cotton experiment immediately ceased operation and Robinson's death touched off a three-year struggle for his wife to recover his back wages and her insurance claims.

Booker T. Washington sent Mrs. Danella Robinson, now residing in Macon, Mississippi, a telegram with the sad new of her husband's death.[64] A grief-stricken Danella Robinson immediately appealed to Booker T. Washington for assistance in obtaining from the Komitee her husband's clothes and belongings, any back pay he had coming, and in recovering the claims on a $2,500 (10,0000 dm), paid-up, life insurance policy her husband carried with the Deutscher Anker Co, Berlin.[65] In making the latter two requests, Mrs. Robinson precipitated an anguished epilogue to this episode, which would last until 1912. There was a stipulation in the insurance policy that in order to recover the claims the holder must have a statement from the German government that the insured was in fact dead.

Booker T. Washington immediately went to work, using all of his influence, to help Mrs. Robinson with her claim on her husband's back wages and with the insurance. Unfortunately, John Robinson's body, he was informed by the Komitee, sank so fast it could not be found.[66] Later the Komitee informed Booker T. Washington that they were waiting for the Imperial Government officer in Togo to send the death certificate. As soon as it arrived it would be forwarded to the insurance company and Mrs. Robinson could be paid. They also suggested that it would cost more to send John Robinson's belongings to the United States than they were worth. The Komitee proposed that Robinson's personal effects be sold, which was customary in cases like this.[67] Meanwhile, through Booker T. Washington, the Kolonial Komitee and the insurance company had requested several items from Danella Robinson in order to settle the claims. She sent them the insurance policy, a letter from the probate judge in Bennettsville, South Carolina (certifying John Robinson's date of birth), and a "Power of Attorney properly signed."[68]

The months passed by and, in spite of Booker T. Washington's involvement, little progress was made on the settlement of Mrs. Robinson's claim. It appeared that the insurance company was willing to pay off but was waiting for the death certificate confirming that John Robinson was dead. The German Governor in Togo could not, in turn, release the death certificate until the dead body was located—which it could not be. The situation seemed to be at an impasse. Suggestions of complicity between the officers of the German government in Togo and the insurance company to deprive Mrs. Robinson of her legitimate claims are given support by the next development.

The Kolonial Komitee wrote to Booker T. Washington, the middleman, in September 1910, indicating that there were new complications in the John Robinson matter. It seems that the entire issue was now placed in the hands of a lawfully appointed trustee, "whose duty it would be to distribute the money amongst the heirs." More important-and the *coup de grace*, the Komitee continued,

> As far as we are informed there are some children of the
> late Mr. Robinson living in Togo, who would also have a
> claim upon part of the insurance money. Such claims, of
> course, would have to be carefully examined by the
> trustee and you may rest assured that everything possible
> will be done by this officer to study the interest of the
> widow.[69]

In other words, John Robinson—they were claiming—had fathered some children in Togo without the knowledge of his wife in the United States.

The new difficulties set the tone for the contents of a great deal of correspondence exchanged between the Kolonial Wirtschafliches Komitee, Booker T. Washington (sometimes now Emmett Scott who began writing for Washington), and Mrs. Danella Robinson, throughout 1911 and into 1912.[70] Time, distance (Togo, Germany, United States), and communications limitations were not in Mrs. Robinson's favor (she lived in rural Mississippi), while they worked to the advantage of the Germans. The more time passed, the more remote it seemed that her claims would ever be satisfied. Desperate, she asked Booker T. Washington whether it would be wise to institute a law suit against the insurance company, and whether the German lawyer she retained, at Washington's suggestion, could be trusted. She was fearful of the lawyer's complicity in what she felt was already a conspiracy to deprive her of what was hers, and she would have to pay him a fee.[71] In what may have been his last letter concerning this affair, Booker T. Washington recommended that she sue. Washington encouraged her to pay the $160 (800 dm) lawyer's fee, and felt that Fuchs (the lawyer) had shown good faith by stating his fee beforehand, and believed that what the lawyer was proposing seemed bona fide. He also cautioned, "the longer you wait the harder it becomes to collect the money. This, however, is only my opinion in the matter. In the last analysis you must be guided by your own judgment."[72] It is unclear whether or Mrs. Robinson ever took this piece of advice from Booker T. Washington. It is also unclear exactly how long she continued to hope that her claim would be satisfied. Nevertheless, it seems to be fairly certain that she was beaten down by attrition and eventually gave up, closing the book on this twelve-year Tuskegee–Togo *sui generis* encounter.

One of the most profound aspects of this Tuskegee-in-Togo episode was its social impact. For example before the Tuskegeans went to Missahoa, the local people seldom used wagons for transportation. Upon arrival in Togo, Calloway and the others attempted to induce the Africans to pull their wagons. The local inhabitants refused, partly because of their ignorance of the modern methods of transporting goods and partly because of their reluctance to deviate from customary labor practices. Consequently, the most important items were loaded on the heads of the Africans, as was the custom, and carried inland. By 1906, however, John W. Robinson exclaimed, "the local people refused to freight by head."[73] With the coming of these African-American cotton growers to the Missahoa region of Togo, the time-honored practice of transporting heavy items on the head was ended.

The opening of public highways, making possible better methods of transportation in Togo, was another result of the experiment in cotton growing. When the effort began five years earlier, "there was not a good public road in the colony. . . . Today [1906] there are nearly 1,000 miles of good public road and nearly the entire transportation is carried on by means of vehicles . . ."[74]

A final important social development had to do with the dress of the local people which Robinson called a "civilizing influence." He summed up its affect in this way:

> In a single village where our work is centered, the entire population was practically naked two years ago. Today fifty per cent of them are fairly well clothed and entirely in cotton goods.[75]

NOTES

1. Anthony G. Hopkins, *An Economic History of West Africa* (New York, 1937), 137–138, 219.

2. See Kwamina B. Dickson, *A Historical Geography of Ghana* (Cambridge, Massachusetts, 1969), 120–132.

3. An excellent study of British involvement with cotton growing in West Africa has been written by John Robert Hose entitled, "Britain and the Development of West African Cotton 1845–1960," Ph.D. thesis, Columbia University, 1970. For these early British efforts to grow cotton in West Africa, see the introduction, pages 5–21.

4. *Ibid.*, 202.

5. *Ibid.*, 314.

6. Most of the preceding information comes from Hose's dissertation especially chapters five and six: "The Work of the British Cotton Growing Association—1900–1914" and "Nigeria and the Empire Cotton Growing Association—1914–1960."

7. *Colored American Magazine* (October, 1909), 261; Mary E. Townsend, *The Rise and Fall of Germany's Colonial Empire* (New York, 1930), 255–260.

8. Baron Herman to Booker T. Washington (BTW) November 3, 1900. The date of this letter should be September 3, 1900 as indicated by the text, BTW Papers (177). I will continue the practice begun by Louis Harlan, "Booker T. Washington and the White Man's Burden," *American Historical Review* (January, 1966), 441–467, reprinted in Okon E. Uya (ed.), *Black Brotherhood: Afro-Americans and Africa* (New York, 1971), 130–153, and continued by St. Clair Drake, "Negro Americans and the African Interest," in John P. Davis (ed.), *The American Negro Reference Book* (Englewood Cliffs, New Jersey, 1969), 662–705, of noting container numbers in the Booker T. Washington Papers in parentheses, even though it poses some problems. The Booker T. Washington Papers are quite a large collection, over 1,000 containers, and oftentimes unlabeled, except by letter—e.g., in this case "H." Each *folder* might have twenty-five, fifty, or more pieces of correspondence. Therefore, someone searching for this particular Baron Herman letter would have to conduct a painstaking search of all of the folders in container (177), and this will be the case with all other correspondence cited. An alternative to this would be to label the folders, e.g. H-1, H-2, etc. However, that has not been done as yet. Also, that might make citing the correspondence a little cumbersome, e.g. (177, H-1).

In addition to that problem, many careless individuals have used the Booker T. Washington Papers, much of the correspondence is misfiled, and the Papers are in an early stage of chaos. Important correspondence is torn, written on, and often filed under the writers first name rather than the last, or filed under the correct last name but in the wrong year. In any case, although Louis Harlan has edited the Booker T. Washington Papers (Urbana, Illinois, 1972–1989), these distressing problems for the researcher are not likely to be resolved with this valuable collection of manuscripts until the entire collection is microfilmed, which necessarily requires systematic cataloging and indexing. According to one archivist at the Library of Congress, this is not likely in the near future. The standard work on Booker T. Washington is Louis Harlan's two volume biography, *Booker T. Washington: The Making of a Black Leader 1856–1901* (New York, 1972) and *Booker T. Washington: The Wizard of Tuskegee 1901–1915* (New York, 1983), where coverage of the Togo episode can be found, 267–269.

9. The foregoing includes a summary of the contents of the lengthy letter (six typewritten pages) from Baron Herman to Booker T. Washington, November, Sept. 3, 1900 (177).

10. BTW to Baron Herman, September 20, 1900 (282a). This letter can be found in *Principal's Office Correspondence 1897–1903* (letterbook), 486–489. There was also reference to a September 18, 1900 letter, which could not be located.

11. *Ibid.*

12. *Ibid.*

13. Cablegram, Kolonial Komitee (KWK) to BTW, October 6, 1900 (177).

14. KWK to BTW, October 11, 1900 (177); also, KWK to BTW, December 11, 1900 (177). On the announcement of the agreement between Tuskegee and the German firm to send a team to Togo, see the following newspapers; Nashville *American* (October 21, 1900), Providence *Bulletin* (October 24, 1900), Cleveland *World* (October 23, 1900), New York *Herald* (October 20, 1900), New York *World* (October 28, 1900), New York *Press* (November 4, 1900), all in BTW Papers (1032) 466–469. *Colored American Magazine* (November, 1900), 49–50, reported the details of the agreement between Tuskegee and the Kolonial Komitee.

15. Harlan, "Booker T. Washington . . ." in Uya (ed.), *Black Brotherhood*, 131.

16. This opposition necessarily includes an exodus to Africa, since the 1890s was the zenith of African-American interest in emigration to Africa.

17. Booker T. Washington, "The Storm Before the Calm," *Colored American Magazine* (September, 1900), 206; also, *Colored American Magazine* (June, 1906), 373, for more on Washington's African views.

18. Booker T. Washington, "The African at Home," *Colored American Magazine* (October, 1909), 261–273.

19. Regarding this International Council, Washington stated, "One of the objectives of the International Council would be the formation of a permanent society, which should stand, in its relations to the civilized world, as a sort of guardian of the native peoples of Africa, a friendly power, an influence with the public and in the councils where so often, without their presence, or knowledge, the destinies of the African

peoples and of their territories are discussed and decided." *The Tuskegee Student* (November 27, 1909), 1, 4. Ideologically, although perhaps a bit paternalistic, this statement and others like it certainly suggests that Booker T. Washington entertained some aspects of the Pan-African idea.

20. Washington's involvement here essentially included his being sought by colonial authorities for advice on racial matters in southern Africa. He was invited to visit southern Africa and, after consultation with Theodore Roosevelt and others, he declined, but held out the prospect that he might consider a visit sometime in the future. He was also frequently consulted on educational policy for South Africans and several South African students attended Tuskegee Institute. His advice was usually fashioned after his ideology of accommodation regarding Blacks in the United States. See Harlan, "Booker T. Washington . . ." in Uya (ed.), *Black Brotherhood*, 136–137. On South African students at Tuskegee and other colleges and universities in the United States, see the Ph.D. dissertation by Richard Ralston, "A Second Middle Passage: African Student Sojourns in the United States During the Colonial Period and Their Influence Upon the Character of African Leadership," UCLA, 1972, especially chapters 1, 4 and 6.

21. Booker T. Washington became actively involved with the situation in the Congo Free State when the atrocities of King Leopold and the Belgians there came to the attention of the world. Essentially, he attempted, through his American contacts, to bring pressure on the Belgians for reforms in the Congo. Washington lectured and wrote about outrages in the Congo. However, it is suggested and confirmed that some of Washington's published writings were actually written by Dr. Robert E. Park of the Congo Reform Association. There is also evidence that Park, from time to time, was on the Tuskegee payroll. A good deal of the correspondence between Booker T. Washington and Robert E. Park concerning the Congo can be found in BTW Papers (30), (33). See also Booker T. Washington, "Cruelty in the Congo Country," *Outlook* (October 8, 1904), 375–377, which was probably written by Park. There is a Ph.D. dissertation at Howard University (1975, history) by Sylvia Jacobs, "Black Americans and European Imperialism in Africa, 1870–1920." A section of that dissertation, "Black American Response to the Congo Controversy, 1904–1908," was read at Howard University's conference on Afro-Americans and Africans, Historical and Political Linkages (July, 1974, Washington, D.C.) That dissertation has been revised and published as *The African Nexus: Black American Perspectives*

on the European Partitioning of Africa, 1880–1920 (Westport, Connecticut, 1981). See the same author's *Black Americans and the Missionary Movement in Africa* (Westport, Connecticut, 1982). Finally, on the Congo there is an enlightening discussion of George Washington Williams' involvement in the Congo in John Hope Franklin, "George Washington Williams and Africa," in Lorraine Williams (ed.), *Africa and the Afro-American Experience* (Washington, D.C., 1973), Howard University, History Department, 13–29.

22. The Liberian crisis between 1908 and 1914 absorbed more of Booker T. Washington's time, effort, and energy than any of his other Africa interests. For the details on the nature and extent of the crisis, see Basil Mathews, *Booker T. Washington: Educator and Interracial Interpreter* (Cambridge, Massachusetts, 1948), chapter 16; Benjamin Brawley, *A Social History of the American Negro* (New York, 1921), 172–212; and J.A. Mower, "The Republic of Liberia," *Journal of Negro History* (July, 1947), 265–306. See also chapter 6 in this book.

23. In the Anglo-Egyptian Sudan, Booker T. Washington and Tuskegee were involved in a fashion similar to that in Togo. In this case, five Tuskegeans, Cain W. Triplett, John P. Powell, Poindexter Smith, Orie R. Burns, and J.B. Twitty, from 1904–1907, went to the Sudan to develop an experimental cotton plantation. The individual behind the Sudan project was a U.S. businessman named Leigh Hunt, and his motives were purely business. The experiment collapsed after Hunt's withdrawal and after tragedies occured that were similar to those of the Togo venture. The Sudan episode would make another interesting case study of African-Americans and cotton growing in Africa. Pertinent correspondence for the Sudan, between Washington and Leigh Hunt can be found in BTW Papers (29). The correspondence between Washington and the Tuskegee graduates involved in the Sudan and vice-versa can be located in BTW Papers (294) and (357). See also Arthur Gaitskell, *Gezira: A Story of Development in the Sudan* (London, 1959), 51–52, 75–76; J.R. Duncan, *The Sudan: A Record of Achievement* (London, 1952), 122–124; Louis Harlan, "Booker T. Washington . . ." in Uya (ed.) *Black Brotherhood*, 135–136.

24. BTW to E.D. Whitehead, John W. Robinson, and Shepherd Harris, September 4, 1900 (282a), 460.

25. There is a photograph of the Togo party in *The Tuskegee Student* (March 28, 1901), 1, and the same photograph is reprinted in Louis Harlan (ed.), *Booker T. Washington Papers: Autobiographical Writings*

(Urbana, Illinois, 1970) Illustration #46. The "Agreement" between William Drake and the Kolonial Komitee, dated April 9, 1902 is an example of the type of contract most Tuskegeans who went to Togo had. Drake apparently joined the group two years after the pioneer group left in 1900. BTW Papers (232).

26. Louis Harlan claims that "Nine Tuskegeans worked in Togo for various periods between 1909 and 1909." "Booker T. Washington. . . ," in Uya (ed.) *Black Brotherhood*, 133. Booker T. Washington suggests that there was a total of seven Tuskegeans who worked in Togo:

> Nearly two years ago three of our graduates went to Africa [not including Calloway] under the auspices of the German Government to teach the raising of cotton to the natives of the German colony of Togo. The German officials were so pleased with the work of these men that this year four more have been added to the colony.

The Twenty-First Annual Report of the Principal and Treasurer of the Tuskegee Normal and Industrial Institute, Alabama (for the year ending May 31, 1902), 5–6, Hollis-Burk Frissell Library, Manuscripts Division, Tuskegee Institute, Tuskegee, Alabama; BTW to Alexander McKenzie, April 24, 1903 (22).

Thus far, I have only been able to unearth detailed information (names, contracts, correspondence, etc.) on eight of these individuals, Calloway, Robinson, Harris, Burks, Drake, Simpson, Bryant and Griffin. It is entirely possible that Professor Harlan was including Mrs. Danella Robinson in his total of nine.

27. Calloway to BTW, February 3, 1901 (218), rprt. *The Tuskegee Student* (March 23, 1901), 1; Harris to BTW, rprt. *The Tuskegee Student* (July 13, 1901), 3. For a sample of the press coverage see New York *American* (November 3, 1900), New York *Herald* (November 4, 1900), Chicago Times *Herald* (November 4, 1900); Portland (Oregon) *Oregonian* (November 8, 1900) and Scranton *Truth* (November 8, 1900), all in BTW Papers, (1032).

28. John Robinson to BTW, May 26, 1901 (218).

29. Shepherd Harris to BTW, May 15, 1901, rprt. *The Tuskegee Student* (July 13, 1901), 3; also (August 24, 1901), 1; John Robinson to BTW, May 26, 1901 (218).

30. One hundred pfennigs are equal to one Deutschemark (dm), which in 1900 was about the equivalent of twenty-five cents.

31. C.T. Hagberg Wright, "German Methods of Development in Africa," *Journal of the African Society* (October, 1901), 34–35; Emile Baillaud "Cultivation of Cotton in Western Africa," *Journal of the African Society* (January, 1903), 132–148.

32. Baillaud, "Cultivation of Cotton. . . ," 136–137.

33. *Ibid.*, 134.

34. *Ibid.*, 135.

35. *Ibid.*, 136.

36. James Calloway to unidentified source, no date, BTW Papers (218).

37. Alan Burks to BTW, February 15, 1902 (218).

38. John Robinson to BTW, May 26, 1901 (218).

39. *The Tuskegee Student* (April 28, 1906), 25–26.

40. James Calloway to BTW, June 2, 1901 (218); see also, "Mr. Calloway Writes of His African Trip," *The Tuskegee Student* (November 23, 1901), 1, for an instructive account of the group's experiences in the African hinterland. See also James Nathan Calloway, "Tuskegee Cotton Planters in Africa," *Outlook* (March 29, 1903), 772–776, and the interview with Calloway in *Indianapolis Freeman* (March 15, 1902), 1, as well as his "African Sketches," *Southern Workman* (November, 1902), 618–621.

41. *The Tuskegee Student* (August 24, 1901), 1.

42. All of the above quotes come from James Calloway's letter to an unidentified source, BTW Papers (218), reprinted in *The Tuskegee Student* (April 20, 1901), 2–3. Louis Harlan states that the author is unidentified and that the date of this letter is January 13, 1901: "Booker T. Washington. . . ," in Uya (ed.), *Black Brotherhood*, 133, note 10. Because the letter was reprinted in *The Tuskegee Student*, cited above (note 27), the author can definitely be identified as Calloway. However, I found no date for the letter. For complaints about climate and references to Burks's sickness, see also James Calloway to BTW, April 20, 1901 (218).

43. Shepherd Harris to BTW, November 3, 1901 (218). The year on this letter is very unclear. As best I can ascertain it appears to be 1901.

44. John Robinson to BTW, April 20, 1902 (218).

45. *The Tuskegee Student* (April 20, 1901), 2; KWK to BTW, May 1, 1902 (232). The British were also apparently engaged in a similar effort to recruit Black American cotton farmers from the southern United States for West Africa at this time, since the following advertisement appeared in *The Tuskegee Student* (November 8, 1902), 3; (December 20, 1902), 3; (January 1903), 3; (January 17, 1903), 3:

WANTED

Wanted—Negro cotton field hands to grow cotton in West Africa. Comfortable homes and just treatment guaranteed. Deserving applicants please write to: New Cotton Fields, Limited, 42 Devonshire Chambers, Bishopsgate Street London, England.

See also "Cotton Raising in German Africa," *The Evening Star*, BTW papers (299) for references to British and Belgian cotton-growing efforts in Africa.

46. James Calloway to BTW, May 8, 1902 (218).

47. *Ibid.*

48. KWK to BTW, July 15, 1902 (232).

49. KWK to BTW, October 21, 1902 (232).

50. *Ibid.*

51. John Robinson to BTW, January 25, 1904 (294).

52. Unidentifiable officer of the KWK (Dr. Grimer?) to John Robinson, April 8, 1904 (294); BTW to John Robinson, October 21, 1904 (294).

53. "Member of Togo Team Returns to U.S," Albany *Knickerbocker* (April 29, 1905), and same type of story in Philadelphia *Public Ledger* (April 29, 1905), both in BTW Papers (1041), 77.

54. *The Tuskegee Student* (March 12, 1904), 2.

55. John Robinson to BTW, rprt. *Southern Letter* (August, 1904) 3; also, *The Tuskegee Student* (April 8, 1905), 3.

56. John Robinson to BTW, January 25, 1904 (294); BTW to John Robinson, October 21, 1904 (294); KWK to John Robinson, April 8, 1904 (294); *Tuskegee Student* (March 12, 1904), 2.

57. For the history of Tuskegee Institute, now Tuskegee University, see L. Albert Scipio, *Tuskegee: The Pre-War Days* (Silver Spring, Maryland, 1987); and Anson Phelps-Stokes, *Tuskegee Institute: The First*

Fifty Years (Tuskegee, Alabama, 1931). Also useful is Booker T. Washington's classic, *Up From Slavery.*

58. Robinson's speech was reprinted in a special edition of *The Tuskegee Student*, commemorating the twenty-fifth anniversary celebration, (April 28, 1906), 25; rprt. *Colored American Magazine* (May, 1906), 335–339.

59. *Ibid.*

60. *Colored American Magazine* (May, 1906) 355.

61. Most of the preceding is from a September 1906 letter from John and Danella Robinson to an unidentified source, rprt. *The Tuskegee Student* (March 30, 1907), 1.

62. John Robinson to BTW, October 21, 1908 (380). Ironically in 1908, some months before Robinson had resolved to leave German West Africa, signaling the end of this phase of the experiment, a German named Emil Leir (?) wrote to Booker T. Washington, January 14, 1908 (375), requesting his aid in getting Black Americans to assist Germany in the development of their African colonies. The fascinating proposal put forth by this German suggested that since American Blacks were the victims of intense prejudice in the United States, they should emigrate to Germany (where they would not find such discrimination), intermarry, and then cooperate in German colonial politics. They should become German citizens and then such a population (including the offspring of intermarriages) "would be the best medium to spread german [*sic*] manners in the African colonies." African-Americans would also, it was suggested, be welcomed in every level of German society depending on background, education, affluence, etc. Finally, Leir requested a Prospectus from Tuskegee and the names and addresses of some influential Blacks and some important Black newspapers to which he could write regarding his proposal. There is no indication that Booker T. Washington answered this letter.

63. KWK to BTW, September 14, 1909 (53).

64. BTW to Danella Robinson, September 30, 1909 (183).

65. Danella Robinson to BTW, October 1, 1909 (53). I feel some compulsion to note here that Mrs. Robinson was impressively articulate in addition to being very astute. Her many letters to Booker T. Washington regarding her husband's death and the insurance claims are well written, insightful, and a delight for the researcher. However,

that did not help her with her claims, and perhaps it even prolonged her agony.

66. BTW to KWK, October 30, 1909; KWK to BTW, undated (probably sometime in November) (53); KWK to BTW, October 20, 1909 (53).

67. KWK to BTW, November 26, 1909; KWK to BTW, December 2, 1909 (53).

68. Danella Robinson to BTW, April 14, 1910 (53).

69. KWK to BTW, September 9, 1910 (53).

70. All of this correspondence can be found in BTW Papers (53), Folder #1 and ranges from 1909–1912.

71. Danella Robinson to BTW, March 25, 1912 (62).

72. BTW to Danella Robinson, April 6, 1912 (62).

73. John W. Robinson's speech at the twenty-fifth anniversary celebration of Tuskegee Institute was printed in *The Tuskegee Student* (April 28, 1906), 25.

74. *Ibid.*

75. *Ibid.*

CHAPTER VIII

Pan-African Conferences

The three most important conferences between 1900 and 1919 involving individuals and organizations throughout the Black world were held in London in 1900, at Tuskegee Institute in 1912, and in Paris in 1919. The role played by African-Americans was significant at each gathering, although, less important in London than at Tuskegee or in Paris. Each conference also made a strong contribution to the evolution of the Pan-African idea among African-Americans who placed Africa at or near the top of their ideological agenda.

The Pan-African Conference (1900)

Formal planning for the 1900 Pan-African Conference actually began with the formation of the African Association in 1897, even though the idea for a convocation of the world's Black people generated some interest before this time.[1] The organizer of the conference was Henry Sylvester Williams,[2] a native of Trinidad studying law in England.[3] One immediate concern of the conference was the situation of Africans in South Africa. At the same time an expanded objective as indicated in the report of the Pan-African Congress, articulated a concern for the treatment, uplift, and future of all people claiming African descent in the world—Africa, North America, South America, and the "Islands of the Sea." "Truly a galaxy of remarkable men" participated in a series of preparatory meetings in June of 1899. Among them were James T. Holly, Episcopal bishop of Haiti and energetic supporter of emigration for Blacks from the United

States to Haiti; Rev. James (Holy) Johnson, valiant African nationalist and Pan-African churchman from West Africa; Bishop Henry McNeal Turner, courageous champion of Black emigration to Liberia in the 1890s; Dr. Majola Agbebi, founder of one of the earliest independent African churches in West Africa; plus Booker T. Washington, the "Sage of Tuskegee." Surprisingly, none of these race stalwarts was able to attend the actual conference in 1900[4] but they all "rendered valuable service" and some agreed beforehand to become local representatives of the Pan-African Association, born at the conference.

There are several persuasive explanations for the selection of London as the site of this historic call to gather. London was the umbilicus of the giant British Empire, "the empire on which the sun never set." Moreover, the curious combination of the British brand of "civilization and colonialism," although strange bedfellows, plagued many Africans and descendants of Africans as well as other people in the world. London was also the residence of the principal convener of the conference, Henry Sylvester Williams. Finally, the year 1900, and perhaps even the dates July 23–25, was conveniently chosen to coincide with the Universal Paris Exposition and the World Christian Endeavor Convention in London, because this would make it possible for considerably more delegates to attend than would ordinarily do so.

It was at this London Pan-African Conference of 1900 that the first recorded reference to Pan-Africanism may have been made public, in "a letter of November 11, 1899 written by Williams . . . to J.M. Bourne, a member of the African Association. . ."[5] Bourne, who was a White South African, registered his protest in characteristic fashion over the convening of the conference, arguing that it was contrary to the aims of the African Association. It was also at this 1900 conference that W.E.B. DuBois, as chairman of the Committee on Address to the Nations of the World, uttered his prophetic dictum, celebrated by scholars and intellectuals ever since and which later appeared in the *Souls of Black Folk* (1903):

> The problem of the twentieth century is the problem of the color line, the question of how far differences of race, which show themselves chiefly in the color of the skin and the texture of the hair, are going to be made, hereafter, the basis of denying to over half the world the right of sharing to their utmost ability the opportunities and privileges of modern civilization.[6]

The keynote speaker for the conference was Dr. Mandell Creighton, Bishop of London, and representatives came from Africa, the United States, and the West Indies. The conference per se opened with Bishop Alexander Walters, from the United States, presiding and delivering the opening remarks, because the keynoter was late. For the most part, the three-day meeting centered on the formal presentation of ideological and position papers treating the Pan-African theme. All of these papers in one way or another addressed the struggle for universal political, social, economic and human rights for Black people. The demand for justice and dignity repeatedly echoed through the stately chambers of Westminster Town Hall. Heated charges of imperialism and colonialism were directed at the British and other European governments, who were engaged in the ruthless exploitation of members of the African family, on the African continent and around the world. Appeals for equity and pleas for a resurrection of humanism were articulated by the most gifted of the conferees. The Rev. Henry Smith of London suggested that Blacks should avoid permitting "any differences in the various shades of color in black or quadroon or octoroon, they should all work together."[7] The prevailing paternalist thinking of the times found a spokesperson in Dr. Creighton, the guest speaker, who reminded the gathering that Great Britain had assumed responsibility for people of color throughout the world and they would dispense self-government to them and others as the British felt they were ready for it.

When DuBois spoke, his diatribe outlined the view that obstacles to Black opportunity, "were not simply an injustice and a drawback to the Blacks it hindered human evolution."[8]

Out of this historic first Pan-African conference was born the Pan-African Association, to be headquartered in London but with branches elsewhere in the world. Alexander Walters was selected as President, Rev. Henry (Box) Brown, the ex-slave from the United States who escaped from southern slavery by sending himself north in a box,[9] was named Vice President; Dr. R.J. Colenso became the General Treasurer, Benito Sylvain was elected General Delegate for Africa; and Henry Sylvester Williams, Esq. was announced as the General Secretary.[10] In addition to these officers, an executive committee was formed and a host of officers for overseas branches were selected. W.E.B. DuBois, who has erroneously been described as the "Secretary of the first Pan-African conference" by several writers and historians[11] was in fact the Vice President of the Association for the United States of America. Indeed, it has been suggested that because DuBois played such a minor role at the 1900 conference, "he was unimpressed with it."[12] Allegedly DuBois, by his failure to acknowledge this conference until an article appeared in the *Chicago Defender* in 1945, created the impression that he was the originator of the Pan-African idea.[13]

At the 1900 conference, it was also decided that general meetings would be held every other year. For 1902 and 1904, meetings were scheduled for the United States and Haiti, respectively. It was also decided to offer honorary membership in the Pan-African Association to the leaders of the world's three sovereign Black states—Abyssinia (Ethiopia), Liberia, and Haiti. The conference further agreed to send the "Address to the Nations of the World" to every country that had people of African descent as residents. A memorial was sent by the conference to Queen Victoria protesting the treatment of Africans in Southern Africa. Through her representative, Joseph Chamberlain, Secretary of State for the Colonies, Queen Victoria replied in predictable fashion: "Her Majesty's government will not overlook the interest or welfare of the native races."[14] Of course, the business of oppression and exploitation went on uninterrupted and as usual.

Henry Sylvester Williams, in his capacity as General Secretary of the Pan-African Association, following up the mandate of the 1900 conference, traveled to Jamaica, Trinidad, and the United States between 1900 and 1902. His purpose was to promote the organization and to stimulate interest in the forthcoming conferences scheduled for the United States and Haiti. Even more, Williams articulated the sentiments during this first decade of the twentieth century, which were later to be repeated by several Pan-African spokespersons (Garvey, Kwame Nkrumah, Malcolm X), that only Blacks could truly represent the interests and sentiments of other Blacks. He expected that the journal he published, *The Pan-African*, would reinforce the seed of Pan-Africanism. However, few issues were published and like countless other periodicals and journals of its ilk, *The Pan-African* was indeed fugacious. While in the United States Williams attended the annual meeting of the Afro-American Council. He never met with DuBois but did confer with Bishop Alexander Walters and there was little indication that the work of the Pan-African Association was being seriously pursued by others. The organizational activity of these Black Americans concentrated on the work of the Afro-American Council, which was founded in 1898 as the successor to the defunct National Afro-American League, originally founded in 1890. Additional organizational activity in the United States at this time focused on the American Negro Academy, founded by the sagacious Rev. Alexander Crummell in 1897. The Academy itself, although specifically concerned with the elitist notions of developing what Crummell and others considered cultured men to guide the Black masses to higher levels of civilization, was, like the Afro-American Council and other Black organizations of the time, primarily interested in justice and equality for Black citizens of the United States. Their concern for Blacks beyond the national boundaries seldom got past the discussion stage.

It has been claimed that following the London Conference, "Pan-Africanism was dead for a decade"—that is, until the Paris Congress called by DuBois in 1919.[15] This view, however, does not appear to be totally supported by events of the period. Certain it is that there was interest in Africa, which perhaps cannot be strictly defined as Pan-Africanism but which did sustain interest in Africa and Africa's affairs, and kept the germ of Pan-Africanism alive. Within the ranks of the progressive Niagara Movement (1905),[16] for one example, in which DuBois played a major role, a Pan-African League Department was established. This was evidently a part of the effort to create a branch of the Pan-African Association in the United States.[17] This branch disappeared when the Niagara Movement was absorbed by the formation of the NAACP.

Through Walters and DuBois especially, African-Americans were not only involved in the London conference (1900) but they played key roles. In any event, Walters's Africa interest seems to have peaked with the London conference or shortly thereafter. DuBois, with the publication of his "The African Roots of War" and *The Negro*, by 1915 was engrossed in the effort by Black American intellectuals to ignite a cultural-psychological renaissance for the glory of Africa's past and people. Four years later it was DuBois again, as catalytic agent for Pan-Africanism, who—along with the initiative taken by Blaise Diagne—made the 1919 Congress possible. DuBois went on to provide the greatest degree of individual continuity for Pan-Africanism, his involvement spanning some sixty years.

The International Conference on the Negro (1912)

Part of the contents in the official announcement, as outlined by Booker T. Washington, for the International Conference on the Negro, originally scheduled for January 1912 but actually held April 17–19, 1912, at Tuskegee Institute,[18] was the following:

For some years past I have had in mind to invite here from different parts of the world—from Europe, Africa, the West Indies and North and South America—persons who are actively interested, or directly engaged as missionaries, or otherwise, in the work that is going on in Africa and elsewhere for the education and upbuilding of the Negro peoples.[19]

Washington went on that the purpose of this gathering was to make available to those engaged in providing any kind of service to the Black world—but especially Africa—helpful information on Blacks in the United States, the Caribbean region, and South America. The meeting would also provide the climate for a general interchange of ideas regarding the systematizing of organizational work in educating Africans and in training teachers for that work. Those in attendance were expected to get a close look at the methods employed at Tuskegee in order to consider adoption of the Tuskegee model for their respective areas.

The planners of the conference hoped that governments interested in Africa and the West Indies would attend or send representatives. A special invitation went out to missionaries because of their known interest in Africa. In this sense the conference was reminiscent of the Atlanta Congress on Africa (1895) sponsored by the Stewart Foundation. Several of the same individuals who delivered papers on Africa in Atlanta were in attendance and presented papers at Tuskegee. The conference was clearly dominated by the missionary theme and homiletic principles, and abstained from confronting political or ideological issues. The monotonous repetition of "spread the gospel" and "save the heathen" was continued here.

Despite the fact that the meeting was called the International Conference on the Negro, its emphasis was overwhelmingly on Africa. The printed program for the three-day conference divides the sessions into "Conditions," "Missions," and "Methods." The morning and afternoon sessions of Wednesday, April 17, were devoted exclusively to papers on Africa. Examples of the topics discussed were, "Africa and America, Past and Present," by Rev. D.D. Martin of the Stewart Foundation; "Africa Today—A Survey of Present Condition," by Cornelius Patton of the American Board of Foreign Missions; "Condition and Progress of Natives of Sierra Leone," by J. Denton of Fourah Bay College; and "Educational Conditions on the Gold Coast," by Rev. Mark C. Hayford (Casely-Hayford's brother), who was representing the Gold Coast.[20]

The evening session on Wednesday considered the West Indies, but a special session was held on Liberia. The discussion that ensued followed the same pattern as Wednesday morning and afternoon, being led mainly by Christian ministers.

Thursday, April 18, was "Missions" day. The topics covered were "The Native and Missions," "The Work of Colored Missions," "Industrial Education and Missions," and "Mission Boards and Mission Schools." There were no fewer than seventeen presentations by people like E.D. Morel, J.W.E. Bowen, Rev. Alexander Walters and at least one representative each from German East Africa: Rev. V. Johanssen; British East Africa, O. Scouten; Portuguese East Africa, W.C. Terrill, and Southern Nigeria, W.L. Brown.

On Friday, April 19, the day reserved for "Methods," the two major topics were "Education of the Primitive Man" and "Principles and Application." Dr. Robert E. Park, former secretary of the Congo Reform Association, headed the list of discussants for the final day.[21]

Accounts vary regarding attendance and representation at the conference, but the most reliable ones indicated that twenty-one foreign countries (or colonies) and thirty-six different missionary societies, representing sixteen different religious denominations, were in attendance.[22] Consequently, the conference was truly international in scope, with individual representatives from every area of the world that had a significant number of Black people. There were Whites in attendance, as well as Black delegates from colonized West

Africa, East Africa, South Africa, and the Caribbean Islands. There were also Black and White participants from South America and the United States. *The Foundation*, the publication of the Stewart Foundation for Africa, based in Atlanta, Georgia, published a front-page photograph of some of the delegates and enthusiastically supported the conference.[23]

Initially, Booker T. Washington indicated that one of the objectives of the conference was to organize "a permanent society which shall be sort of a sponsor to the civilized world . . . for Africans."[24] This "International Society" was to number among its membership, scientists, explorers, missionaries, and all others directly or indirectly involved with Africa. The idea was to assist Africa and represent the continent and its interests before the nations of the world. There were, moreover, plans for subsequent international conferences. It was agreed at the final session of the 1912 conference that Washington, who served as chairman of the first conference, would head a planning committee composed of Emmet Scott, Hollis B. Frissel, and Robert E. Park, for the second confab. Three additional members were to be added at a later date, and they were charged with the responsibility for making the necessary arrangements for a Second International Conference on the Negro, to be held in three years. The mandate was to gather representatives from every country in which Africans or people of African descent constituted a considerable portion of the population.[25]

Even though the idea for an "International Society," to provide whatever kind of assistance it could for Africa, and the plans for a Second International Conference were good and visionary, there is no evidence that it ever went beyond the planning stage. The second conference was never held and there is no indication that an organization growing out of the first International Conference, and specifically established with an African interest, was ever formed. To what extent Booker T. Washington's death in 1915 was a factor in either of these plans is unclear. But if a consideration at all, it is likely that his death was a stronger impediment to the idea of an "International Society," since that required the stronger stimulus, than to the realization of another conference.

The 1912 conference enjoyed the approval both of Blyden and Casely-Hayford, but apparently not that of DuBois. In fact, DuBois was conspicuous by his absence at this conference, but that absence can be attributed most to the open ideological conflict in which DuBois and Booker T. Washington were then embroiled. Some of Casely-Hayford's comments read to the conference, brought the three-day conference as close as it came to expressed nationalist or Pan-Africanist sentiments. He advocated African-Americans and Africans joining forces for a "national aim, purpose and aspiration."[26] Bylden, who was dead at the time of the conference, had sent his greetings beforehand indicating that he was impressed with the fact that a Black school (Tuskegee) was so well known in the world that it could call a meeting of this kind without anyone regarding it as strange or unusual.[27] Nevertheless, Booker T. Washington does not seem to have departed from the attitude that characterized the "White man's burden," nor to have shed the accomodationist quality of his leadership with Africa or Black America. If nothing else, the conference made possible a marketplace for the cross-fertilization of ideas among Africans from Africa, the West Indies, South America, and the United States. In sustaining the African interest in a small way, it also became part of the foundation from which came more militant action in later years.

The Pan-African Conference (1919)

In sharp contrast to the International Conference on the Negro was the 1919 Pan-African Congress held in France. The political poignancy of this Congress can be seen, for instance, in the proposals for African self-government, or at least participation in governing until eventually Africa would be ruled by Africans. This 1919 Congress was inestimably important as part of the foundation for African nationalism. It was, in a sense, the "smoking gun" that presaged the demise of the colonial system. Nevertheless as underscored by Immanuel Geiss, in some ways the Congress was retrogressive vis-à-vis the 1900 conference in London.[28] For example, there was no detailed report of the Congress similar to that of the 1900 meeting.[29] Second there was no comprehensive list of those who participated or the roles they played.[30] Finally, concerns over land expropriation, forced labor, and education in Africa were really first mentioned at the 1900 conference. Geiss further reminds us that many writers who have discussed the Paris Congress (1919) accepted uncritically DuBois's self-adulation of his role in Pan-Africanism, and the dearth of sources available for constructing a history of the Congress. Most of those sources he calls the "handiwork" of DuBois.[31]

In 1911 DuBois had attended the Universal Races Congress in London and enjoyed an opportunity to interact with the few Africans present. The initiative for this Races Congress was taken by the New York humanitarian, Felix Adler, although one source suggests that DuBois originated the idea.[32] The intent of the Congress was to improve relations among the races of the world through personal interaction. Scholarly papers were presented and DuBois in particular dealt with "The Negro Race in the United States of America." The conference experience gained at the 1900 gathering in London and at the Races Congress in 1911 both helped DuBois in his organizing role with the 1919 Congress.

The Pan-African Congress of 1919 was held in Paris, France, from February 19 to February 21. W.E.B. DuBois, the prime mover at the Congress, traveled to France on the steamship *Orizaba* representing *Crisis* magazine, the organ of the NAACP. This interracial protest group financed the entire affair and commissioned DuBois to call a "Pan-African Congress."[33] A second Black individual, Dr. R.R. Moton (Booker T. Washington's successor at Tuskegee), representing the President of the United States and the Secretary of War, went to France primarily to investigate allegations of discrimination and mistreatment of Black soldiers in the United States Army stationed in France. Lester A. Walton, a correspondent for the New York *Age*, and the third Black on board the steamer, which was also carrying President Woodrow Wilson's "peace party," went to France to gather information about Black troops for *Age* readers.[34] He subsequently provided first-hand accounts of the Pan-African Congress for the *Age*.[35]

The Pan-African Congress of 1919 received comparatively good coverage in the New York *Age*. Its most dramatic headlines were released in the February 1, 1919, which stated strikingly, PLAN PAN-AFRICAN CONGRESS. The story below the headlines discussed plans under way for the Congress and played up the role of African-Americans, chiefly DuBois.[36] The February 22, 1919 issue of the *Age* carried an on-the-scene report from the Congress and claimed that a world Black population of 157,000,000 was being represented there. It cautioned that the stability of the League of Nations depended on Black interests being safeguarded.[37] Finally, in a March 1, 1919, "Extra" the *Age* underscored the fact that the Congress passed a resolution to go before the peace conference under way in Paris and asked for the creation of an international code to protect of the world's African people.

> At the opening session of the Pan-African Congress held here last week, a resolution was passed for presentation to the Peace Conference proposing that the allied and associate powers establish an international code for the protection of Negroes. The resolution covers regulation of the investment of capital, the granting of concessions, political or religious liberty and demands that Negroes have equitable representation in all of the international institutions of the League of Nations.[38]

It was with the assistance of Blaise Diagne of Senegal, the first African to sit in the French Chamber of Deputies, that the Congress was eventually held. There was some fear on the part of the American delegation attending the peace conference in Versailles that the Pan-African Congress would be used as a forum to embarrass the United States. The Americans suspected that DuBois, for example, would bring up the subject of the injustices and discrimination that African-Americans experienced in the United States and would point particularly to the brutality of lynching. DuBois attempted to assure Woodrow Wilson that the Congress did not intend to deal with the problems of Blacks in America, but could not get beyond Wilson's chief adviser, Colonel Edward House, who was "sympathetic but non-committal."[39] One result of these American fears was that Black delegates from the United States hoping to attend the Congress were denied passports.[40]

Blaise Diagne had earlier become a favorite of Georges Clemenceau, Prime Minister of France, because of his vigorous recruiting efforts of African troops for France during World War I. Those African soldiers fighting for the French on the western front were partly responsible for stopping the German offensive at the Battle of the Marne in July 1918. When DuBois persuaded Diagne to attempt to secure a meeting place for the Congress and Diagne approached Clemenceau, permission was given to hold the Congress in Paris. The French Minister cautioned Diagne not to "advertise" the Pan-African Congress because it might upset some of the allies at the peace conference but to "go ahead."[41]

All of the sessions of the 1919 Congress were to be held in the Grand Hotel on the Boulevard des Capucines in Paris. An office of the Congress was also maintained at the Hotel de Maulte, 63 Avenue Richelieu. Blaise Diagne was Chairman of the Congress, W.E.B. DuBois was Secretary and Ida Gibbs Hunt (USA) was Assistant Secretary. These three individuals, along with E.F. Fredericks (a lawyer from Trinidad,[42] whose official role is not clear) made up the Executive Committee of the Congress.[43] There were fifty-seven delegates to the Congress representing Africa, the West Indies, and the United States. The largest number (sixteen) came from the United States; in addition there were thirteen from the French West Indies, seven from

Haiti and France, three from Liberia, two from the Spanish colonies and one each from the Portuguese colonies, San Domingo, England, British Africa, Egypt, Belgian Congo, Algeria, Abyssinia, and French Africa.[44]

The speeches delivered and the papers read at the Congress were directed mainly at colonial rule in Africa. However, they were only mildly critical of colonialism, and Blaise Diagne even extolled French colonial rule. The atrocities of the Belgians and Portuguese in Africa were glossed over and Black American spokespersons only half-heartedly indicated their dissatisfaction with the United States. Most of the attention at the Congress was drawn to a petition to the League of Nations requesting the allied powers to place the former German colonies of Tanganyika, Cameroons, Togo, and South West Africa under international supervision. It was hoped that eventually these "Trust territories" would become self-governing. The claim that this petition formed the basis for the "Mandates System" of the League of Nations has been disputed as an "obvious exaggeration."[45]

The principal resolutions of the 1919 Congress were that a code of law be established guaranteeing the international protection of Africans. Also, it was resolved that the League of Nations establish a permanent bureau to supervise the application of these laws for the political, social, and economic welfare of Africans. Finally, it was "demanded" that Black people of the world, and Africans in particular, be governed by the following guidelines:

1. The Land.—The soil and its natural resources shall be reserved and held in trust for the natives; and that they shall have effective ownership of such land as they can profitably develop.

2. Capital.—The system of concessions shall be so regulated as to prevent the exploitation of the natives and the exhaustion of the natural wealth of the country. These concessions should always be temporary and subject to State control. Note should

be taken of the growing needs of the natives and part of the profits should be used for work relating to the moral and material development of the natives.

3. Labour.—Slavery and corporal punishment shall be abolished, and forced labour, except in punishment of crime, and conditions of labour shall be prescribed and regulated by the State.

4. Education.—It shall be the right of every native child to learn to read and write his own language, and the language of the trustee nation, at public expense, and to be given technical instruction in some branch of industry. The State shall also educate as large a number of natives as possible in higher technical instruction in some branch of industry. The State shall also educate as large a number of natives as possible in higher technical and cultural training and maintain a corps of native teachers.

5. Health.—It ought to be understood that existence in the tropics requires special safeguards as well as a scientific system of public hygiene. The State ought to take responsibility for medical treatment and health conditions, without prejudice to missionary and private initiative. A service of medical assistance, provided with doctors and hospitals, shall be established by the State.

6. The State.—The natives of Africa must have the right to participate in the Government as fast as their development permits, in conformity with the principle that the Government exists for the natives, and not the natives for the Government. They shall at once be allowed to participate in local and tribal government, according to their ancient usage, and this participation shall gradually extend, as education and experience proceed, to the higher offices of state; to the end that, in time, Africa is ruled by consent of the Africans. Whenever it is proved that African natives are not receiving just treatment at the hands of any State or that any State deliberately excludes its civilized citizens or subjects or Negro descent from its

body politic and culture, it shall be the duty of the
League of Nations to bring the matter to the notice of
the civilized world.[46]

The Paris resolutions do not seem to have been either
revolutionary or threatening to the White world. The New York
Herald characterized them as "nothing unreasonable,"[47] and it
was generally felt that they were moderate.[48] Demands for the
abolition of slavery, corporal punishment, and forced labor,
along with improvements in education, protection from
economic exploitation and expropriation of land, and supervision by the League of Nations in Africa, were all quite
fashionable for the time. Several of these concerns had already
been aired at the 1900 conference in London. The demand that
Africans be allowed to first participate in the running of their
own affairs and to take over the running of those affairs "as fast
as their development permits" had also been voiced at the
London conference as "responsible government for Africa."[49]

The Allied Powers meeting at Versailles did not seriously
consider this Pan-African manifesto submitted by Blacks
meeting in Paris. They agreed in "principle," but their agreement
was not translated into meaningful action. Land expropriation
and economic exploitation in Africa continued. So did forced
labor and many aspects of slavery. There were only token
improvements in education, and African participation in
government varied with the colonial power involved, but was
always held to a minimum. One scholar believed, "The men who
were settling the affairs of Europe at Paris were talking *realpolitik*
and Africa was merely one of the bargaining counters."[50]
Nonetheless, despite its non-revolutionary character, the 1919
Congress was important in the evolution of Pan-Africanism. It
followed the precedent set by the 1900 London conference of
providing a global stage for at least venting the concerns of the
world's Black people. The Congresses of the 1920s, the
Manchester Congress (1945), and Ghana's independence
(1957)—milestones in the beginning of the end of colonial rule—
all drew major inspiration from the 1919 Pan-African Congress.

NOTES

1. Accounts of the 1900 conference can be found in Owen C. Mathurin, *Henry Sylvester Williams and the Origins of the Pan-African Movement, 1869–1911* (Middletown, Conn., 1976); in the autobiography of Alexander Walters, *My Life and Work* (New York, 1917), chapter 20; Benito Sylvain, *Du Sort Des Indigenes Dans Les Colonies D'Exploitation* (Paris, 1901); S.E.F.C.C. Hamedoe, "The First Pan-African Conference of the World," *Colored American Magazine* (September 1900), 223–231; J.R. Hooker, "The Pan-African Congress 1900," *Transition* 46 (October/ December, 1974) 20–24; Clarence G. Contee, "W.E.B. DuBois and the African Nationalism: 1914–1945," Ph.D. dissertation, American University, 1969, chapter 2; Milfred C. Fierce, "Henry Sylvester Williams and the Pan-African Conference of 1900," *Geneve-Afrique* 14, no. 1 (1975), 106–114; *Report of the Pan-African Conference*, Fisk University Library.

2. For Williams's life, see J.R. Hooker, *Henry Sylvester Williams: Imperial Pan-Africanist* (London, 1975), and two essays by Clarence G. Contee, "Henry Sylvester Williams: Pioneer Pan-Africanist," *Black World* (March, 1974), 32–37 and *Henry Sylvester Williams and Origins of Organizational Pan-Africanism: 1897–1902* (Washington, D.C., 1973).

3. In the March 22, 1906, issue of the New York *Age* (p. 2), the editor, T. Thomas Fortune, made the claim that H.S. Williams got the idea for a Pan-African conference from him during his visit to the United States in the 1890s. He went on to suggest that the entire movement, the conference and the Pan-African Association were failures because the leadership was not "sufficiently influential to draw together a representative body of people." This claim was not confirmed by Bishop Alexander Walters, an influential African-American involved in this early phase of Pan-Africanism. See Walters, *My Life and Work*, 253.

4. Booker T. Washington was expected to attend the conference as late as June 1990. When it became clear that Booker T. Washington would not attend, Henry Sylvester Williams writing on stationery with a "Pan-African Committee" letterhead asked him to contribute a paper on the "industrial development of our people in the light of current history." Washington does not appear to have responded to this letter

nor did he contribute a paper. Henry Sylvester Williams to BTW, June 1, 1900 and June 29, 1900 (187).

5. Mathurin, *Henry Sylvester Williams*, 102.

6. Walters, *My Life and Work*, 257.

7. Mathurin, *Henry Sylvester Williams*, 128.

8. *Ibid.*

9. See John Hope Franklin, *From Slavery to Freedom* (New York, 1988), 169–170.

10. *Report of the Pan-African Conference 1900*, 18.

11. Among them are August Meier and Elliot Rudwick, *From Plantation to Ghetto* (New York, 1968), 201. They also mistakenly report that the London Conference (1900) was "dominated by the personality of DuBois." Other accounts that announce DuBois as the "Secretary" include DuBois's own *Autobiography of W.E.B. DuBois* (New York, 1968), 438; St. Clair Drake, "Negro Americans and the Africa Interest," *America Negro Reference Book* (Englewood Cliffs, New Jersey, 1969) 681; George Shepperson, "Introduction," IX, XII, W.E.B. DuBois, *The Negro*,, rev. ed. (New York, 1970).

12. Mathurin, *Henry Sylvester Williams*, 116–117, 144–146.

13. "Other than a passing mention in 1920 in *Darkwater* and in May, 1921 in the *Crisis*," *ibid.* See Chicago *Defender*, September 22, 1945. For more on this DuBois omission, see Clarence Contee, "W.E.B. DuBois and African Nationalism: 1900–1945," chapter 1.

14. Walters, *My Life and Work*, 257; George Padmore, *Pan-Africanism or Communism* (New York, 1971), 96; George Shepperson, "Notes on Negro American Influences on the Emergence of African Nationalism," *Journal of African History* (1960), 306–307; W.E.B. DuBois, *The World*, 8; Hooker, *Pan-African*, 24.

15. DuBois, *The World*, 8; Rayford Logan, "The Historical Aspects of Pan-Africanism: A Personal Chronicle," *African Forum* 1 (Summer, 1965), 91; Padmore, *Pan-Africanism*, 91.

16. See Elliot Rudwick, "The Niagara Movement," *Journal of Negro History* (July, 1957), 177–200; Emma Lou Thornbrough, "The National Afro-American League, 1887–1908," *Journal of Southern History* (November, 1961), 494–512; and DuBois, *Autobiography*, chapter 14.

17. Shepperson, "Notes. . . ," 222n; Contee, "W.E.B. DuBois. . . ," 55–56; *Voice of the Negro* (October, 1906), 409–411.

18. See *The Tuskegee Student* (March 23, 1912), (April 13, 1912), (April 20, 1912), (May 4, 1912) for detailed accounts of the conference proceedings. Worthwhile is Robert E. Park, "Tuskegee International Conference on the Negro," *Journal of Race Development* (July, 1912–April, 1913), 117–120.

19. Printed announcement "International Conference on the Negro," BTW Papers, Library of Congress, Manuscripts Division, Box 917, folder marked "International Conference on the Negro."

20. "Program" for International Conference on the Negro," BTW Papers (917).

21. There is a summation of each day's activities, evidently a press release, in the BTW Papers (917). They are undated, unsigned and typewritten.

22. This record of attendance comes from a press release in the BTW Papers (917), undated, unsigned and typewritten, but reprinted with some modifications in New York *Age* (April 12, 1912), 1, 5. For differing accounts see *The Tuskegee Student* (February 3, 1912), 1 and (April 27, 1912), 1, 304. Complete lists of the more than one hundred individuals planning to attend the conference can be seen in BTW Papers (917); *The Tuskegee Student* (April 13, 1912), 2–4; New York *Age* (April 12, 1912), 5–6.

23. *The Foundation* (June 1912), p. 1. See, also, issues of *The Foundation* between January and April, 1912, publicizing the conference. Louis Harlan purports that most of the delegates at the conference were White and that there were few Africans. Immanuel Geiss echoes Harlan, writing that the delegates were "mostly Whites; three Afro-West Indians and some Afro-Americans." I was unable to find the "list of arrivals" cited by Harlan, whom Geiss footnotes, in the BTW Papers. However, the printed "Program" does not confirm conclusively this "White majority" and the photograph in *The Foundation* shows fourteen Blacks and twelve Whites. Of these fourteen Blacks, seven are Afro-West Indians. Louis Harlan, "Booker T. Washington and the White Man's Burden," in O.E. Uya (ed.), *Black Brotherhood*, 152; Immanuel Geiss, *Pan-African* 219, 218–221.

24. Memorandum addressed "To the Agent of the Associated Press—Atlanta, Georgia," no date, unsigned, typewritten, but

apparently authored by Washington or his secretary, Emmet J. Scott. BTW Papers (917). BTW expressed these same ideas in "Industrial Education in Africa," *Independent* (March 15, 1906), 616–619.

25. *The Southern Letter* (May, 1912), 3; *The Tuskegee Student* (April 27, 1912), 1; "Memorandum of a Meeting of the Committee Appointed to Nominate a Committee to Arrange for a Second International Conference in 1915," BTW Papers (917), undated, unsigned, typewritten.

26. New York *Age* (April 12, 1912), 5.

27. *Ibid.*, 1.

28. Geiss, *Pan-African*, 230–240.

29. The 1900 Report is in the DuBois Papers at the Fisk University Library.

30. For the 1900 conference list see Walters, *My Life and Work* chapter 20; Geiss, *Pan-African*, 182–183.

31. Geiss, *Pan-African*, 230–240.

32. Arna Bontempts, *One Hundred Years of Negro Freedom* (New York, 1961), 217.

33. W.E.B. DuBois, *The World and Africa* (New York, 1961), 217.

34. New York *Age* (February 1, 1919), 1.

35. New York *Age*, especially (February 22, 1919), 1 and (March 1, 1919), 1.

36. New York *Age* (February 1, 1919), 1.

37. New York *Age* (February 22, 1919), 1.

38. New York *Age* (March 1, 1919), 1.

39. *Ibid.*; Padmore, *Pan-Africanism*, 99–100.

40. Padmore, *Pan-Africanism*, 100 and 101; J.B. Webster and A.A. Boahen, *History of West Africa* (New York, 1972), 284; Geiss, *Pan-African*, 237.

41. DuBois, *The World*, 9–10.

42. J.A. Langley, *Pan-Africanism and Nationalism in West Africa 1900–1945* (London, 1973), 63. Geiss, *Pan-African*, 236 claims Fredericks was from Sierra Leone.

43. Langley, *Pan-Africanism*, 63.

44. *Crisis* (March, 1919), 271–274; Langley, *Pan-Africanism*, 63; Geiss, *Pan-African*, 238–239; Padmore, *Pan-Africanism*, 101.

45. For the dispute, Geiss, *Pan-African*, 233; for the claim, DuBois, *The World*, 11; Padmore, *Pan-Africanism*, 101. See also Rayford Logan, *The African Mandates in World Politics* (Washington, D.C., 1948) IV, 42; George L. Beer, *African Questions at the Paris Peace Conference* (New York, 1923), 285–286.

46. The resolutions can be found in their entirety in Langley, *Pan-Africanism*, 65–66; DuBois, *The World*, 11–12; Padmore, *Pan-Africanism*, 102–103; Colin Legum, *Pan-Africanism: A Short Political Guide* (New York, 1965), Appendix I, 151–152. There are some minor discrepancies in the above accounts, but most interesting and for reasons that are unclear, DuBois, Padmore, and Legum omit the Health section of the resolutions.

47. Quoted in DuBois, *The World*, 12.

48. Geiss, *Pan-African*, 239.

49. *Ibid.*

50. Langley, *Pan-Africanism*, 66.

Conclusion

The events of the first two decades of the twentieth century marked an increase in the interest in Africa of African-Americans compared with the decades prior to 1900. In addition to the emigrationist and missionary interest, which was most characteristic of the nineteenth century and continued into the twentieth century, a poignant Black intellectual interest also developed after 1900. African-Americans showed interest in various commercial schemes along with a concern over Africa's continued abuse by European nations, and they sincerely attempted to do something about it. The flames of African-American interest in and interaction with Africa were further fanned between 1900 and 1919, and the Pan-African idea grew to maturity. The idea of race brotherhood, even a limited feeling of *quid pro quo*, although still comparatively small, became more widespread among American Blacks than at any time before 1900. The planting of the seed of Pan-African thought in the consciousness of a few African-Americans, marketed within the Black world as part of the "commerce in ideas," actually set the stage for a viable movement decades later. There is ample evidence, as demonstrated in this thematic investigation of African-American interest in Africa, that after the turn of the century the Pan-African idea among key Black-Americans not only became enlivened but was spreading. What is more, after 1919 the Pan-African movement began to show distinct signs of its transition away from the idea stage toward visible action.

An extraordinary feature of this little known, but tremendously important phase of African-American history is the fact that an interest in Africa and the plight of Africans, however small, could find sympathy, even encouragement, among elites in a group of people who were exhausting every means at their disposal merely to survive themselves. By 1915 African-Americans were the defenseless victims of intimidation, disfranchisement, lynchings, and almost universal circumscription. Fifty years removed from slavery in the South, Black Americans were essentially a powerless people. They were making a desperate dash for the cities of the United States in the South and the North only to find that neither would be their promised land. Every major institution in American society at this time (the church, labor unions, universities, the armed forces, media, government) inelegantly perpetuated the stereotype of innate Black inferiority. Social Darwinism and pseudoscientific racism enjoyed their heyday precisely at this time, as well. In spite of this, or perhaps because of the tenuous socioeconomic and related circumstances prevailing in the United States for Black people, some looked to Africa for sustenance.

When the new century opened, to say that Africa was a mystery, a chimera, to all but a handful of Blacks in a country on the way to becoming a world power, may be an understatement. The *zeit geist* of the times made possible a savage, implacable propaganda campaign against African-Americans, Africans, and Africa. Many Black people themselves, as well as others, were convinced, beyond doubt, that the "dark continent" was only to be scorned. Some African-Americans responded to their own social rejection with compounded chagrin over Africa. Europeans and the White majority in the United States assumed that technological superiority was axiomatic with cultural, social, political, and every other kind of superiority. Africa and its people, according to the racists, were the epitome of backwardness, barbarism, and repugnance. Given this hostile context, most African-Americans found very little with which they wanted to identify in Africa.

Certain it is, however, that the Africa interest, the Pan-African idea, expanded at this time. We are able to discern not only horizontal change in the Africa interest, but vertical change as well, from the nineteenth century interest. The intellectuals, DuBois, Woodson, Bruce, Schomburg, Johnson, Ellis, and others—provoked mainly by eroding conditions in Africa and Black America and Africa's none too subtle besmirching—were mobilized to defend the proud heritage of Africa and Black people that had been exorcised from the pages of history. Their uncompromising response to Africa's detractors was a boon to the Africa interest. Through their writings, the organizations they formed, and their own Pan-African proclivities, these unyielding intellectuals labored for a more accurate image of Africa. Certain too, it is, that Black American intellectuals significantly influenced African intellectuals. The indispensability of this period in the ideological birth of Pan-Africanism and the contributions of these Black intellectuals have been acknowledged by every important student of the Pan-African idea and movement, from George Shepperson to E.U. Essien-Udom to J.A. Langley. Furthermore, it is possible to observe the beginning of the end of colonialism in Africa commencing with the ideas and actions emanating from the two most important Pan-African meetings held during the period under investigation.

The activities of Black missionaries in Africa are significant in every respect. Their motives were inspired most by Christian enterprise or the Social Gospel, and they genuinely wanted to help Africa. They candidly felt that evangelizing in Africa was the best way to do it. Those who went out under the auspices of the Stewart Foundation as well as under the aegis of the independent Black churches often dedicated their lives to Africa. They were guilty of reinforcing many of the stereotypes of Black inferiority, but were merely victims of the racist thought of the times. Their methods are more to be questioned than their intentions. Too often, Black missionaries helped foster a passive attitude among Africans that ensured a long life of exploitation. At the same time, the Black American missionary reputation as "agitators" was sometimes enough to inspire radical action among Africans. And it is noteworthy that, almost without exception, African-American missionaries were well educated and expressed principled feelings of brotherhood with Africans. They deserve much of the credit for keeping the idea of Africa's existence alive in the consciousness of African-Americans within their ambit.

Recurrent interest in a physical return to Africa was exemplified best by "Chief Sam." Bishop Turner remained the leading ideologue for a Black exodus from the United States, but the action phase of his movement peaked in the 1890s. He went on trying to organize various schemes but had no real success, sending no ships to Africa. Small groups and individual Blacks emigrated to Africa, especially to Liberia, but the demise of the American Colonization Society and the coming of World War I added to the prevailing reservations that most African-Americans had regarding emigration, and underscored the lack of appeal of back-to-Africa crusades.

The cotton-growing episode in Togo illustrated one example of African-Americans interacting in West Africa outside Liberia. The experiment did not meet with the expectations of the Germans or the Tuskegeans and had its share of tragedies. The Togo experience also demonstrated what at least some Germans had in mind for the management of its African colonies—the importation and employment of the progeny of ex-slaves from the United States in some capacity. The Tuskegeans who worked in Togo, much like James Nathan Calloway (supervisor of the project), saw primarily class differences between Africans and African-Americans. Most of the Tuskegeans, although they were by no means a politicized group, recognized the ebony kinship between Blacks in the United States and Blacks in Africa. However, that was not the motive for their willingness to attempt to grow cotton in West Africa. Their presence in Togo is best explained by the business acumen of German entrepreneurs.

Given the special set of circumstances surrounding Liberia's founding, the comparatively high level of interest in and interaction with that West African Republic is understandable. The ruling elite, Americo-Liberians, traced their family backgrounds mainly to Georgia in the United States. There was missionary interest and commercial interest, and, led by Booker T. Washington and the New York *Age*, African-Americans attempted, through diplomacy, to pump any kind of relief they could into that prostrate polity during its period of severe crisis. The rescue mission, as admirable as its intentions were, was short-lived. Liberia continued to be threatened with European interposition and to have critical economic, political, and social difficulties.

The New York *Age* was Liberia's and Africa's most persistent defender among the Black press during this period. Its coverage outdistanced all other newspapers and periodicals and was unprecedented. Africa was found regularly in *Age* front-page stories, which did not avoid political realities. The *Age* not only accepted the principle of the Pan-African idea, but gave it enthusiastic endorsement though headlines and editorials.

As in domestic affairs, Booker T. Washington and W.E.B. DuBois assumed center stage in African-American concerns for Africa. Between the 1900 London conference and the 1919 Paris Congress, DuBois was engaged in the campaign to generate "Africa pride" in African-Americans through an emphasis on the African background. He also took part in the effort to ease Europe's economic and political strangle-hold on Africa. Booker T. Washington, known primarily as a domestic Black leader, was variously engaged in Africa's affairs. He was a regular correspondent with Africans, and his name and that of Tuskegee Institute were familiar in some of the remotest areas of Africa. The Liberia episode and the Togo experiment were both extensively directed by him. South Africa, the Congo, Sudan, and several parts of West Africa specifically bore witness to his influence. African students studied at Tuskegee, and many who did not study there were nevertheless agents of the Tuskegee idea. There are even indications that, on occasion, Booker T. Washington—for all his accommodation and acquiescence to White leadership and the status quo in both African-American and African affairs—entertained some aspects of the Pan-African idea.

The dynamism of Marcus Garvey and the subsequent Pan-African congresses led by W.E.B. DuBois dominated the Africa interest in the 1920s. The Garvey-led Universal Negro Improvement Association established branches of the organization in Africa and throughout the world, and sponsored its own Pan-African-oriented conventions in New York City. UNIA failed in its attempt to secure land in Liberia but their effort did not lack vigour. Right up to the time Garvey was incarcerated, in 1925, the clarion cry, "Africa for the African" was a prominent feature of the UNIA program. There were UNIA branch offices in Lagos, Nigeria, and Garvey's brand of nationalism had political consequences in Liberia, Sierra Leone, and the French-speaking areas of West Africa. French and Belgian officials in equatorial Africa (especially the Congo) often considered the influence of Garveyism responsible for local disturbances. In essence, although Garvey never set foot on African soil, the political vibrations from the movement he led were felt in South Africa, Central Africa, and West Africa. To be sure, Garveyism was a force to be reckoned with in the African nationalist body-politic.

Drawing on the experience gained and lessons learned in London in 1900 and at Paris in 1919, DuBois, with support from the NAACP, organized Pan-African congresses in London, Brussels, and Paris (1921), London and Lisbon (1923), and New York (1927). The 1921 Congress was the most radical of this series, since there was an eloquent and outspoken denunciation of imperialism in Africa and racism in the United States—the twin blights that infested most of the Black world. Nevertheless, Garveyism, with its distinct economic goals, tended to impress West African nationalist leaders (notably the National Congress of British West Africa) much more than did the celebrated, but at this point ineffective, movement being led by W.E.B. DuBois.

In the 1930s the Great Depression replaced the good times of the 1920s and affected the entire world. In the United States,

Black people suffered most, notwithstanding their excitement over Franklin D. Roosevelt's New Deal. Garvey was deported from the United States in 1927 following his release from the federal prison in Atlanta, Georgia. His departure precipitated a power struggle within UNIA ranks that led to factionalism and a severe weakening of the organization, and its earlier *élan* was never recovered. Meanwhile, DuBois broke with the NAACP over the issue of his new support for voluntary Black segregation. His Africa interest by now was clearly subordinated to domestic issues. In 1937, under the leadership of Paul Robeson the Council of African Affairs was established to look out for the interests of Africa, only to become a victim of the Cold War paranoia of the next decade. The episode that attracted the most attention in the Black American community, insofar as Africa, was concerned, between the two world wars, was Italy's cowardly attack on Ethiopia in 1935.

The Italian invasion of Ethiopia in October of 1935 inspired a pro-Ethiopian movement among a limited number of African-Americans, which was a good barometer of the Pan-African sentiment among Blacks. African-Americans protested and demonstrated in an attempt to get the United States government to intercede in this conflict on Ethiopia's behalf. The Black press was vigilant, with its lead stories and editorials designed to whip up support for Ethiopia. Even Joe Louis's boxing ring victory over Primo Carnera represented what Black nationalists hoped was a preview of Ethiopia's eventual victory over its fascist invaders. Since 1896 and the battle of Adowa, the first outbreak of hostilities between Ethiopia and Italy—at which Italy was soundly defeated—Black American and pro-Ethiopia sentiment was minimal. By the time of Italy's merciless invasion at the beginning of World War II, the Pan-African idea had indeed come a long way.

The Pan-African Congress at Manchester, England, in 1945, is generally considered, by students of the subject, to have been the *ne plus ultra* of Pan-Africanism, a coalescing of the idea and the movement creating positive force. The strategy developed there to organize African people through trade unions and political parties achieved rapid results. The objectives of autonomy and immediate national independence witnessed their first success with Ghana's independence, the first domino, a decade later. Younger men and women, and more Africans took over the leadership of Pan-Africanism and merged the movement with nationalism. The 1945 Congress further inspired an awakening of African political consciousness already primed by the impact World War II had on colonial possessions around the globe. W.E.B. DuBois was Black America's only participant at Manchester, and although he received all of the deference commensurate with his monumental role in the growth of Pan-Africanism, most of the organizational work was carried out by individuals like George Padmore, Kwame Nkrumah, and Jomo Kenyatta. By the time the Congress ended, it was apparent that the Black world had seized the initiative, and prevailing attitudes would soon be jarred by the now-pressing imperatives of self-determination and Black liberation in Africa.

During the first nineteen years of the twentieth century, neat ideological symmetry was missing among the African-Americans actively involved with West Africa or other parts of Africa. The simultaneous reality both of the interest in and the action concerning Africa among Black Americans debunks DuBois's view that Pan-Africanism was dead for a generation.

The evolution of the Pan-African idea between 1900 and 1919 was a major phase of Pan-Africanism. It represents a link between the loosely organized, unsophisticated, "New World" interest in Africa and the increasing political perspicacity of the post-World War I era. This multifaceted African-American interest in Africa during the first two decades of the twentieth century has secured for itself, through its sincerity and perseverance, a cherished place in the history of the world's African people.

Bibliography

Manuscript Collections

1. Booker T. Washington Papers (BTW), Manuscript Division, Library of Congress, Washington, D.C.

2. Booker T. Washington Papers (BTW), Hollis Burke Frissell Library, Tuskegee Institute, Tuskegee Alabama.

3. John Edward Bruce Collection, Schomburg Research Center, New York Public Library.

4. Stewart Foundation Papers, Interdenominational Theological Center, Atlanta, Georgia.

5. J.W.E. Bowen Papers, Interdenominational Theological Center, Atlanta, Georgia.

6. Wilbur Thirkield Papers, Interdenominational Theological Center, Atlanta, Georgia.

7. T. McCants Stewart Papers, Moorland Spingarn Research Center, Howard University, Washington, D.C.

8. Alain Locke Papers, Moorland-Spingarn Research Center, Howard University, Washington, D.C.

Newspapers

1. New York *Age*

2. Indianapolis *Freeman*

3. *The Tuskegee Student*

4. *The Southern Letter*

5. *Southern Workman*

6. *Voice of the Negro*

7. *Voice of Missions*
8. *Voice of the People*

Periodicals

1. *Colored American Magazine*
2. *Crisis: A Record of the Darker Races*
3. *The Foundation*
4. *Quarterly Bulletin*
5. *Liberia Bulletin*
6. *African Repository*
7. *A.M.E. Church Review*
8. *Moon*
9. *Horizon*
10. *Mission World*

Dissertations, Theses, and Manuscripts

Coan, Joesphus. "Expansions of Missions of the African Methodist Episcopal Church in South Africa, 1896–1908." (Hartford Seminary, 1961), Ph.D.

Contee, Clarence G. "W.E.B. DuBois and African Nationalism, 1900–1945." (American University, history, 1969), Ph.D.

Hose, John Robert. "Britain and the Development of West African Cotton 1845–1960." (Columbia University, history, 1970), Ph.D.

Kimbro, Dennis Paul. "Towards a Model of Pan-Africanism." (Northwestern University, political science, 1984), Ph.D.

Lipede, Abiola Ade. "Pan-Africanism in Southern Africa, 1900–1910." (University of York, political science, 1960), Ph.D.

McPheeters, Alphonso. "The Origin and Development of Clark University and Gammon Theological Seminary." (University of Cincinnati, 1944), Ed.D.

Magubane, Bernard. "The American Negro's Conception of Africa: A Study in the Ideology of Pride and Prejudice." (U.C.L.A., sociology, 1967), Ph.D.

Marah, Karefah. "Social History of Practical Pan-Africanism and the Education of Teachers in African Countries." (Syracuse University, Education, 1982), Ph.D.

Markakis, John. "Pan-Africanism: The Idea and the Movement." (Columbia University, political science, 1965), Ph.D.

Mathurin, Owen Charles. "Henry Sylvester Williams and the Origins of the Pan-African Movement, 1869–1911." (unpublished manuscript—Trinidad, 1972).

Page, Carol A. "Henry McNeal Turner and the 'Ethiopian Movement.'" (Roosevelt University, history, 1973), M.A.

Ralston, Richard. "A Second Middle Passage: African Student Sojourns in the United States During the Colonial Period and Their Influence Upon the Character of African Leadership." (U.C.L.A., history, 1972), Ph.D.

Scott, William R. "A Study of Afro-American and Ethiopian Relations, 1896–1941." (Princeton University, history, 1971) Ph.D.

Taylor, Prince A. "A History of Gammon Theological Seminary." (New York University, education, 1948), Ph.D.

Williams, Walter. "Black American Attitudes Toward Africa: The Missionary Movement, 1877–1900." (University of North Carolina, Chapel Hill, history, 1974), Ph.D.

Yates, Walter Ladell. "The History of the African Methodist Episcopal Zion Church in West Africa, Liberia, Gold Coast (Ghana) and Nigeria, 1900–1939." (Hartford Seminary, 1967) Ph.D.

———. "The History of the African Methodist Episcopal Zion Church in West Africa, Liberia and Gold Coast (Ghana) 1880–1900." (Hartford Seminary, 1963), M.A.

Published Articles and Essays

Alot, Magaga. "Dar Es Salaam Notebook." *Africa: An International Business, Economic and Political Monthly* (August, 1974), 17–18.

Andrain, Charles F. "The Pan-African Movement: The Search for Organization and Community." *Phylon* (Spring, 1962), 5–17.

Asante, S.K.B. "Re-Birth of Pan-Africanism." *Africa; An International Business, Economic and Political Monthly* (September, 1974), 29–30.

Ayandele, E.A. "An Assessment of James Johnson and His Place in Nigerian History." *Journal of the Historical Society of Nigeria* (1964), 486–516.

Azikiwe, Nnamdi. "In Defense of Liberia." *Journal of Negro History* (January, 1932), 30–50.

Baillaud, Emile. "Cultivation of Cotton in Western Africa." *Journal of the African Society* (January, 1903), 132–148.

Batten, Minton. "Henry M. Turner, Negro Bishop Extraordinary." *Church History* (September, 1938), 231–246.

Bennet, Lerone, Jr. "Pan-Africanism at the Crossroads." *Ebony* (September, 1974), 148–160.

Berman, Edward H. "Tuskegee in Africa." *Journal of Negro Education* (Spring, 1972), 99–112.

Bittle, William and Gilbert Geis. "Alfred Charles Sam and an Africa Return: A Case Study in Negro Despair." *Phylon* (Summer, 1962), 178–194.

Bruening, William H. "Racism: A Philosophical Analysis of a Concept." *Journal of Black Studies* (September, 1974), 3–17.

Calloway, James N. "Tuskegee Cotton Planters in Africa." *Outlook* (March 29, 1902), 772–776.

Clark, J. Dunmore. "A Eye Opener—Based on Twelve Years' Experiences on the West Coast of Africa and Seven Years as a Missionary in the A.M.E. Church." *A.M.E. Church Review* (October, 1916), 63–68.

Contee, Clarence, ed. "Worley Report on the Pan-African Congress of 1919." *Journal of Negro History* (April, 1970).

———. "Henry Sylvester Williams: Pioneer Pan-Africanist." *Black World* (March, 1974), 32–37.

———. "The Emergence of DuBois as an African Nationalist." *Journal of Negro History* (January, 1969), 48–62.

Coulter, E. Merton. "Henry M. Turner: Georgia Negro Preacher-Politician During the Reconstruction Era." *Georgia Historical Quarterly* (December, 1964), 371–410.

Davis, Lenwood G. "Pan-Africanism: An Extensive Bibliography." (Part II) *Geneve Afrique*, Vol. 12, No. 1 (1973), 601–621.

DuBois, W.E.B. "Liberia and Rubber." *New Republic* (November 18, 1925), 326–330.

———. "The African Roots of War." *Atlantic Monthly* (May, 1915), 707–714.

———. "The Future of the Negro Race in America." *East and the West* (January, 1904), 4–19.

Duigan, Peter. "Pan-Africanism: A Bibliographic Essay." *African Forum* (Summer, 1965), 105–107.

Drake, St. Clair. "Pan-Africanism: What Is It?" *Africa Today* (January–February, 1959), 6–10.

———. "Negro Americans and the Africa Interest." *American Negro Reference Book.* (Englewood Cliffs, New Jersey, 1969), 662–705.

Ejimofor, Cornelius. "Black American Contributions to African Nationalism and African Influence on U.S. Civil Rights." *Journal of Afro-American Issues* (Fall 1974), 332–347.

Elkine, W.F., ed. "Influence of Marcus Garvey on Africa: A British Report of 1922." *Science and Society* (Summer, 1968), 321–323.

Ellis, George W. "Liberia in the New Partition of West Africa." *Journal of Race Development* (January, 1919), 175–200.

———. "Political and Economic Factors in Liberian Development." *Journal of International Relations* (1915), 65–90.

———. "Liberia in the New Partition of West Africa." *Journal of Race Development* (January, 1919), 260–268.

Essien-Udom, E.U. "The Relationship of Afro-Americans to African Nationalism." *Freedomways II* (Fall, 1962), 391–407.

Esedebe, P.O. "Dating Pan-African Conferences." *Africa: An International Business, Economic and Political Monthly* (November, 1974), 36–38.

Falkner, Roland Post. "The United States and Liberia." *American Journal of International Law* (1910), 529–545.

Fierce, Milfred C. "Defining and Dating Pan-Africanism." *Africa: An International Business, Economic and Political Monthly* (August, 1973), 56–57.

————. "Henry Sylvester Williams and the Pan-African Conference of 1900." *Geneve-Afrique*, Vol. 14, No. 1 (1975), 106–114.

————. "Selected Black American Leaders and Organizations and South Africa, 1900–1977: Some Notes." *Journal of Black Studies*, Vol. 17, No. 3 (1987), 305–306.

Fisher, Miles Mark. "Lott Cary, The Colonizing Missionary." *Journal of Negro History* (October, 1922), 380–418.

Fuller, Hoyt W. "Notes from a Sixth Pan-African Journal." *Black World* (October, 1974), 70–88.

Garrett, James. "A Historical Sketch: The Sixth Pan-African Congress." *Black World* (March, 1975), 4–20.

Geiss, Immanuel. "Notes on the Development of Pan-Africanism." *Journal of the Historical Society of Nigeria.* (Volume III, n.d.), 719–740.

Hamedoe, S.E.F.C.C. "The First Pan-African Conference of the World." *Colored American Magazine* (September, 1900), 223–231.

Hamilton, Charles. "Pan-Africanism and the Black Struggle in the U.S." *The Black Scholar* (March, 1971), 10–15.

Harding, Vincent. "W.E.B. DuBois and the Black Messianic Vision." *Freedomways* (1969), 44–54.

Harlan, Louis. "Booker T. Washington and the White Man's Burden." *American Historical Review* (January, 1966), 441–467.

Higgins, Billy D. "Negro Thought and the Exodus of 1879." *Phylon* (Spring, 1971), 39–52.

Hoadley, J. Stephen. "Black Americans and U.S. Policy Toward Africa: An Empirical Note." *Journal of Black Studies* (June, 1972), 489–502.

Hooker, J.R. "The Pan-African Congress 1900." *Transition* 46(October/December, 1974), 20–24.

Horne, David L. "The Pan-African Congress: A Positive Assessment." *The Black Scholar* (July–August, 1974), 2–11.

Isaacs, Harold. "The American Negro and Africa: Some Notes." *Phylon* (Fall, 1959), 219–233.

James, C.L.R. "Attack on the Sixth Pan-African Congress." *Race Today* (October, 1974), 282–283.

———. "Historical Development of the Sixth Pan-African Congress." *Black Books Bulletin* (Fall, 1974), 4–9.

Kirk-Greene, A.H.M. "America in the Niger Valley: A Colonization Centenary." *Phylon* (Fall, 1962), 225–239.

———. "Garveyism and African Nationalism." *Race* (October, 1969), 157–171.

———. "Pan-Africanism in Paris, 1924–1936." *Journal of Modern African Studies*. (April, 1969), 69–94.

Klima, Vladimir. "Duboisuv Pan-Afrikanism." *Novy Orient* (Czechoslovakia), Vol. 38, No. 5 (1983), 138–143.

Langley, J.A. "Chief Sam's Africa Movement and Race Consciousness in West Africa." *Phylon* (Summer, 1971), 164–178.

———. "Garveyism and African Nationalism." *Race* (October, 1969), 157–171.

———. "Pan-Africanism in Paris, 1924–1936." *Journal of Modern African Studies* (April, 1969), 69–94.

Locke, Alain. "Apropos of Africa." *Opportunity* (February, 1924), 36–40.

Logan, Rayford. "Carter G. Woodson." *Phylon*. (4th Quarter, 1945), 315–321.

———. "The Historical Aspects of Pan-Africanism: A Personal Chronicle." *African Forum* (Summer, 1965), 90–104.

Lynch, Hollis R. "Pan-Negro Nationalism in the New World Before 1862." *Boston University Papers on Africa* , Vol. 2 (1966), 149–179.

McAdoo, Bill. "Pre-Civil War Black Nationalism." *Progressive Labor* (June–July, 1966), 36–38.

Madhubuti, Haki. "The Latese Purge: The Attack on Black Nationalism and Pan-Africanism by the New Left, the Sons and Daughters of the Old Left." *The Black Scholar* (September, 1974), 50–58.

Mehlinger, Louis. "Attitude of the Free Negro Toward African Colonization. *Journal of Negro History* (July, 1916), 271–301.

Miller, Kelly. "An Estimate of Carter G. Woodson and His Work in Connection with the Association for the Study of Negro Life and History Inc." (Washington, D.C., 1926).

Montiero, Anthony. "The Sixth Pan-African Congress: Agenda for African Afro-American Solidarity." *Freedomways* (4th Quarter, 1974), 295–302.

———. "DuBois and Pan-Africa." *Freedomways* (1965), 166–187.

Moore, Richard B. "Africa Conscious Harlem." *Freedomways* (1963), 315–334.

Moses, Wilson J. "Civilizing Missionary: A Study of Alexander Crummell." *Journal of Negro History* (April, 1975), 229–251.

Mower, J.A. "The Republic of Liberia." *Journal of Negro History* (July, 1947), 265–306.

Nowicka, Ewa. "Historia Pan Afrikanizmu a Ruchy Umyslowe Wsrop Czarnet Ludnosci Stanow Zjednozonych Ap." *Kultura i Spoleczenstwo* (Poland) Vol. 24 (1980): 271–290.

Ofari, Earl. "A Critical View of the Pan-African Congress." *The Black Scholar* (July–August, 1974), 12–15.

Okoye, Felix. "The Afro-American and Africa." in *Topics in Afro-American History*. (Buffalo, New York, 1971), 37–58.

Park, Robert E. "Tuskegee International Conference on the Negro." *Journal of Race Development* (July, 1912–April, 1913), 117–120.

Parrington, Paul. "The Moon, Illustrated Weekly: Precursor of The Crisis." *Journal of Negro History* (July, 1963), 206–216.

Porter, Dorothy. "Early American Negro Writings: A Bibliographical Study." *Bibliographical Society of America Papers* (3rd Quarter, 1945), 192–268.

———. "Organized Educational Activities of Negro Literary Societies, 1828–1846." *Journal of Negro Education* (1936), 556–576.

Redkey, Edwin. "Bishop Turner's African Dream." *Journal of American History*. (September, 1967), 271–290.

Rodney, Walter. "Class and Nationalism in Africa." *Race Today* (August, 1974), 231–233.

Rogers, Ben. "William E.B. DuBois, Marcus Garvey and Pan-Africa." *Journal of Negro History* (April, 1955), 154–165.

Romero, Patricia. "W.E.B. DuBois, Pan-Africanists and Africa," 1963–1973." Paper presented at the Third International Congress of Africanists, Addis Ababa, Ethiopia, December 9–19, 1973.

Said, Abdulkadir N. "The Sixth Pan-African Congress." *New Directions* (1974), 10–15.

Scally, Sister Anthony. "The Carter G. Woodson Letters in the Library of Congress." *Negro History Bulletin* (June/July, 1975), 419–421.

Sherbakov, N.G. "Pan-Afrikanizm I Pan-Afrikanskaia Konferentsiia 1900 G" *Narody Azii I Afriki* (USSR), Vol. 1 (1983), 81–89.

Schomburg, Arthur A. "Racial Integrity: A Plea for the Establishment of a Chair of Negro History in Our Schools and Colleges," (Negro Society for Historical Research Occasional Paper Number 3 (1913).

Scott, Emmett J. "Is Liberia Worth Saving?" *Journal of Race Development* (January, 1911), 277–301.

———. "The American Commissioners in Liberia." *Colored American Magazine* (September, 1909), 204–210.

Seraile, William. "Black American Missionaries in Africa, 1821–1925." *Social Studies* (October, 1972), 198–202.

Shepperson, George. "The African Diaspora or the African Abroad." *African Forum* (1966), 76–91.

———. "Abolitionism and African Political Thought." *Transition 12* (1964), 22–26.

———. "Ethiopianism and African Nationalism." *Phylon* (1953), 9–18.

———. "Notes on Negro American Influences on the Emergence of African Nationalism." *Journal of African History* (1960), 299–312.

———. "Pan-Africanism and 'Pan-Africanism': Some Historical Notes." *Phylon* (Winter, 1962), 346–358.

———. "The Story of John Chilembew," *Negro History Bulletin* (January, 1952), 2–8.

Sherwood, H.N. "Early Negro Deportation Projects." *Mississippi Valley Historical Review* (March, 1916), 484–508.

———. "Paul Cuffe." *Journal of Negro History* (April, 1923), 153–229.

———. "Paul Cuffe and His Contribution to the American Colonization Society." *Proceedings of the Mississippi Valley Historical Association for the Year 1912–1913* (1913), 370–402.

Stewart, T. McCants "Conditions in Liberia." *A.M.E. Church Review* (July, 1915), 7–14.

Stuckey, Sterling. "DuBois, Woodson and the Spell of Africa: Black Americans and Africa Consciousness." *Negro Digest* (February, 1967), 20–24, 60–74.

Thorne, J. Albert. "An Appeal Addressed to the Friends of the African Race." (1896), n.p.

Wahle, Kathleen O'Mara. "Alexander Crummell: Black Evangelist and Pan-Negro Nationalist." *Phylon* (Winter, 1968).

Walker, Walter. "The Liberation Crisis." *Colored American Magazine* (April, 1909), 209–211.

Washington, Booker T. "Cruelty in the Congo Country." *Outlook* (October 8, 1904), 375–377.

———. "Industrial Education in Africa." *Independent* (March 15, 1906), 616–619.

———. "The Storm Before the Calm." *Colored American Magazine* (September, 1900), 203–207.

———. "The African at Home." *Colored American Magazine* (October, 1909), 261–273.

Weisbord, Robert G. "Africa, Africans and the Afro-American: Images and Identities in Transition." *Race* (January, 1969), 305–321.

Williams, Walter. "Black American Attitudes Toward Africa, 1877–1900." *Pan-African Journal* (Spring, 1971), 173–194.

———. "Black Journalism's Opinion About Africa During the Late Nineteenth Century." *Phylon* (September, 1973), 224–235.

Wright, C.T. Hagberg. "German Methods of Development in Africa." *Journal of the African Society* (October, 1901), 34–35.

Books and Pamphlets

Abraham, Willie E. *The Mind of Africa* (Chicago, 1962), University of Chicago Press.

Adams, C.C. *Negro Baptists and Foreign Missions* (Philadelphia, Pennsylvania, 1944), Foreign Missions Board, N.B.C.

Adams, E.A., ed. *Yearbook and Historical Guide to the African Methodist Episcopal Church* (Columbia, South Carolina, 1955), Bureau of Research and History A.M.E. Church.

Agyeman, Opoku. *The Pan-Africanist Worldview* (Independence, Missouri, 1985), University of Missiouri Press.

Ajala, Adekunle. *Pan-Africanism: Evolution, Progress and Prospects* (New York, 1974), St. Martin's Press.

Ajayi, J.F.A. and Crowder, M., ed. *History of West Africa*, Vol. I (New York, 1972), Columbia University Press.

Alleyne, Cameron Chesterfield. *Gold Coast at a Glance* (New York, 1931), Hunt Printing Co.

American Society of African Culture, ed. *Africa Seen by American Negro Scholars* (New York, 1963), American Society of African Culture.

————. *Pan-Africanism Reconsidered* (Berkeley, 1962), University of California Press.

Anderson, Robert Earle. *Liberia: America's African Friend* (Chapel Hill, North Carolina, 1952), University of North Carolina Press.

Aptheker, Herbert, ed. *Annotated Bibliography of the Published Writings of W.E.B. DuBois* (Millwood, New York, 1973), Kraus-Thompson.

————. *The Correspondence of W.E.B. DuBois, 1877–1934*, Vol. I (Amherst, Massachusetts, 1973), University of Massachusetts Press.

Ayandele, E.A. *Holy Johnson: Pioneer of African Nationalism, 1836–1917* (New York, 1970), Humanities Press.

————. *The Missionary Impact on Modern Nigeria 1842–1919: A Political and Social Analysis* (New York, 1967), Humanities Press.

Azikiwe, Nnamdi. *Liberia in World Politics* (London, 1934), A.H. Stockwell Co.

————. *Renascent Africa* (1937; rprt. New York, 1969), Negro Universities Press.

Bancroft, Frederick. *Colonization of the American Negro* (Norman, Oklahoma, 1957), University of Oklahoma Press.

Baraka, Imamu Amiri. *African Congress: A Documentary of the First Modern Pan-African Congress* (New York, 1972), William Morrow and Co.

Bell, Howard, ed. *Minutes of the Proceedings of the National Negro Conventions, 1830–1864* (New York, 1969), Arno Press.

————. *Survey of the Negro Convention Movement, 1830–1861* (New York, 1969), Negro Universities Press.

Bergman, Peter. *The Chronological History of the Negro in America* (New York, 1969), Harper & Row.

Berman, Edward H., ed. *African Reactions to Missionary Education* (New York, 1975), Teachers College Press, Columbia University.

Berry, Lewellyn. *A Century of Missions of the African Methodist Episcopal Church 1840–1940* (New York, 1942), Guttenberg Printing Co.

Biddiss, Michael D., ed., *Gobineau: Selected Political Writings* (New York, 1970), Harper and Row.

Bittle, William and Gilbert Geis. *The Longest Way Home: Chief Alfred C. Sam's Back to Africa Movement* (Detroit, Michigan, 1964), Wayne State University Press.

Bixler, Raymond W. *The Foreign Policy of the United States in Liberia* (New York, 1957), Pageant Press.

Blyden, Edward. *A Voice From Bleeding Africa on Behalf of Her Exiled Children* (Monrovia, Liberia, 1856).

———. *Christianity, Islam and the Negro Race* (London, 1888).

———. *Vindication of the Negro Race* (Monrovia, Liberia, 1857).

Boahen, A.A. and J.B. Webster. *A History of West Africa: The Revolutionary Years, 1815 to Independence* (New York, 1970), Praeger.

Bowen, J.W.E. *Africa and the American Negro: Addresses and Proceedings of the Congress on Africa 1895* (rprt. Miami, Florida, 1969), Mnemosyne Publishing Inc.

Bracey, John, et al. *Black Nationalism in America* (New York, 1970), Bobbs-Merrill Co. Inc.

Bradley, David. *A History of the A.M.E. Zion Church* (Nashville, Tennessee, 1970), Parthenon Press.

Brawley, Benjamin. *A Social History of the American Negro* (New York, 1921), Macmillan Co.

Brawley, James P. *Two Centuries of Methodist Concern: Bondage, Freedom and Education of Black People* (New York, 1974): Vantage Press.

Broderick, Francis L. *W.E.B. DuBois: Negro Leader in a Time of Crisis* (Stanford, California, 1959), Stanford University Press.

Brotz, Howard, ed. *Negro Social and Political Thought 1850–1920* (New York, 1966), Basic Books, Inc.

Brown, George N. *The Economic History of Liberia* (Washington, D.C., 1941), Associated Publishers.

Buell, R.L. *International Relations* (New York, 1926), Henry Holt and Company.

————. *The Native Problem in Africa*, 2 Vols. (New York, 1928). Macmillan Company.

Calendar of Manuscripts in the Schomburg Collection of Negro Literature, 3 Vols. (New York, 1943), Compiled by the Historical Records Survey, Works Projects Administration, New York City.

Campbell, Penelope. *Maryland in Africa: The Maryland State Colonization Society, 1831–1857* (Urbana, Illinois, 1971), University of Illinois Press.

Camphor, Alexander Priestly. *Missionary Sketches and Folklore* (Cincinnati, Ohio, 1909), Jennings and Graham.

Casely-Hayford, J.E. *Ethiopia Unbound: Studies in Race Emancipation* (1911; rprt. London, 1969), Frank Cass.

Cauther, Baker. *Advance: A History of Southern Baptist Foreign Missions* (Nashville, Tennessee, 1970), n.p.

Chrisman, Robert and Nathan Hare. *Pan-Africanism* (New York, 1974), Bobbs-Merrill

Clarke, John Henrik, ed. *Harlem: A Community in Transition* (New York, 1964), Citadel Press.

————. *Marcus Garvey and the Vision of Africa* (New York, 1974), Random House.

Cobb, Charlie. *African Notebook: Views on Returning Home* (Chicago, 1972), n.p.

Cole, Henry Benoni. *Who Are the Liberians?* (Cape Coast, Gold Coast, 1946), Mfantisiman Press.

Cronon, Edmund D. *Black Moses: The Story of Marcus Garvey and the Universal Negro Improvement Association* (Madison, Wisconsin, 1969), University of Wisconsin Press.

Crummell, Alexander. *Africa and America: Addresses and Discourses* (1891; rprt. New York, 1969), Negro Universities Press.

————. *The Future of Africa: Being Addresses, Sermons, Etc., Etc., Delivered in the Republic of Liberia* (New York, 1862), Charles Scribner.

————. *The Relations and Duties of Free Colored Men in America to Africa* (Hartford Connecticut, 1861), Case, Lockwood and Company.

Davis, John P., ed. *The American Negro Reference Book* (Englewood Cliffs, New Jersey, 1968), Prentice-Hall.

Davis, Stanley A. *This is Liberia* (New York, 1953), William Frederick Press.

Dean, Harry. *The Pegro Gorino: The Adventures of a Negro Sea Captain in Africa and on the Seven Seas in His Attempt to Found an Ethiopian Empire* (Boston and New York, 1929), Houghton-Mifflin.

Delaney, Martin R. *The Condition, Elevation and Destiny of the Colored Races of the United States* (1852; rprt. New York, 1969), Arno Press.

————. and Robert Campbell. *Search for a Place: Black Separatism and Africa* (1860; rprt. Ann Arbor, Michigan, 1969), University of Michigan Press.

Dorn, Edwin and Walter Carrington. *Africa in the Minds and Deeds of Black American Leaders* (Washington, D.C., 1991), Joint Center for Political and Economic Studies.

Downing, Henry Francis. *Liberia and Her People* (New York, 1925), n.p.

DuBois, W.E.B. *The Autobiography* (New York, 1968), International Publishers.

————. *Darkwater: Voices from Within the Veil* (1920; rprt. New York, 1969), Schocken Books.

————. *Dusk of Dawn: An Essay Toward an Autobiography of a Race Contest* (1940; rprt. New York, 1968), Schocken Books.

————. *The Negro* (1915; rprt. New York, 1970), Oxford University Press.

————. *The World and Africa: An Inquiry into the Part Africa Has Played in World History* (New York, 1965), International Publishers.

Dudley, Samuel M. *The African Methodist Episcopal Zion Church Yearbook 1924–1943* (Washington, D.C., 1943), A.M.E. Zion Book Concern.

Egerton, M.W. *Our Work in Africa* (Baltimore, Maryland, 1901), n.p.

Ellis, G.W. *Negro Culture in West Africa* (New York, 1915), Neale Publishing Co.

Esedebe, P. Olisanwuche. *Pan-Africanism: The Idea and the Movement 1776–1963* (Washington, D.C., 1982), Howard University Press.

Essien-Udom, E.U. *Black Nationalism: A Search for an Identity in America* (New York, 1969), Dell Publishing Co.

Fax, Elton. *Garvey: The Story of a Pioneer Black Nationalist* (New York, 1972), Dodd-Mead.

Ferris, William H. *Alexander Crummell* (Washington, D.C., 1920), n.p.

Fierce, Milfred C. *Africana Studies Outside the United States: Africa, Brazil and the Caribbean* (Ithaca, New York, 1991), Africana Studies and Research Center, Cornell Unviersity.

Foner, Jack. *Blacks and the Military in American History* (New York, 1974), Praeger.

Foner, Philip, ed. *The Life and Writings of Frederick Douglass*, 4 vols. (New York, 1955) International Publishers.

———. *W.E.B. DuBois Speaks: Speeches and Addresses 1890–1919*, Vol. I (New York, 1970), Pathfinder Press.

Fox, Early Lee. *The American Colonization Society, 1817–1840* (Baltimore, Maryland, 1919), n.p.

Frederickson, George. *The Black Image in the White Mind: The Debate on Afro-American Character and Destiny 1817–1914* (New York, 1971), Harper and Row.

Freeman, Edward. *The Epoch of Negro Baptists and the Foreign Missions Board, National Baptist Convention, U.S.A., Inc* (Kansas City, Missouri, 1954), Foreign Missions Board, N.B.C.

Garvey, Amy-Jacques, ed. *Philosophy and Opinions of Marcus Garvey* (New York, 1969), Anthenum.

———. *Garvey and Garveyism* (New York, 1970), Collier-Macmillan.

Geiss, Immanuel. *The Pan-African Movement: A History of Pan-Africanism in America, Europe and Africa* (New York, 1974), Africana Publishing Co.

Gilbert, Peter, ed. *The Selected Writings of John Edward Bruce: Militant Black Journalist* (New York, 1971), Arno Press.

Gossett, Thomas. *Race: The History of an Idea in America* (Dallas, Texas, 1963), Southern Methodist University Press.

Green, Reginald Herbold. *Unity or Poverty? The Economics of Pan-Africanism* (Baltimore, Maryland, 1968), Penguin African Library.

Grove, C.S. *The Planting of Christianity in Africa*, 3 vols. (London, 1954), Lutterworth Press.

Haley, Alex. *Roots* (New York, 1976), Doubleday.

Hanna, William John. *Independent Black Africa* (Chicago, 1964), Rand McNally.

Harlan, Louis. *Booker T. Washington: The Wizard of Tuskegee, 1901–1915* (New York, 1983), Oxford Univeristy Press.

———. *Booker T. Washington: The Making of a Black Leader 1856–1901* (New York, 1972), Oxford University Press.

Harris, Clara E. *The Woman's Parent Mite Missionary Society of the African Methodist Episcopal Church* (n.p., 1935), A.M.E. Book Concern.

Harris, Joseph, ed. *Pillars in Ethiopian History: The William Leo Hansberry African Notebook*, Vol. I (Washington, D.C., 1974), Howard University Press.

———. *Africa and Africans as Seen by Classical Writers: The William Leo Hansberry African History Notebook*, Vol. II (Washington, D.C., 1981), Howard University Press.

Harris, Sheldon, *Paul Cuffe: Black America and the African Return* (New York, 1972), Simon & Schuster.

Hill, Adelaide and Martin Kilson, ed. *Aprpos of Africa: Afro-American Leaders and the Romance of Africa* (New York, 1971), Anchor-Doubleday.

Hill, Robert. *Marcus Garvey: Life and Lessons, A Centennial Companion to the Marcus Garvey and Universal Negro Improvement Association Papers* (Berkeley, California, 1987), University of California Press.

———, ed. *Pan-African Biography* (Los Angeles, California, 1987), University of California Press.

———, and Barbara Bair, ed., *The Marcus Garvey and Universal Negro Improvement Association Papers*, Vols. I–VII (Berkeley, California, 1983–1990), University of California Press.

Hofstadter, Richard, ed., *The Progressive Movement 1900–1915* (Englewood Cliffs, New Jersey, 1963), Prentice-Hall.

Hood, James W. *One Hundred Years of the African Methodist Episcopal Church* (New York, 1895), A.M.E. Zion Book Concern.

Hooker, James R. *Black Revolutionary: George Padmore's Path from Communism to Pan-Africanism* (New York, 1967), Praeger.

———. *Henry Sylvester Williams: Imperial Pan-Africanist* (London, 1975), Rex Collins.

Hopkins, Anthony G. *An Economic History of West Africa* (New York, 1973), Columbia University Press.

Huebrich, Charles Henry. *The Political and Legislative History of Liberia 1877–1945* (New York, 1947), Central Book Company, Inc.

Huggins, Nathan I. *Slave and Citizen: The Life of Frederick Douglass* (Boston, 1980), Little Brown and Co.

Isaacs, Harold. *The New World of Negro Americans* (New York, 1969), Viking Press.

Jacobs, Sylvia. *The African Nexus: Black American Perspectives on the European Partitioning of Africa, 1880–1920* (Westport, Connecticut, 1981), Greenwood Press.

————. *Black Americans and the Missionary Movement* (Westport, Connecticut, 1982), Greenwood Press.

James., C.L.R. *A History of Pan-African Revolt* (Washington, D.C., 1964), Drum and Spear.

Johnson, Sir Harry. *Liberia*, 2 vols. (London, 1906), Hutchinson and Co.

Johnson, Thomas. *Africa for Christ, or Twenty-Eight Years a Slave* (London, 1892), Alexander and Shepard.

Jordan, Artishia Wilkerson. *The African Methodist Episcopal Church in Africa* (New York, 1960), Department of Foreign Missions, A.M.E. Church.

————. *Negro Baptist History* (Nashville, Tennessee, 1930), Sunday School Publishing Board.

————. *Up the Ladder in Foreign Missions* (Nashville, Tennessee, 1930), Sunday School Publishing Board.

Jordan, Lewis. *In Our Stead* (Philadelphia, Pennsylvania, n.d.), Foreign Missions Board, N.B.C.

July, Robert. *The Origins of Modern African Thought* (New York, 1967), Praeger.

Karnga, Winfred Abayomi. *Liberia Before the New World* (London, 1923), F.T. Philips.

Keiser, Robert L. *Liberia: A Report on the Relations Between the United States and Liberia* (Washington, D.C., 1928), United States Government Printing Office.

King, Kenneth. *Pan-Africanism from Within* (London, 1972), Oxford University Press.

————. *Pan-Africanism and Education: A Study of Race Philanthropy and Education in the Southern States of America and East Africa* (London, 1971), Oxford University Press.

Lane, Ann J. *The Brownsville Affair: National Crisis and Black Reaction* (Port Washington, New York, 1971), Kennikat Press.

Langley, J.A., *Pan-Africanism and Nationalism in West Africa 1900–1945: A Study in Ideology and Social Classes* (London, 1973), Oxford University Press.

Legum, Colin. *Pan-Africanism: A Short Political Guide* (New York, 1973), Preager.

Lester, Julius, ed. *The Seventh Son: The Thought and Writings of W.E.B. DuBois* (New York, 1971), Random House.

Liebenow, J. Gus. *Liberia: The Evolution of Privilege* (Ithaca, New York, 1969), Cornell University Press.

————. *Liberia: The Quest for Demoocracy* (Bloomington, Indiana, 1987), Indiana University Press.

Logan, Rayford, ed. *W.E.B. DuBois: A Profile* (New York, 1971), Hill and Wang.

————. *The Betrayal of the Negro: From Rutherford B. Hayes to Woodrow Wilson* (New York, 1969), Collier Books.

Lynch, Hollis R., ed. *Black Spokesmen: Selected Published Writings of Edward Wilmot Blyden* (London, 1970), Frank Cass.

————. *Edward Wilmot Blyden: Pan-Negro Patriot* (London, 1967), Oxford University Press.

MacCartney, William. *Doctor Aggrey: Ambassador for Africa* (London, 1949), S.S.C.N. Press.

McKay, Vernon. *Africa in World Politics* (New York, 1963), Harper and Row.

Martin, Tony. *Race First: The Ideological and Organizational Struggles of Marcus Garvey and the Universal Negro Improvement Association* (Westport, Connecticut, 1976), Greenwood Press.

————. *The Pan-African Connection: From Slavery to Garvey and Beyond* (Canton, Massachusetts, 1983), African World Library.

————. *Marcus Garvey, Hero: A First Biography* (Canton, Massachusetts, 1983), African World Library.

————. *Literary Garveyism: Garvey, Black Acts and the Harlem Renaissance* (Canton, Massachusetts, 1983), African World Library.

————, ed. *African Fundamentalism: A Literary and Cultural Anthology of Garvey's Harlem Renaissance* (Canton, Massachusetts, 1991), African World Library.

————, ed. *The Poetical Works of Marcus Garvey* (Canton, Massachusetts, 1983), African World Library.

Mathews, Basil. *Booker T. Washington: Educator and Interracial Interpreter* (Cambridge, Massachusetts, 1948), Harvard University Press.

Maier, August. *Negro Thought in America 1880–1915: Racial Ideologies in the Age of Booker T. Washington* (Ann Arbor, Michigan, 1969), University of Michigan Press.

————, and Rudwick, Elliott. *From Plantation to Ghetto: An Interpretative History of American Negroes* (New York, 1969), Hill and Wang.

Miller, Floyd J. *The Search for a Black Nationality: Black Colonization and Emigration 1787–1863* (Urbana, Illinois, 1975), University of Illinois Press.

Moses, Wilson J. *Alexander Crummell: A Story of Civilization and Discontent* (New York, 1989), Oxford University Press.

————, ed. *Destiny and Race: Selected Writings of Alexander Crummell, 1840–1898* (Amherst, Massachusetts, 1992), University of Massachusetts Press.

Musson, M. *Aggrey of Achimota* (London, 1946), United Society for Christian Literature.

Mydral, Gunnar. *An American Dilemma: The Negro Problem in Modern Democracy*, 2 vols (New York, 1962), Harper & Row.

Newby, I.A. *Jim Crow's Defense: Anti-Negro Thought in America, 1900–1930* (Baton Rogue, Louisiana, 1965), Louisiana State University Press.

Padmore, George, ed. *History of the Fifth Pan-African Congress* (London, 1963), Hammersmith.

————. *Pan-Africanism or Communism* (New York, 1971), Doubleday and Co.

Painter, Nell Irvin. *Exodusters: Black Migration to Kansas After Reconstruction* (New York, 1979), W.W. Norton.

————. *Standing at Armageddon: The United States, 1877–1919* (New York, 1987), W.W. Norton.

Payne, Daniel Alexander. *History of the African Methodist Episcopal Church* (Nashville, Tennessee, 1891), A.M.E. Department of Foreign Missions.

Pelt, Owen D. and Ralph Lee Smith. *The Story of the National Baptists* (New York, 1960), Vantage Press.

Phelps-Stokes, Anson. *Tuskegee Institute: The First Fifty Years* (Tuskegee, Alabama, 1931), Tuskegee Institute.

Phelps-Stokes Fund. *Educational Adaptations: Report of Ten Years' Work of the Phelps-Stokes Fund, 1910–1920* (New York, n.d.), Phelps-Stokes Fund.

————. *Phelps-Stokes Reports on Education in Africa* (London and New York, 1962), Oxford University Press.

————. *Twenty-Year Report of the Phelps-Stokes Fund, 1911–1931* (New York, 1932), Phelps-Stokes Fund.

Quarles, Benjamin. *Black Abolitionists* (New York, 1969), Oxford University Press.

Redkey, Edwin. *Black Exodus: Black Nationalist and Back-to-Africa Movements, 1890–1910* (New Haven, Connecticut, 1969), Yale University Press.

————. *Respect Black: The Writings and Speeches of Henry McNeal Turner* (New York, 1971), Arno Press.

Reid, Inez Smith and Ronald Walters, ed. *From Gammon to Howard; Proceedings of the African-American National Conference on Africa, 1972* (n.p., n.d.), sponsored by the Black Congressional Caucus.

Richards, Henry J., ed. *Topics in Afro-American Studies* (Buffalo, New York, 1971), Black Academy Press, Inc.

Richings, G.F. *Evidences of Progress Among Colored People* (Philadelphia, Pennsylvania, 1904), George S. Ferguson Co.

Rigsby, Gregory D. *Alexander Crummell: Pioneeer in Nineteenth Century Pan-African Thought* (Middletown, Connecticut, 1987), Greenwood Press.

Rogers, J.A. *World's Great Men of Color*, 2 vols. (1946; rprt., New York, 1972), Macmillan Co.

Rudwick, Elliot M. *W.E.B. DuBois: Propagandist of the Negro Protest* (Philadelphia, Pennsylvania, 1960), University of Pennsylvania Press.

Scipio, Albert L. *Tuskegee: The Pre-War Days* (Silver Spring, Maryland, 1987).

Scott, William R. *The Sons of Sheba's Race: African-Americans and the Italo-Ethiopian War, 1935–1941* (Bloomington, Indiana, 1992), Indiana University Press.

Shatz, Walter, ed. *Directory of Afro-American Resources* (New York, 1970), R.R. Bowker Company.

Shepperson, George and Thomas Price. *Independent African* (Edinburgh, 1958), Edinburgh University Press.

Sibley, James L. *Liberia: Old and New* (Garden City, New York, 1928), Doubleday.

Simmons, William. *Men of Mark* (1887; rprt. New York, 1968), Arno Press.

Singleton, George A. *The Romance of African Methodism: A Study of the African Methodist Episcopal Church* (New York, 1952), Exposition Press.

Sinnette, Elinor Des Verney, *Authur Alfonso Schomburg, Black Bibliophile and Collector: A Biography* (Detroit, Michigan, 1989), Wayne State University Press.

Sithole, Ndabaningi. *African Nationalism*, 2nd edition (New York, 1968), Oxford University Press.

Smith, C.E. *Our Work is Africa* (Richmond, Virginia, n.d.), Foreign Missions Board, Southern Baptist Convention.

Smith, Charles Spencer. *A History of the African Methodist Episcopal Church, 1856–1922*, Vol. I (Philadelphia, Pennsylvania, 1922), Book Concern of the A.M.E. Church.

Smith, Edwin W. *Aggrey of Africa: A Study in Black and White* (London, 1929), n.p.

Southern, Eileen. *The Music of Black Americans* (New York, 1971), W.W. Norton.

Staudenraus, P.J. *The African Colonization Movement* (New York, 1961), Columbia University Press.

Thomas, Lamont. *Paul Cuffe: Black Entrepreneur and Pan-Africanist.* (Urbana, Illinois, 1988), University of Illinois Press.

Thompson, Vincent. *Africa and Unity: The Evolution of Pan-Africanism* (New York, 1969), Humanities Press.

Thornborough, Emma Lou. *T. Thomas Fortune: Militant Journalist* (Chicago, Illinois, 1972), University of Chicago Press.

Tindall, George. *South Carolina Negroes* (Columbia, South Carolina, 1952), University of South Carolina Press.

Toppin, Edgar A. *A Biographical History of Blacks in America Since 1528* (New York, 1971), David McKay Co.

Uya, Okon Edet, ed. *Black Brotherhood: Afro Americans and Africa* (Lexington, Massachusetts, 1971), D.C. Heath and Company.

Vincent, Theodore. *Black Power and the Garvey Movement* (Berkeley, California, 1971), Ramparts Press.

Walters, Alexander. *My Life and Work* (New York, 1917), Fleming H. Revell Co.

Walls, William J. *The African Methodist Episcopal Zion Church: Reality of the Black Church* (Charlotte, North Carolina, 1974), A.M.E. Zion Publishing House.

Weaver, John D. *The Brownsville Raid* (New York, 1970), W.W. Norton.

Weisbord, Robert. *Ebony Kinship: Africa, Africans and the Afro-American* (Westport, Connecticut, 1973), Greenwood Press.

Welch, Claude Emerson. *Dream of Unity: Pan-Africanism and Political Unification in West Africa* (Ithaca, New York, 1968), Cornell University Press.

Williams, George Washington. *A History of the Negro Troops in the War of the Rebellion 1861–1865* (1888; rprt. New York, 1968), Bergman Publishers.

———. *History of the Negro Race in America*, 2 vols. (New York, 1883), G.P. Putnam and Sons.

Williams, Lorraine, ed. *Africa and the Afro-American Experience* (Washington, D.C., 1973), History Department, Howard University.

Williams, Walter. *Black Americans and the Evangelization of Africa, 1877–1900* (Madison, Wisconsin, 1982), University of Wisconsin Press.

Wilson, Henry, ed. *Origins of West African Nationalism* (New York, 1969) Macmillan Co.

Woodson, Carter G. *The African Background Outlined: Or Handbook for the Study of the Negro* (1936; rprt. New York, 1969), New American Libraries Inc.

Woodward, C. Vann. *Origins of the New South 1877–1913* (Baton Rouge, Louisiana, 1951), Louisiana State University Press.

———. *The Strange Career of Jim Crow* (New York, 1974), Oxford University Press.

Wright, Richard Robert, ed. *The Encyclopedia of the African Methodist Episcopal Church* (Philadelphia, Pennsylvania, 1947), A.M.E. Book Concern.

———. *The Bishops of the African Methodist Episcopal Church* (Nashville, Tennessee, 1963), A.M.E. Sunday School Union.

Index

Abbott, Lyman, 183
Aborigines Rights and
    Protection Society
    (ARPS), 42
Abyssinia (Ethiopia), 202,
    212
Adams, Charles Hall, 151
Adeshigibin, Dada, 48
Adler, Felix, 184
Africa
  descriptions of in the
    United States, xvi
  nationalist movements in,
    47
Africa and America
    (Alexander
    Crummell), 23
Africa and the Africans (J.E.
    Casely-Hayford), 62
Africa for Christ (Thomas
    Johnson), 101
"African" (as term used by
    Black Americans), 9
The African Abroad (William
    Ferris), 58
African-American
    intellectual
    community, growth
    of, 37–66
African-American
    missionaries,
    100–101
African and African-
    American Mutual
    Influences, 61–66

African Association, 199, 200
*The African Background
    Outlined* (Carter G.
    Woodson), 49
African Baptist Church, 99
African Civilization Society,
    13
African Institution of Boston,
    4
African intellectuals, 48
African Jubilee Emigration
    Society, 144
African Liberation Day
    programs, xviii
African Methodist Episcopal
    Church (A.M.E.), 9,
    15, 16, 21–22, 86, 99,
    112–18, 175
African Methodist Episcopal
    Zion Church
    (A.M.E.Z.), 9, 21–22,
    52, 99, 106–10, 117
African Pioneer, 126, 137
The African Repository, 9
African Society of London,
    52
African Times, 136
*African Times and Orient
    Review*, 52, 53, 58,
    136
African Union Company
    (AUC), 147–48
African World, 53
Afro-American Council, 109,
    203